Adventure Tourism Management

Adventure Tourism Management

Ralf Buckley
International Centre for Ecotourism Research
Griffith University
Gold Coast, Australia

ELSEVIER

AMSTERDAM • BOSTON • HEIDELBERG • LONDON • NEW YORK • OXFORD
PARIS • SAN DIEGO • SAN FRANCISCO • SINGAPORE • SYDNEY • TOKYO
Butterworth-Heinemann is an imprint of Elsevier

Butterworth-Heinemann is an imprint of Elsevier
Linacre House, Jordan Hill, Oxford OX2 8DP, UK
30 Corporate Drive, Suite 400, Burlington, MA 01803, USA

First edition 2010

British Library Cataloguing in Publication Data
A catalogue record for this book is available from the British Library

Library of Congress Cataloging-in-Publication Data
A catalog record for this book is available from the Library of Congress

ISBN: 978-1-85617-834-1

For information on all Butterworth-Heinemann publications
visit our web site at books.elsevier.com

Printed and bound in Great Britain
10   10 9 8 7 6 5 4 3 2 1

Working together to grow
libraries in developing countries

www.elsevier.com | www.bookaid.org | www.sabre.org

ELSEVIER   BOOK AID International   Sabre Foundation

Contents

Dedication

This book is dedicated to two remarkable athletes who have used extraordinary feats of adventure to promote conservation.

To raise money for Save the Rhino, Christina Franco has run the 6-day Marathon des Sables across the Sahara, and won a ski race to the North Magnetic Pole. In 2009 she skied solo to the North Pole itself.

Wang Shi is a highly successful property entrepreneur who has also climbed the Seven Summits, skied both North and South Poles, and rafted the Yangtze to help raise awareness of river conservation.

Christina Franco, Arctic expedition race

Wang Shi and Travis Winn of Last Descents, Yangtze Great Bend

Preface

People take holidays as a break from the routine from their everyday lives. For some, the best kind of break is to be looked after in luxury. For others, it means broadening their horizons through some new experience or education. But for many, the best kind of holiday is one that brings a sense of adventure, something exciting and memorable. Some people want all of these in the same holiday, and indeed, that is perfectly possible.

Not surprisingly, therefore, a large proportion of the commercial tourism industry has been established specifically to provide people with adventurous experiences. Different people have very different ideas of what makes a good adventure, and the industry is correspondingly diverse. It is also very large, with an annual turnover somewhere in the region of a trillion dollars.

Unlike other major sectors of the commercial tourism industry, however, adventure tourism has received remarkably little research attention. In fact, it appears that there are only two previous books which address adventure tourism explicitly: one by Swarbrooke et al. (2003), which focuses on individual adventure experiences; and one by Buckley (2006a) which focuses on the structure of commercial adventure tourism products. Even including academic books in related areas such as that by Ryan (2003) on *Recreational Tourism* and Baldacchino (2006) on *Extreme Tourism*, and commercial publications such as *The Lonely Planet Blue List*, this is still a remarkably sparse literature for such a large field.

The reasons for this lack of research attention are not clear. Perhaps adventure tourism has not been well defined: but the same certainly applies for ecotourism, and there is no shortage of books on that topic. Perhaps adventure tourism has been analysed under other headings: but in fact, although there is a large literature on outdoor recreation, that literature focuses almost exclusively on private individual recreational practices, with rather little attention to the commercial adventure tourism industry. Perhaps tourism researchers do not see any opportunities for research in adventure tourism to advance theoretical understandings of tourism more generally. In fact, however, surely many such opportunities exist, if only because people in unfamiliar situations behave differently than they do at home, providing significant scope for psychological and behavioural analysis.

Perhaps, therefore, it is simply that as a subsector of the commercial tourism industry, adventure tourism has grown to its current scale rather recently and rapidly. Of course, this depends on just how adventure tourism is defined, but in very broad terms we might recognise three historical phases. In the earliest phase, there were some highly adventurous travellers, but not many of them. In the second phase, the expansion of mass tourism, the number of tourists grew enormously, but most of them were not very adventurous. It is only in this current third phase, as mass tourism has evolved from its model-T beginnings to its highly customised current structures, that commercial adventure tourism has had the opportunity to expand its economic scale, with the proliferation of adventure equipment, clothing, infrastructure and lifestyles as well as retail tours.

Irrespective of the reasons, it does surely seem that adventure tourism has received a great deal less academic attention that it deserves; and the aim of this volume is to contribute to overcoming this deficit. As with the previous volume (Buckley, 2006a), this book focuses on commercial adventure tourism, where predefined products and packages are sold ultimately to retail consumers, through a range of different marketing mechanisms. The approach taken, however, is quite different from that previous volume, which provided detailed descriptive analyses of audited adventure tourism products from around 20 different subsectors, defined by the principal activity concerned.

This volume, in contrast, examines general features of the entire adventure tourism sector simultaneously, with only a few activity subsectors considered in detail as case studies. Individual adventure tourism products are referred to on occasion as examples, but are not described in any detail. Some of the patterns presented here have been derived from further analysis of data published previously in the 2006 volume, whereas others are entirely new. At the time of going to press, one of these 13 chapters had also been published as an article in the journal *Tourism Management*, and part of another overlaps a submission to the journal *Annals of Tourism Research*. The remaining material is not available elsewhere.

This book is written for a variety of different readers. It includes reviews and analyses of research data and previous publications which are generally intended to be reliable, representative, and up-to-date. It is written in a straightforward style using non-technical language, for use by practitioners and university students as well as researchers. It will be most valuable if read in conjunction with the 2006 volume which presents detailed case studies. This follows the same approach as a 2009 book on ecotourism (Buckley, 2009a), which can usefully be read in conjunction with a 2003 book on ecotourism case studies (Buckley, 2003a).

The material presented in this book is intended for readers who already have a general understanding of the tourism industry, whether through practice, research interests, or an undergraduate course in tourism or tourism management. There are many textbooks and research volumes on tourism management more generally, and this book assumes that the reader understands the broad structure of the tourism industry, including marketing and distribution systems and the variety of business models in common use. My aim here is not to review the basics of tourism studies, but to show how and where adventure tourism fits, both in the commercial industry itself and in the various relevant research disciplines.

The 13 chapters are organised into three sections. The first section, chapters 1–3, presents a global overview of the scale and scope, geography, and product and marketing patterns in the adventure tourism industry. The second section, chapters 4–8 inclusive, addresses four major operational management aspects, namely, risk, communications, access, and environment. Climate change is also considered in this section. The third section, chapters 9–12 inclusive, presents four different subsectors representative of different components of the adventure tourism industry: wildlife, marine, boardsports, and helicopter adventure tourism, respectively. In conclusion, chapter 13 identifies key trends and patterns for future practice and research.

About the Author

Ralf Buckley is Professor and Director of the International Centre for Ecotourism Research, established in 1993 at Griffith University, Australia. He has over 700 publications including 185 refereed journal articles; and he has written and edited a dozen academic books, including seven on ecotourism and related topics. He has several decades of experience in various forms of adventure recreation and used to work as a tour guide for a US-based international tour company. His research focuses principally on the various interactions between the tourism industry and the natural environment. His 2006 book on *Adventure Tourism* assembled over 100 audited case studies from over 20 activity subsectors. This volume builds on that foundation by taking a more analytical approach.

List of Tables

List of Figures

PART 1

Global Overview

Exploding wave, Colorado River, USA

CHAPTER 1

Scope and Scale

KEY ISSUES

Scope

- defining adventure tourism
- related terms and sectors
- history of the concept
- activities involved
- structure of the sector
- review of academic and grey literature

Scale

- how to estimate the economic scale of the adventure tourism sector
- components and boundaries
- valuation and estimation measures and methods
- review of actual estimates for particular sectors and places
- range of estimates for the global industry
- adventure tourism as a trillion-dollar sector
- add-ons such as amenity migration and associated property markets

CONTENTS

CHAPTER SUMMARY

Scope

Adventure tourism is a broad term which encompasses all types of commercial outdoor tourism and recreation with a significant element of excitement. It is closely related to nature-based tourism, with some overlap. Whilst nature-based tourism products focus on seeing, however, adventure tourism products focus on doing.

A wide range of outdoor recreation activities have been packaged as commercial adventure tour products, from short, low-key hiking trips to expensive and equipment-intensive tours involving helicopters and expedition cruise vessels.

Adventure tourism is sometimes also taken to include independent travel which provides or is perceived by the travellers themselves as providing, an adventurous experience. At the other end of the spectrum, it may also be taken to include large-scale, fixed-site outdoor sporting facilities such as ski resorts and yacht marinas, and associated retail and residential components. Here, however, the focus is on packaged commercial retail adventure tourism products purchasable by individual consumers.

Scale

There are basically two different approaches to estimate the economic scale of the adventure tourism sector: top-down or bottom-up. The former relies on calculating what proportion of the tourism industry as a whole consists of adventure tourism. The latter relies on estimating the economic scale of every individual adventure tourism operation or at least subsector, and aggregating these into a cumulative figure for the adventure tourism industry as a whole. With perfect data and unambiguous definitions, these two approaches should yield the same result. In practice, since both data and definitions are rather incomplete and unreliable, the two approaches can yield quite different results. The degree to which they correspond, however, can provide an indication of how reliable they may be.

It is only in recent decades that countries have begun to estimate the scale of their tourism industries at all, since historically this was not included as one of the calculation components for GNP. Tourism satellite accounts are now widespread in a number of nations, but still not particularly precise. It is notable, for example, that the peak international tourism industry association, the World Travel and Tourism Council, estimates global tourism turnover at around $7 trillion per year, whereas the peak intergovernmental body, the UN World Tourism Organisation, gives a considerably smaller figure. Even if we can estimate accurately what proportion of the overall tourism industry consists of adventure tourism, therefore, we still have to decide which of these whole-of-sector estimates to use as a starting point.

Even taking those uncertainties into account, it seems clear that adventure tourism is now a large industry sector, with an annual global turnover estimated at around one trillion US dollars. More precise measures depend firstly, on defining exactly what is or is not included; and secondly, on obtaining accurate statistics for different subsectors and components.

RESEARCH REVIEW

Scope

The term adventure tourism is relatively new in academic research. Reviews of the adventure tourism literature less than 5 years ago (Buckley 2006a,b) indicated that of around 350 publications relevant to the field, most had originated either in parks and recreation research, in sport and travel medicine, or in tourism economics. Of these, around 27% were related to environmental impacts, 22% to participant perceptions, 16% to commercial aspects such as product structures, and 11–12% each to economic scale, risks and accidents, and conflicts between different activities. There are still very few books either on adventure tourism specifically (Swarbrooke et al., 2003; Buckley, 2006a) or on related areas such as adventure sports (Hudson, 2002; McNamee, 2007), adventure programming (Priest and Gass, 2005), tourism in adventurous terrain (Godde et al., 2000; Prideaux and Cooper, 2009) or tourism in adventurous regions (Baldacchino, 2006; Snyder and Stonehouse, 2007; Spenceley, 2008).

The scope of adventure tourism has commonly been expressed through lists of specific outdoor activities involved. Buckley (2006a) listed 35–40 such activities, some of them in aggregated categories. In alphabetical order, these were: abseiling, aerobatic aircraft flights, ballooning, black water rafting, bungy jumping, caving, cross-country skiing, diving, downhill skiing and snowboarding, expedition cruises, gliding, hang gliding, heliskiing and heliboarding, hiking, horse riding, ice climbing, jet boating, kiteboarding, mountain biking, mountaineering, off-road 4WD driving, parapenting and paragliding, quad biking and ATV driving, rock climbing, sailboarding, sailing, sea kayaking, skydiving and parachuting, snowshoeing, surfing, whale watching, whitewater canoeing and kayaking, whitewater rafting, wildlife watching and zorbing. This list is by no means exhaustive, and many of these categories could be subdivided.

In that volume, the term adventure tourism was taken to mean 'guided commercial tours where the principal attraction is an outdoor activity that relies on features of the natural terrain, generally requires specialised sporting or similar equipment, and is exciting for the tour clients'. This definition 'does not require that the clients themselves operate the equipment: they may simply be passengers...'. Buckley (2006a) went on to examine critical components of this definition, such as distinctions between tourism and recreation and between fixed and mobile activities. The roles of skills, risks and remoteness in defining adventure have also been referred to by a number of authors, reviewed by Buckley (2006a, 2007a). Typologies of adventure tourism have also been put forward by authors such as Trauer (2006), Mehmetoglu (2007) and Weber (2007).

A number of authors have focussed more on adventure tourists and their motivations, expectation and experiences, than on adventure tourism products and activities (Swarbrooke et al., 2003). Tran and Ralston (2006) found that many adventure tourists are people who are motivated by achievements, whilst Patterson et al. (2007) examined what attracts the baby-boomer generation to adventure tourism. Sung (2007) used mail surveys from 1000 of the 60,000 members of the Adventure Club of North America to classify them numerically into various subgroups. Kane and Zink (2007) described interviews with seven Americans on a commercial kayak tour in New Zealand.

A significant proportion of the research analyses in adventure tourism focus on specific adventure activities rather than the sector as a whole. Examples include: Smith (2006) on commercial expedition yacht cruising; Mograbi and Rogerson (2007) on dive tourism, Buckley (2009b) on whitewater raft and kayak tours; and Costa and Chalip (2007) on skydiving tourism in northern Portugal.

Scale

Economic scale, value and impact have been examined for a number of adventure tourism activities and regions. Techniques and examples of such analyses were reviewed by Buckley (2009a, pp. 82–116, 269–292), who emphasised two particular aspects. The first is selecting which precise components to include or exclude, and how to define them. The second is selecting techniques to estimate the economic size of each component, whether market or non-market. Texts on the economics of outdoor tourism include those of Hanley et al. (2003) and Tisdell (2001, 2005). Reviews of techniques to estimate economic values include Azqueta and Sotelsek (2007) and Bebbington et al. (2007). Reviews of techniques to estimate economic impact include Frechtling (2006), Alpizar (2006), Loomis (2006) and Stynes and White (2006).

Examples of regional scale cross-activity estimates include Mallett (1998) for the USA, Buckley (1998a) for Australia and Page et al. (2005) for Scotland. There are estimates of economic scale or impact for: mountain biking (Chavez, 1996a,b; Fix and Loomis, 1997); off-road driving (Bowker, 2001); climbing (Hanley, 2002; Hanley et al., 2001, 2003; Grijalva et al., 2002); whitewater rafting and kayaking (Bowker et al., 1996; English and Bowker, 1996a,b; Northeast Natural Resource Centre, 1997; Buultjens and Davis, 2001; Siderelis and Moore, 2006); diving (Cope, 2003; Green and Donnelly, 2003) and whale watching (Duffus and Dearden, 1993; Davis and Tisdell, 1996, 1998; Hoyt, 2000; Parsons et al., 2003; Woods-Ballard et al., 2003; Rodger and Moore, 2004).

The economic scale, value and impacts of various types of wildlife adventure tourism in Africa have been examined by, e.g. Borge et al. (1991) and Mmopelwa et al. (2007) in Botswana; Barnes et al. (1992, 1999) and Barnes and Jager (1996) in Namibia; Archabald and Naughton-Treves (2001) in Uganda; and Blom (2000) in the Central African Republic. In North America, the economics of bear-watching tourism were examined by Clayton and Mendelsohn (1993) in Alaska, and by Lemelin and Smale (2006) for polar bears in Hudson Bay. In Indonesia, Walpole and Goodwin (2000) examined the economics of tourism based on watching Komodo dragons, with particular attention to pricing policies. There are many more economic studies of tourism based on wildlife and nature (Buckley, 2009a), but most of these would not necessarily qualify as adventure tourism.

BIG PICTURE

Scope

Adventure tourism can be defined in various ways, and there is as yet no officially accepted or generally agreed universal definition. From the perspective of the individual tourist, anything which they personally consider adventurous can be counted as adventure tourism. Different individuals, however, or even the same individual at different ages, may have widely different perceptions of how adventurous a particular activity may be, depending on prior experience, skills and interests. From a supply-side perspective, a wide range of different commercial tourism activities may be marketed as adventure tourism. There are also many activities where particular products are marketed as adventure and where other essentially identical products have been marketed and analysed under different names and labels. Certain types of wildlife tourism, for example, or marine tourism, or indeed ecotourism, may equally be treated as adventure tourism, whereas others probably would not.

Like any other component of the commercial tourism industry, adventure tourism includes accommodation, transport and activities. Most commonly, perhaps, it is the activities that spring to mind when we think of adventure tourism, but there are also examples of transport and even accommodation, which are considered adventurous in themselves. Indeed, in some cases, transport or accommodation itself becomes the activity, as in the case of Overlander tours through Africa or Asia, or the Arctic Ice Hotel in northern Sweden.

The Oxford Dictionary defines adventure as 'unexpected or exciting experience; daring enterprise, hazardous activity'. Its Australian equivalent, *The Macquarie Dictionary*, gives several meanings, including 'an exciting experience' and 'an undertaking of uncertain outcome; a hazardous enterprise'. The US equivalent, *Websters*, also gives a series of definitions, including 'a remarkable experience', 'the encountering of risks; hazardous enterprise', and 'a bold undertaking, in which hazards are to be met and the issue hangs upon unforseen events; a daring feat'. All these definitions thus include elements of excitement, of uncertainty, and of risk and danger.

To create marketable products that can be sold repeatedly to a retail clientele so as to run a profitable business, however, each of these elements must be managed quite stringently. Clients may indeed want excitement, but they generally do not want to be terrified, and the balance between the two must be managed carefully for the particular clients and activities. Clients may want to feel that to some degree they are venturing into the uncertain and unknown, but they still want the trip to end as scheduled so that they can catch the plane home. They may also want the perception of risk, but they do not actually want to lose their equipment, or suffer illness, injury or worse. In addition, from a tour operator's perspective, such adverse outcomes would be very bad for business, not to mention insurance premiums. The management of actual and perceived risk is thus a key component of many adventure tourism operations.

The ways in which these different aspects of an adventure experience are managed depend on the type of activity, the type of clients, and the location and logistics. A 10-day ski holiday package in Colorado, USA or Queenstown, New Zealand certainly incorporates excitement, uncertainty and risk, and ski resorts are commonly included in the adventure tourism sector (Hudson, 2002). Both the circumstances and the clients, however, would commonly be very different for a 10-day exploratory heliski traverse of

Greenland, where all three adventure factors are far greater. Dry-suit diving from an expedition cruise vessel in the Antarctic is very different from resort diving in the Red Sea or even a live-aboard dive charter in the Coral Sea or the Indian or Pacific Oceans. Issues of risk and liability management are critical to most forms of commercial adventure tourism, and are therefore considered in more detail in Chapter 4.

Formal definitions of adventure tourism have been put forward by a number of authors, as outlined earlier; but to determine the scope of the current volume, it is the interpretation of these definitions, rather than their precise wording, which is most critical. In particular, there are some very large-scale components, which may or may not be included, depending on the interpretation adopted. We can usefully distinguish four different types or components, as follows. The first is independent travel which qualifies as tourism in the economic statistics sense, which involves at least some commercial transport and accommodation, and which includes at least some activities which the traveller concerned treats as adventurous. The second consists of fully packaged guided commercial adventure tours, departing on defined dates from specified gateways. The third consists of fixed-site adventure activities which are available both to tourists and local residents, but where tourists make up a significant proportion of the clientele. Ski resorts provide the best-known example. And the fourth consists of all the ancillary businesses and economic sectors which are linked to adventure tourism through various mechanisms, notably recreational equipment, adventure-branded clothing, and a significant proportion of the amenity-migrant property market, where people who have visited an area previously as adventure tourists then move there permanently as amenity migrants.

There are overlaps between each of these four categories, both in economic and social terms. An individual person may take part in adventure activities sometimes independently, and sometimes as part of a commercial tour. They may buy equipment or clothing which is used sometimes for individual recreation, sometimes to take part in a commercial adventure tour, sometimes for fixed-site adventure sports and sometimes for none of these purposes. An individual unit of residential accommodation may be available for tourists part of the year, and occupied by the owner during the remainder. Similarly, neighbouring units in strata-titled or condominium-style property developments may be used on the one hand for short-term adventure tourism accommodation and on the other hand for long-term amenity migrants.

From a tourism management perspective, however, this four-way division provides a useful classification, because management issues and tools differ markedly between them. Individual tourists travelling for adventure recreation rely principally on generic mass tourism transport and accommodation, and make use of publicly accessible areas of land and water such as national parks and national forests, and marine parks and other reserves. Unless they make up a significant proportion of visitors to a particular place, they have little influence on the transport and accommodation offered, or on the activities permitted in particular areas. Commercial adventure tour operators, in contrast, can negotiate with travel and accommodation providers on a wholesale basis; or they may construct, buy or lease their own special-purpose accommodation or transport, from back-country huts to five-star lodges, dugout canoes to expedition cruise vessels complete with helicopters. They may form industry associations and marketing syndicates, which have significantly greater political power than individual adventure travellers, especially if they form coalitions with other interested industry sectors on particular political issues such as motorised access to public protected areas. They see themselves clearly as a component of the commercial travel and tourism industry, and expect to have their views heard by government tourism portfolios.

For fixed-site adventure sports infrastructure with a strong dependence on tourists, such as ski resorts or yacht and dive marinas, the key consideration is the very large initial or staged capital investment required to establish the facility. From the perspective of the owner or operator, it is critical to maintain a continuing cash flow based on that investment at that site. This may involve: intensive marketing in conjunction with other sectors of the tourism industry; growth, including access to additional land; expansion into new revenue streams such as large-scale retail or residential property operations; or refurbishments to improve competitive position. From the perspective of the land owner or land management agency, large-scale investments in fixed-site facilities are generally only made on the basis of a long-term lease, and once the facility is operational there will be very strong pressure to permit any expansions needed to maintain profitability. Management options are thus largely restricted to modifying how the facility operates rather than whether it continues to do so. For the equipment, clothing and property development sectors, sales associated with adventure tourism are only part of their overall market portfolio, and in many cases only a minor part. Only a small proportion of 4WD vehicles, for example, are routinely used off-road; and only a small proportion of surf-branded clothing is actually worn by surfers. On the other hand, few people would buy a kayak or a snowboard unless they have planned to use it.

The main focus of this volume is on the core of the commercial adventure tourism industry, the tour operators who sell and run pre-packaged retail tour products featuring outdoor adventure activities as the key component.

This is the second of the four groups outlined above. Some of these products are all-inclusive, even providing specialist clothing as well as equipment, and wines and liqueurs with meals. At the other extreme, some provide only a guide, with the customer providing everything else and making all the travel arrangements. Some do not even provide a guide, but only an itinerary and a shuttle service. Each of these models has a market in different circumstances, depending on the needs and resources of the customers concerned. Commercial adventure tourism products, however, do not operate in isolation. Some of them are available only to clients who are skilled in the adventure activity concerned, and have learned these skills through independent adventure recreation. Some rely on fixed-site adventure sport facilities, either as a base or to provide part of the product. Most of them need specialist equipment and many also need specialist clothing, whether owned by the clients, rented from an outdoor equipment store, or provided by the tour operator. Because of these links, research literature on outdoor recreation and sports, the psychology of risk taking, occupational safety, legal liability, emergency services, wilderness medicine and many other fields may be relevant at least in part to the study of adventure tourism.

A wide range of different outdoor activities have been included in adventure tourism products. Activities on land may include hiking, mountain biking, horse riding, quad bikes and ATVs, and off-road 4WD tours. Some wildlife watching tours, whether on foot, on horseback or in safari vehicles, are also considered adventurous. A wide range of adventure tours involves kayaking, canoeing or rafting either on whitewater rivers, wilderness float trips, blackwater cave rivers, lakes or oceans. Sailing and yachting, powerboats and expedition cruise vessels, jet skis and jet boats, and a wide variety of other watercraft may also form the basis for commercial adventure tours, along with surfing, bodyboarding, sailboarding and kiteboarding. Diving and snorkelling tours are now widespread in cold as well as warm water, and a few tours operate submarines or semi-submersibles. Skiing, snowboarding, snowshoeing, sledding, dog sledding, snowmobiling, cat skiing and heliskiing are all offered as commercial adventure tours. Aerial adventure activities include parachuting, parapenting and hang gliding whether solo or tandem; ballooning, gliding, light aircraft tours, microlight aircraft, helicopters and even jetfighter aircraft. Rock climbing, ice climbing and mountaineering have also spawned an entire set of rope-based adventure activities, from abseiling and canyoning to bridge swings and bungy jumping.

Almost any kind of excitement-based activity which people have tried for private recreation, is also packaged as a commercial adventure tour. Most expensive of all is space tourism, currently within the financial reach of a very small market indeed (Page, 2007; Pizam, 2008).

Different adventure activities are packaged in very different ways as commercial adventure tourism products. Such packaging is determined partly by the practical aspects of the activity concerned; partly by the logistics of access, especially to remote areas; and partly by operators' perceptions of the preferences of their particular target markets. Some products are put together as single-day or half-day packages, which can be purchased by tourists at gateway towns or adventure destinations, essentially as an impulse buy. That is, they can be bought even on the morning of departure or at least up until the evening before, with no specialist skill or equipment requirements. There are examples of this type of product across a very wide range of adventure activities, including whitewater rafting, sea kayaking, horse riding, mountain biking, diving, ballooning, scenic flights and even heliskiing. These products may also be available as part of a larger package assembled and sold by retail tour operators with a broader portfolio of products, in addition to individual local purchases. At the other extreme, there are many multi-day commercial adventure tourism products which can only be purchased well in advance, either because supply is restricted through access or logistic issues, and demand exceeds supply; or because the tour needs a minimum number of clients in order to run, and the operator needs to know well in advance of the departure date so as to make logistic arrangements, especially for remote areas. Tours of this type are more likely to be fully inclusive, but this is not always the case.

Scale

Adventure tourism is a worldwide industry with a total annual turnover of around US$1 trillion (Buckley, 2009a). In the USA alone, the scale of the outdoor tourism sector has been estimated at US$730 billion per annum (Outdoor Industry Association, 2007). There seem to be several reasons for the strong growth of the adventure subsector within the tourism industry. Outdoor recreation in developing nations has become increasingly commercialised, as populations become more and more urbanised. Recreational equipment has become more specialised and expensive. And as large developing nations, such as China and India, have become wealthier, they have generated large domestic adventure tourism industries.

Defining the economic scale of the adventure tourism industry depends on what components are included and how they are measured (Buckley, 2009a). There are three critical considerations regarding the components included. The first is whether independent private travel for adventure recreation should be included. Most tourism statistics include travel for private purposes such as visiting friends and relatives. This component should therefore also be included in economic estimates of adventure tourism, but it is often difficult to quantify. In China, for example, it has been estimated that there are two billion domestic tourists each year (Buckley et al., 2008a), but there is apparently no English language information on what proportion of these trips might qualify as adventure. Similarly, in many developed nations, many people travel to hike, hunt, fish or photograph wildlife and scenery (Outdoor Industry Association, 2005), but there is limited information on their expenditure patterns.

The second critical consideration is whether to include fixed-site adventure sports, such as resort-based skiing and snowboarding or marina-based diving and yachting, and if so, what proportion of property and construction costs to include under the heading of adventure tourism. Most mountain and coastal resorts incorporate significant residential and retail components, and only some of this is used for adventure tourism, some of the time. The third consideration is how to account for equipment which is used only sometimes for adventure tourism, such as privately owned 4WD vehicles. None of these three questions has a right or wrong answer; they are issues of definition or accounting protocol. Each of them, however, makes a big difference to estimates of economic scale.

There are two main approaches to measure the economic scale of the adventure tourism subsector. These may be described broadly as bottom-up or top-down. The bottom-up approach relies on aggregating the retail turn-over of commercial adventure tour operators offering particular activities in particular regions. Examples are NNRC (1997) for whitewater recreation in Vermont, Fix and Loomis (1997) for mountain biking near Moab, Hoyt (2000) for whale watching worldwide, and Green and Donnelly (2003) for dive tourism in the Caribbean. These estimates generally do not include travel to the departure point of the tours concerned, or expenditure on private recreation in the same region and subsector, or the costs of privately owned equipment. They are thus generally underestimates.

The top-down approach relies on disaggregating estimates of total tourism turnover for a particular region so as to ascribe a particular propor-tion to adventure activities specifically. This is generally only possible if surveys of individual tourists are carried out to establish what activities they undertake, and if possible for how long and at what cost. Estimates derived using this approach depend heavily on the figures used to calculate the total scale of the tourism sector; and also on the reliability of data used to disag-gregate this total. For example, surveys may provide some data on what proportion of a country's residential population or inbound tourists engage in a particular adventure activity at some time, but without accurate estimates of total time or money invested.

With consistent definitions and complete data, top-down and bottom-up approaches should yield similar estimates for the economic scale of the adventure tourism subsector. In practice, however, data are generally incomplete. Both top-down and bottom-up estimates for the scale of outdoor tourism in Australia, most of which qualifies as adventure tourism, indicate that it comprises around one-quarter to one-third of the tourism industry as a whole. Estimates from other countries suggest significantly higher proportions in smaller developing nations whose economies rely heavily on international inbound tourism; and smaller proportions for heavily populated developed nations where tourism relies more heavily on urban attractions, and a much higher proportion of tourist expenditure is on food, drink and accommodation.

At a global scale, it appears that the outdoor and adventure subsectors make up about one-fifth of the global tourism and travel sector (Buckley, 2009a), which in turn comprises about 11% of the global economy (WTTC, 2007). These figures indicate that the global scale of the adventure tourism subsector is around US$1 trillion annually, and perhaps significantly more. The degree to which it has been affected by the global economic downturn in 2008/09 had not yet been estimated as this volume went to press.

LOOKING BACK

1. Is adventure tourism a recognisable industry sector of the tourism industry, and if so, how can it be defined? How is it distinguishable from outdoor sports and recreation?

2. What academic disciplines are relevant to studying adventure tourism, and how can they be applied? Which are most significant, and why?

3. How did adventure tourism originate, how has it evolved, and how has it changed in recent decades?

4. What components can potentially be counted to contribute to the total economic value of adventure tourism? Which are likely to be largest, and which are commonly included? How much does the total economic value of the subsector depend on exactly how it is defined?

5. Pick one adventure tourism activity for which economic statistics are available. Summarise those statistics and critique their likely accuracy and reliability. What techniques and approaches would potentially be available to make a more accurate and up-to-date

estimate? What alternative methods might be available to 'triangulate' or crosscheck such an estimate? Would the approaches you suggest be technically and financially feasible?

6. Estimates of the tourism value of individual sites or areas depend heavily on the types of activity carried out there. Explain why. Is this reasonable, or how could valuation techniques be improved to overcome the difficulty?

Iconic site, Colorado Grand Canyon, USA

CHAPTER 2

Geography

KEY ISSUES

- global distribution of different adventure tourism sectors
- icon sites for particular adventure tourism activities
- natural cf. human factors affecting geography
- terrain and weather
- access time and costs
- risks and rescue opportunities
- interaction of factors
- maps for particular subsectors
- factors that lead to changes in geography

CONTENTS

CHAPTER SUMMARY

Adventure tourism may be distinguished not only by skill, excitement, risk and remoteness, but also by its geography. Each adventure activity has a hierarchy of icon sites worldwide where aficionados want to practice their pursuits, whether as private recreation or commercial tourism. So too do other types of tourism, whether urban- or nature-based, but the geography of adventure tourism is as yet largely unstudied.

For the adventure sector, the icon sites are reinforced and perpetuated through specialist outdoor magazines, which publish lists and rankings. Icon sites can change quickly, partly through new discoveries and partly through fashion. More extreme sites in more remote areas with less infrastructure not only have higher risks but also higher personal and social rewards, and this drives the geographical expansion.

The icon sites for most adventure tourism activities are widely scattered worldwide, reflecting the optimum natural conditions for the activities rather than proximity to population. The majority of adventure tourism operators, however, are clustered near mainstream tourism gateways where there is a continual supply of clients. This reflects the overall structure of the adventure tourism sector, with a large number of high-volume, low-skill, low-price, short-duration products on offer in accessible areas, and a small number of low-volume, high-skill, high-price, long-duration products in remote and less accessible areas.

RESEARCH REVIEW

The geography of adventure tourism deserves academic attention in the same way as the geography of tourism and recreation more generally (Higgins, 1996; Lew and Hall, 1998; Franklin and Crang, 2001; Butler, 2004; Hall and Page, 2006). Rather little of the published research literature in adventure tourism, however, examines the global geography of the adventure activity concerned (Buckley, 2006a; Gibson, 2008). The geographies of mountain biking and ice climbing in North America have been described by Schaefers (2006) and Johnson and Godwin (2006), respectively. The global geography of commercial horse riding was outlined by Ollenburg (2006), mountaineering tourism by Hales (2006), whale watching tourism by Hoyt (2000) and shark watching tours by Carwardine and Watterson (2002). Geographic patterns, however, were not the primary focus in any of these reviews.

The opportunities and constraints on adventure tourism have been examined for particular geographic areas such as Nepal (Zurick, 1992), South Africa (Rogerson, 2007), the Mekong River Basin (Laws and Semone, 2009) and the polar regions (Snyder and Stonehouse, 2007). Small-scale geographic patterns at adventure tourism destinations have also received some attention. Cater (2006a), for example, pointed out that adventure tourism operations near Queenstown, New Zealand, are concentrated along particular corridors. Geographical aspects have sometimes been considered in analysing adventure tourism accidents (Bentley and Page,

2001) and marketing (Waitt, 1997; Jenkins, 2003). Generally, however, rather little of the research on tourism geographies has focussed on the adventure subsector.

BIG PICTURE

An adventure tourist is simply a tourist taking part in an adventure activity, i.e. one whose principal purpose is excitement. Whilst it is possible for adventure activities to take place in urban and indoor settings, the vast majority are in outdoor settings, many of them relatively remote. These settings, and particularly the terrain and climate, are integral and critical to the adventure tourism activity and product. And for most adventure tourism activities, the best opportunities occur only in a limited selection of sites worldwide. That is, adventure tourism has a geography, and that geography is a core part of the industry sector. Indeed, the geography of different adventure tourism activities is well known to tour operators, to magazine editors, and to aficionados of the activity concerned.

Given the shortage of research in this area, this chapter presents two new sets of geographical data, one global and the other at continent-wide scale, and analyses the factors which determine them. The former focuses only on key or icon sites and destinations for three adventure tourism activities. The latter covers all outdoor tour operators, regardless of company size or range of activities offered.

Global icon sites

Information on icon sites for different adventure tourism activities is available from two main sources: editorial and advertising materials in specialist magazines; and websites and printed marketing materials for individual tour operators. In particular, some companies provide, package and resell local tour products so as to offer a comprehensive global range of destinations and experiences, and their marketing materials thus give a good indication of popular sites for the activity concerned.

These sources are not comprehensive. In particular, adventure activity sites which are easily accessible from mainstream mass tourism destinations, are unlikely to be offered by specialist tour companies or featured in specialised magazines. The number of international visitors who travel to surf in Hawaii, Australia's Gold Coast or the south coast of South Africa, for example, is far larger than the number who travel to surf in Tonga or Samoa, but a larger proportion of the latter use commercial tour providers, and it is therefore these destinations which feature in their marketing materials. A map derived from such materials, therefore, provides only part of the picture. From the supply side, such a map does indeed show a commercial geography of tour operators, the places where they make their money. From the demand side, however, it underemphasises the high-volume adventure destinations, and overemphasises the low-volume and more expensive destinations aspired to by many, but visited by few.

This section examines the global geography of iconic sites for three commercial adventure tourism activities: heliskiing, surfing and whitewater paddling. General descriptions and individual case studies for these sectors were provided by Buckley (2006a). Heliskiing is taken to include heliboarding, i.e. riding a snowboard on slopes accessed by helicopter. It does not include cat skiing where access is by tracked oversnow vehicles, even though some heliski operators also run powder cat tours. Nor does it include helicopter shuttles between fixed-site ski resorts with conventional lifts and tows. Some heliski operations are based at or near such resorts, typically using the same accommodation. Others, however, are in more remote areas and operate out of their own purpose-built lodges. Some of these lodges are accessible by road, some only by helicopter. A recent addition is boat-based heliskiing where accommodation is in luxury live-aboard yachts equipped with helipads, providing access to otherwise inaccessible coastal skiing terrain such as that in the coastal ranges of western Canada and Alaska.

Surfing is taken to include tow-in options where a jetski is used to allow surfers to catch waves that would be too large and fast to paddle onto unassisted. Special surfboards with footstraps are commonly used for tow-in surfing, but once the surfer is on the wave the tow-rope is dropped and propulsion is provided by the wave and gravity alone, as for unassisted paddle-in surfing. This provides a distinction from sailboarding and kiteboarding, where the primary motive power is from the wind rather than the surf. These latter activities are therefore not included with surfing.

Whitewater paddling is a broad term, which refers to running rivers that have whitewater rapids: either in rafts, inflatable kayaks, hardshell kayaks or canoes (Buckley, 2009b). Rafts include both conventional, oval-floored designs, and catarafts with inflatable pontoons and a rigid frame. Both designs may be rigged either as paddle rafts, oar rafts, or, in a few rivers, as motorised rafts. In a paddle raft, each client has a single-bladed paddle, and they act as a team to steer and propel the raft under the direction of a guide, who sits at the rear with a long-shafted steering paddle. In an oar raft, steering and propulsion are provided by a single centrally seated rower, using long-handled oars mounted in a rowing frame. Clients in oar rafts usually ride simply as passengers. Motorised whitewater rafts, used for example on the

Colorado Grand Canyon, are large rafts with a small outboard motor mounted in an engine well at the rear of the craft and used only to provide steerage way. They are thus very different from inflatables used for ocean rescue and similar purposes, which have powerful motors capable of driving them at speed over breaking waves.

By far the majority of commercial whitewater tours use either oar or paddle rafts, depending principally on the size of the river. With suitably skilled guides, even completely inexperienced clients can safely raft rivers that include technically difficult rapids. Commercial canoe trips using open undecked canoes, in contrast, are commonly restricted to rivers with relatively mild whitewater. For hardshell kayaks, the principal commercial market is in providing guides and logistic support for relatively skilled kayakers to paddle technically demanding rivers in remote areas. This market also includes the much smaller number of skilled hardshell canoeists, who paddle craft with a similar hull to a whitewater kayak, but with a different paddle and seat configuration.

For all three of these adventure activities, different tour operators offer products for clients with different prior skill levels, but with corresponding differences in scope. Heliski operators in New Zealand, for example, offer single-day packages aimed at intermediate-level skiers with little or no previous heliskiing experience. Some of the Canadian heliski lodges, in contrast, are open only to skilled skiers and boarders who have previously visited lodges elsewhere with easier terrain. These operations are hence able to offer their clients steep descents of heavily treed slopes, or narrow couloirs between cliffs. Highly skilled guides and helicopter pilots are essential in such areas because of avalanche risks. Heliski operations in Alaska specialise in particularly steep runs, on slopes too steep to hold snow for a major slab avalanche. In such areas, however, skiers and boarders have to pick lines so as to avoid being swept off their feet by snow sloughing downslope from previous turns.

The principal icon sites for each of these three activities are shown in Figure 2.1, drawn from the author's own experience (Buckley, 2006a) and from marketing materials produced by the major specialist tour operator in these activity subsectors. The discussion below aims to elucidate the factors that set these patterns.

To understand the geography of heliskiing, we must appreciate that there are several different market subsectors searching for rather different products. To think of heliskiers and heliboarders simply as rich, skilled skiers and boarders would be inaccurate. Some, indeed, are extremely wealthy and spend most of their year heliskiing at different sites in North and South Hemispheres. Some are rich but short of time, and are attracted by opportunities

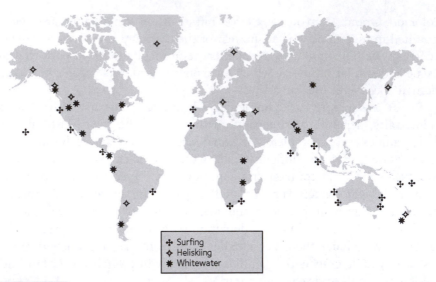

FIGURE 2.1 *Global distribution of adventure tour destinations for surfing, heliskiing and whitewater rafting.*

seen as exclusive, such as special trips in Greenland or boat-based tours in western Canada. Some are relatively unskilled resort skiers who buy a low-cost, three-run, one-day heliski package as a one-off experience. The majority, perhaps, are keen and experienced skiers and boarders who save up for a short heliski holiday once every couple of years as an opportunity to ski untracked powder away from the resort lift lines. And a few are fanatical powder skiers on a lifetime search for the world's lightest and driest snow.

In addition to skill and wealth, heliskiers may be influenced by factors such as access, security and alternative opportunities. Relative to the number of skiers, there are proportionately fewer heliski operators in the Alps than the Rockies. One reason may be that more European resorts allow lift access to unpatrolled slopes outside the resort boundaries. Another may be that the higher population density causes greater local opposition to helicopter noise. As a result, many European and also Japanese skiers go heliskiing in the Canadian Rockies by choice; and this is where the world's two largest heliski operations are based (Canadian Mountain Holidays, 2009; Mike Wiegele Helicopter Skiing, 2009). Other heliski operations in North America are based in Alaska, Utah, Nevada, Colorado, and coastal British Columbia (boat based). In the European region, there are heliski operations in the Alps and the Caucasus. Further east, there is a heliski operation in the Indian Himalayas, and others in Kamchatka in Russia's far east. In the Southern Hemisphere, there are heliski operations in the Andes near the ski resorts of

Chile and Argentina, and several high-volume operations in the South Island of New Zealand. The geography of heliski operations is hence determined by a combination of factors, including seasonality, access and safety as well as snow quality and terrain.

Similar considerations apply in commercial surf tourism. At the lower end of the skill and price range, there are surf schools catering to backpackers in various well-known surfing destinations. Many competent surfers also travel to surf, but since most surfing areas are also mainstream coastal tourism destinations, they do not need to take specialist surf tours and are not identified as surf tourists. Such destination areas include, e.g. southwest USA, west-coast Mexico and central America and parts of Chile and Brazil; the Atlantic coastlines of France and Spain; much of southeast and southwest Australia; parts of Indonesia and Noumea; and islands such as Hawaii, Tahiti, Fiji and Reunion. There are specialist surf tour companies that organise package tours to all of these areas, and also to less heavily frequented destinations such as northwest Western Australia, west-coast North Africa and Namibia, and islands such as the Maldives, Tonga and Samoa. The distinguishing feature of all these areas is that they can also be accessed by independent travelling surfers who book their own flights and make their own accommodation and local transport arrangements.

Some of the world's best-known surf breaks, however, are accessible only by boat. For these destinations, it can be difficult and time-consuming to make independent arrangements for boat hire. As a result, these areas are serviced principally by specialist surf tour operators who sell fully catered and guided package tours aboard live-aboard surf charter yachts. Such tours operate in, e.g. the Mentawai Islands off western Sumatra in Indonesia; the southern atolls of the Maldives and the Montebello Islands off the west coast of Australia. These trips are relatively expensive, but keen surfers may save up for several years in order to afford one. The attraction is straightforward: prime conditions, no crowds. For this reason, these live-aboard surf charters are also very popular with older, cash-rich, time-poor surfers.

To attract such clients, it helps to provide alternative opportunities and activities for their non-surfing family members, and this has lead to a recent proliferation of surf resorts. These resorts are commonly on tropical reef islands with good surf, where access is difficult or restricted so that the resort can offer uncrowded waves to its clients. Commonly, these resorts also offer fishing, diving, sea kayaking and similar activities for non-surfing guests and for days when the surf is poor. Examples include Tavarua, Nagigia and Lalati in Fiji; Savaii and Salani in Samoa; and recently constructed resorts in the Mentawai Islands in Indonesia. There are also icon surfing sites where conditions are too difficult and dangerous except for highly skilled surfers.

These are not yet visited by commercial tour operators, but that may change in future. Examples include waves such as Peahi in Hawaii, Mavericks in California, Teahupo'o in Tahiti, Shipstern in Tasmania, Cortez Bank in the mid-Atlantic and Cyclops in Western Australia.

Rivers with paddleable whitewater rapids occur almost worldwide wherever there is enough rain and sufficient gradient. The smaller the river, the steeper the gradient which can be paddled with a reasonable level of safety and excitement. Different rivers are used in different ways by people with different interests and equipment, and this is reflected in the geography of the subsector. Kayakers may make repeated visits to so-called park-and-play sites with one or two well-known rapids close to town, or they may travel to remote areas to make a multi-day first descent down an unknown gorge. Some commercial rafting companies offer family float trips down gentle riffles, whereas others take backpackers over technically difficult and potentially dangerous drops. Some trips take half a day, others several weeks. Some involve tight manoeuvring through technical rapids on small steep rivers, using four-person paddle rafts; others run giant oar or motor rigs down high-volume rivers with rapids that are substantial but widely spaced. Many North American rivers are so popular that there are quota and permit systems, some with lead times of months, years or even decades (Buckley, 2009b).

In developed nations, therefore, most rivers with good whitewater rapids are paddled routinely by recreational rafters and kayakers. Indeed, high-quality whitewater is one of the main attractions for many amenity migrants in North America. Whether or not particular rivers are used for commercial tourism depends partly on permit systems, but principally on the supply of tourists, particularly for one-day trips. Such short trips are commonly seen simply as one activity available at an adventure tourism destination. It is only for the longer and more famous river journeys, such as the Colorado Grand Canyon in the USA or the Nahanni in Canada, that people will plan their holiday specifically to take that trip.

In most of the developing world, the majority of commercial whitewater tour clients are overseas visitors from developed nations. Particular rivers are internationally famous for whitewater rafting and kayaking. Many commercial clients will plan their whitewater trip as part of a holiday package, though there are always some who sign up on the spot. The relative proportions commonly depend on the length of the whitewater trip. Most clients for the one-day whitewater run on the Zambezi in Zimbabwe or Zambia, for example, take these trips at short notice, since the trips operate out of the well-known multi-activity adventure destinations of Victoria Falls or Livingstone. Taking a commercial multi-day raft or kayak tour on rivers such as the Rio Futaleufu in southern Chile, or the Karnali River in Nepal, requires a specific commitment of time and travel to an area that is otherwise off the beaten tourist track. For a commercial first descent or river expedition in, e.g. Bhutan or Tibet, even more advanced planning is required.

A recent but significant addition to the geography of whitewater tourism is the growth of domestic interest within newly industrialised nations. There is now a fledgling but very fast-growing whitewater rafting and kayaking industry in countries such as China, some of the southeast Asian nations, and no doubt also in countries such as Chile and Costa Rica. Indeed, such patterns may well represent the next wave in the development of adventure tourism more generally. Just as local kids learn to surf on borrowed boards wherever international surf tourists visit regularly, they are also learning to paddle in borrowed kayaks wherever there are rivers with an established whitewater tourism industry.

The geography of whitewater tourism can thus be understood by considering it in several different segments as follows. The best-known, highest-volume operations are single-day adrenalin runs near multi-activity adventure tourism destinations such as Cairns in Australia, Queenstown in New Zealand, Victoria Falls in Zimbabwe, Chamonix in Switzerland or Moab in the USA. There are internationally famous multi-day river trips such as the Grand Canyon of the Colorado. And there are rivers in more remote areas, which are run commercially only in semi-expedition style, with departures only on demand, and equipment brought in only as required.

Patterns at continental scale

The second set of data is more restricted in geographical scope but more comprehensive in its coverage of operators. For the past 15 years, we have maintained a database of outdoor tour operators throughout Australia. This was originally established in the early 1990s by searching electronic versions of classified telephone directories for all states and regions. Every few years, we sent a mail questionnaire to all operators on this database, so as to track changes in the economic scale of the sector. As part of this exercise we can identify turnover in the sector and adjust the database accordingly. This provides information that we can use to map the geography of adventure tourism within one continent. A similar exercise could be carried out for other continents, but to date no such maps seem to have been published.

The Australian database provides three relevant sets of information. First, the database as a whole includes the addresses of company headquarters, so we can map where they are based. For small, single-site, single-activity operators, the base is commonly at the operating site, or at least the nearest gateway town. For large, multi-site, multi-activity operators, however, the address of the headquarters gives no indication of the operational areas, so this subset contains an inherent bias. The other two subsets derive only from respondents to the survey, i.e. a sample of the total. For these, we know what types of outdoor adventure activity they offer, and the actual operating site or sites identified to various levels of precision. We also have data on the annual turnover of the survey respondents and *per capita* prices charged for different activities. These data are sufficiently robust to map the main operating areas for adventure tour operators throughout Australia and to compare annual revenue and number of operations at a state-by-state level with confidence.

The relative proportions of operators and revenue in each state are presented in Table 2.1. The main patterns may be summarised as follows: The eastern states of Queensland, New South Wales and Victoria have the largest numbers of operators. The larger states, namely Queensland, New South Wales, South Australia and the Northern Territory generate most revenue. Western Australia is a conspicuous exception, but this reflects the arid climate and low population density across much of the state. Relative to area, the two smallest states of Victoria and Tasmania have by far the most active outdoor tourism sectors.

The main areas for outdoor tourism operations in Australia are shown in Figure 2.2. These operating areas are known only for survey respondents, not the entire national database. They are approximate, since different respondents specified their operating areas with greater or lesser precision. Each

| Table 2.1 | Proportions of Outdoor Tour Operators in Each Australian State and Territory |

State or Territory	Area 10^6 km^2	Area % Total	Percent of Operators	Ratio to Area	Percent of Revenue	Ratio to Area
Qld	1.7	22	20	0.9	24	1.1
NSW*	0.8	10	21	2.1	18	1.8
Vic	0.24	3	21	7.00	11	3.7
SA	1.0	13	13	1.0	19	1.5
WA	2.5	33	15	0.45	7	0.2
NT	1.3	17	4	0.24	18	1.1
Tas	0.07	1	6	6.0	3	3.0
Australia	7.7	100	100	1.0	100	1.0

*Including Australian Capital Territory

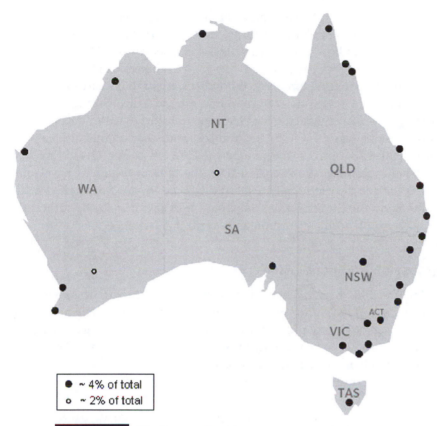

FIGURE 2.2   *Distribution of outdoor tour operators in Australia.*

solid circle represents roughly the same proportion of total operators. Note that these are not weighted by size, so the map shows the distribution of tour operators, not tour clients. In some parts of the country, such as the area around Cairns from Port Douglas to Mission Beach, the circle does indeed represent a relatively precise location. In others, such as outback New South Wales, the circle is shown at the approximate centroid of a broad geographical region. Similarly, the circle in Tasmania represents Tasmania as a whole, not only the central highlands. Some of the operators included in this figure offer tours that are more nature oriented, others more adventure oriented. Most include components such as hiking, biking, climbing, horse riding, or four-wheel-driving in scenic areas.

Three main patterns may be discerned. Firstly, the distribution of outdoor tour operators broadly matches that of the Australian population. Most of them are east of the Great Divide, the low mountain spine that runs roughly north–south a little inland of the eastern coastline. Secondly, there are certain areas that support a high level of adventure activity, despite a relatively small local population. Cairns, northeastern New South Wales, the northern tablelands of New South Wales, and especially the Kimberley region in northwest Western Australia provide good examples. And thirdly, despite the national marketing emphasis on outback Australia, relatively few tours actually operate there. There are a few around Alice Springs in central Australia, a few in the goldfields area near Kalgoorlie in Western Australia, a few in South Australia's Flinders Ranges, and some in inland New South Wales, which in practice means anything inland of the Great Divide. In a nutshell, this map shows that whilst Australia does indeed have tourist regions outside the metropolitan areas, they tend to be where there is a range of different tourist attractions, such as north Queensland, rather than a single type of scenic attraction as in central Australia.

Discussion and conclusions

As illustrated by the activities outlined above, adventure tourism has a well-defined geography, and for many adventure activities that geography is critical to understand how the sector operates. People prefer to go to particular places for various adventure activities. These places are not perceived as equally valuable; indeed, for most adventure activities there is a global hierarchy of icon sites. The adventure tourism industry makes its money principally by getting people to those sites safely and comfortably, and by providing accommodation, catering, equipment and local expertise once they arrive.

The hierarchy of icon sites for each activity depends ultimately on particular features of the natural terrain and climate. At any given time, however, only some of these sites support commercial adventure tourism operations, and only a small proportion support high-volume adventure tourism. The factors that determine which particular potential sites are actually in use at any given time are social, economic and political: human rather than natural. They include, for example, the cost and time in getting to the area; the variety of alternative activities available there; industry safety standards and political security; the standard of accommodation and service available; and information available to potential clients, including fashion as well as technical aspects. There are various feedback mechanisms, both positive and negative, as the reputations of individual places wax or wane and tourist numbers increase or decrease.

Some adventure tour operators specialise in low-price, high-volume, short-duration trips, which are only feasible once sites are well known and heavily patronised. Others specialise in high-price, low-volume, longer-duration trips to more remote areas, which appeal only to aficionados of the activity concerned. If an area becomes generally popular and accessible, such clients will want to go somewhere else. These companies specialise in overcoming local political and logistic difficulties so as to provide their clients with an efficient, reliable, safe and comfortable trip in areas where people without local knowledge and contacts would find it difficult to obtain any of these things.

Local knowledge, however, can only take one so far. In some countries there are wars, active terrorists, local unrest, government bans on foreigners or high levels of criminal violence. Even adventure tourists are likely to avoid such destinations. As global political patterns change, therefore, particular countries that may offer the terrain and climate for specific adventure activities can move on and off the map of places which people actually want to visit. During Idi Amin's violent dictatorship, for example, Uganda was largely off limits for tourists of any kind. Currently, however, Uganda's White Nile has become a very popular destination for whitewater rafting and kayaking. During the Maoist insurrection in Nepal, the country's well-known whitewater rivers lost popularity because of political unrest. Until recently, permits to run rivers in China were very difficult to obtain. Now they are easier to get, but still severely overpriced. In a few years, perhaps, it may become much easier to obtain permission. Meanwhile, however, most of the best whitewater in China is being dammed for hydroelectric power – as in many countries including Chile, Australia, New Zealand and the USA. The geography of adventure tourism is not independent of other sectors.

Results presented above are merely a first sample of the kind of geographical data and analysis potentially available for the adventure tourism industry. The main aim is simply to show that a geographical approach is useful and indeed long overdue. Visitor statistics identifying countries of origin and destination provide only part of the picture. The physical and political features of the places where adventure activities are, or can be, practiced, are a more fundamental consideration.

The geography of adventure tourism, as outlined above, is not particularly complex, but nor is it trivial. A geographic approach is valuable in analysing product patterns, financial flows and social situations in the adventure tourism sector. And to analyse the geographic patterns in any adventure tourism activity, it requires some understanding of the different types of participants and what they want; the natural environments they need and where to find them; and the various social, political and economic factors that block or facilitate travel to each of these potential destination areas. This is a fruitful area for further research.

LOOKING BACK

1. Pick any specific adventure tourism activity and describe where it is carried out both (a) globally and (b) in the continent or country where you live yourself. What factors influence these patterns, both (a) physical geographic factors and (b) human geographic factors? Is the geography of that activity, both in your own country or continent and globally, likely to change in future or remain stable, and why?

2. It has been suggested that adventure tourists are less concerned than mainstream urban or resort tourists with regard to risks associated with travel in general, such as disease, terrorism and political unrest. Do you think this is correct? And if so, give examples. How does this factor affect the geography of adventure tourism?

3. How important is language to the geography of adventure tourism? Is it a significant barrier, or can commercial operators overcome it completely?

Baoshan Stone Town, China – where
Genghis Khan crossed the Yangtze

Products, Pricing, and Marketing

KEY ISSUES

Products and pricing

- size of individual adventure tour operators

- business models for successful companies

- design of commercially successful products in different activity sectors

- in different countries and cultural contexts

- for different socioeconomic market segments

- price structures for different products

- relation between prices and time/cash calculus

- relation between prices and degree of risk and remoteness

- price patterns between and within activity subsectors

Marketing

- who buys adventure tour products — cash-rich, time-poor cf time-rich, cash-poor

- crossovers between activities, and between recreation and tourism

- crosslinks between adventure tourism, clothing, equipment, and entertainment

- matching product design, market segment, and marketing medium

- broad advertising: television programmes, newspaper editorial, magazines, equipment catalogues, product placements
- focused marketing: traditional travel agents, www websites, email push lists, tour product catalogues, marketing syndicates, social networking sites

CHAPTER SUMMARY

Products and pricing

To test whether commercial tourism products in different adventure activity sectors have different functional characteristics, I took part in tours offered by 75 operators worldwide and analysed: price per person per day, duration, prior skill requirements, remoteness, group size and client-to-guide ratios. There is an enormous range of variation. Some activities overlap but some are clearly distinguishable, on commercial as well as operational criteria. Products can be arranged on a scale from low-volume, high-difficulty, high-price to high-volume, low-difficulty, low-price. There are recognisable signatures for some subsectors, but not all.

Prices per person per day range from less than a hundred to over a thousand dollars, and in a few cases higher still, depending on equipment needed, remoteness, the degree of luxury, and the client-to-guide ratio. Product structures range from little more than a set of directions, to all-inclusive luxury in exclusive privately owned surroundings. There are discernible recurrent patterns, for example, in tour duration and client-to-guide ratio, for some activities in some areas, but by no means all.

Marketing

Marketing strategies amongst adventure tourism enterprises reflect the pyramidal structure of the sector. High-volume, low-skill, low-price, short-duration products on offer at highly accessible mass-market adventure tourism destinations rely heavily on pavement advertising, shopfront sales, and walk-in customers, boosted by brochures distributed liberally in bars, backpacker hostels, hotel lobbies, and airport arrivals halls. In some destinations they cross-market extensively with other adventure tour operators, with outdoor equipment stores, and with nightclubs and music venues.

Low-volume, high-skill, high-price, long-duration adventure tours in remote areas, however, rely heavily on repeat business and word-of-mouth referrals from former clients, with selective mail and email solicitations and lead times of up to a year. Cross-marketing occurs principally where guides work for several different operators, who may offer different activities. Between these extremes, adventure tours are sold by much the same means as other types of travel products, using catalogues, trade shows, advertisements and editorial coverage in magazines, agent familiarisation trips, and so on. For some activities there is also a degree of cross-marketing with the fashion and entertainment industries, but at a very broad level.

RESEARCH REVIEW

Products and pricing

Academic research in adventure tourism has generally been slow to examine the changing structure, pricing and marketing of actual retail adventure tourism products (Buckley, 2006a, 2007a, 2009a). Indeed, this applies even for non-commercial adventure recreation (More and Averill, 2003). There is a growing research literature on specific commercial adventure activities at particular geographic locations, but the focus is on human experiences rather than product design. Even if the product itself is not the primary concern, however, a number of such studies describe the operational aspects to provide context, and a small proportion address the product structure directly.

Outdoor adventure pursuits, as activities rather than products, have been analysed over an extended period by authors such as Ewert (1989). The social processes by which such activities are commercialised and commodified, the roles of guides in such processes, and the ways in which commercial tours have become integrated into private recreational patterns have been addressed by, e.g. Johnson and Edwards (1994), Livet (1997), Beedie and Hudson (2003), Hudson and Beedie (2006), Smith (2006), and Cater and Cloke (2007).

Most available analyses of terrestrial adventure tour products and subsectors fall into five categories: mountaineering and climbing; skiing and snowboarding; river rafting and kayaking; riding and biking; and wildlife watching. Global reviews of mountaineering tourism and ice-climbing were presented by Hales (2006) and Johnson and Godwin (2006), respectively. More localised analyses are available for: the Alps (Wyder, 1987; Giard, 1997; Bourdeau et al., 2002); the Himalayas (Zurick, 1992; Bisht, 1994; Kayastha, 1997); New Zealand (Booth and Cullen, 2001; Davidson, 2002); and Japan (Suzuki and Kawamura, 1994). The fixed-site ski industry was described by Hudson (2002); the heliski industry by Buckley (2006a, pp. 251–234); and the cross-country skiing sector by Buckley (2006a, pp. 235–244). Skiing in

Sweden was analysed by Fredman and Heberlein (2003). Mountain biking tourism was reviewed by Schaefers (2006), with an additional case study by Goeft and Alder (2000). River rafting and kayaking has been described by Arnould and Price (1993) and Buckley (2006a, pp. 32–110; 2009b). Camel riding tours were described by Shackley (1996a), and horse riding tours reviewed by Ollenburg (2006). Wildlife tourism is considered further in Chapter 9; product descriptions include Shackley (1996b); Sournia (1996) in West and Central Africa; a thorough analysis by Lamprey and Reid (2004) for the Maasai Mara area of East Africa; operational descriptions of a number of southern African products by Buckley (2006a, pp. 352–379; 2009a); and an analysis of tiger watching in India by Sekhar (2003).

Polar tourism has some similarities with high-altitude mountain tourism, because of the cold; and some similarities with marine tourism, because the majority of tours use expedition cruise ships for access and accommodation (Buckley, 2006a, pp. 153–161). The most comprehensive review is a volume edited by Snyder and Stonehouse (2007), with chapters by Bertram et al. (2007), Lamers et al. (2007), and Landau and Splettstoesser (2007) addressing product structure specifically.

Marine tourism more generally has been examined in several recent books (see Chapter 10); notably Cater and Cater (2007), Jennings (2003, 2007a), and Higham and Lück (2008). Diving and dive sites have been described in: Hawaii (Tabata, 1989); the Caribbean (Hawkins and Roberts, 1992, 1993, 1994; Hawkins et al., 1999; Williams and Polunin, 2000); Egypt (Prior et al., 1995); Spain (Mundet and Ribera, 2001); and Australia (Davis and Tisdell, 1995, 1996, 1998; Davis et al., 1997). Whale shark watching tours in Australia are described by Davis et al. (1997), and snorkelling to see stingrays by Shackley (1998a). Boat tours to watch large saltwater estuarine crocodiles in northern Australia were described by Ryan (1998) and Ryan and Harvey (2000). Whale watching has been examined in: western Canada (Duffus and Dearden, 1993; Duffus, 1996); the St Lawrence River in eastern Canada (Blane and Jaakson, 1994); Australia (Scott and Laws, 2004); New Zealand (Constantine, 1999; Curtin, 2003); Ireland (Berrow, 2003); and Scotland (MacLellan, 1999; Parsons et al., 2003; Woods-Ballard et al., 2003). Surf tourism has also received some attention, e.g. from Buckley (2003a, 2003b), Dolnicar and Fluker (2003), Lazarow et al. (2008), and Corne (2009).

Marketing

Tourism marketing is an extensive and heavily researched topic (Holloway, 2004; Fyall and Garrod, 2005; Goeldner and Brent Ritchie, 2005; Cooper et al., 2008), but little of this literature addresses the marketing of adventure tourism products specifically. Buckley and Araujo (1997) found that around 100 tourism businesses in the Gold Coast area, a major international beach holiday destination in Australia, relied heavily on brochures and flyers as a large part of their marketing campaign. About 15% of these featured outdoor adventure tourism products, particularly four-wheel-drive and horse riding tours. The former, in particular, featured illustrations of landscapes, plants, and animals. Page et al. (2006) examined the promotion of adventure tourism in Scotland, and Buckley et al. (2006a) described the proliferation of the term 'adventure capital' as a marketing device. Cater (2006a) and Schott (2007) examined the marketing of adventure tourism in the self-proclaimed world adventure capital of Queenstown, New Zealand; and Blumberg (2008) described how a mountain guide visiting from Switzerland successfully transplanted the Queenstown multi-sport adventure destination concept to Interlaken. Johnson and Godwin (2006), however, argue that the town of Chamonix in the European Alps has provided an extensive array of commercially guided outdoor adventure activities for longer than either Queenstown or Interlaken. Lynch et al. (2007) noted that many adventure tourism enterprises are short-lived, and Buckley (2008a) examined how a commercial tourism marketing publication has taken up concepts such as adventure, cultural, and ecotourism or responsible tourism.

BIG PICTURE

Products and pricing

This chapter examines price, duration, group size, skill requirements, and remoteness for a set of commercial adventure tours offered by 75 operators worldwide and involving various activities and locations (Table 3.1). The data are derived from on-site field audits of the products concerned. The individual products were described in detail by Buckley (2006a), and the approach by Buckley (2007a). The parameters examined are: price, duration, remoteness, group size, client-to-guide ratio, and prior skill requirements. These are all considerations which may affect purchasing decisions in various ways.

A total of 78 individual audits are available, but there are <10 individual tour products for any 1 activity type, and the selection of products in each subsector is not necessarily representative. Some of the products considered, for example, include upmarket accommodation and meals, whereas others only include the activity itself. Prices are also influenced by currency exchange rates. Results are therefore presented principally in a graphical manner, with limited statistical analysis as appropriate.

Table 3.1	Adventure Tour Operators Audited

Adrift, Uganda	Africa Wildlife Safaris, Uganda
AJ Hackett Bungy, New Zealand	Allardice's Ultimate Descents, Nepal
And Beyond, South Africa	And Beyond, Tanzania
And Beyond, Zanzibar	Aurora Expeditions, Svalbard
Balloon Down Under, Australia	Blackfeather, Canada
Boojum Expeditions, Mongolia	Canadian Mountain Holidays, Canada
Carlos Colares, Brazil	Delphis Diving, Maldives
Dhonveli Beach Resort, Maldives	Earth Science Expeditions, China
Endless River Adventures, Costa Rica	Expediciones Chile, Chile
Expeditions Inc, USA	Explore Kamchatka, Russia
Explorer Shipping, Antarctica	Harris Mountains Heliski, New Zealand
Himachal Helicopter Skiing, India	John Gray's Sea Canoe, Thailand
Jump the Beach, Australia	Kaikoura Helicopters, New Zealand
Kenya Wildlife, Kenya	King Dive, Australia
Lalati Dive Resort, Fiji	Last Descents, Tibet
Mentawai Sanctuary, Indonesia	Methven Heliski, New Zealand
Mike Wiegele Heli Skiing, Canada	Nagigia Surf Resort, Fiji
National Outdoor Leadership School, Alaska	National Outdoor Leadership School, Australia
Natural Habitat Adventures, Canada	Natural High, New Zealand
Ningaloo Blue, Australia	OARS, USA
Ocean River, New Zealand	Oregon Peak, USA
Paddy Pallins, Australia	Queenstown Rafting, New Zealand
Quicksilver Dive, Australia	Raft and Rainforest, Australia
Raging Thunder, Australia	Raleigh Expeditions, Australia
Rangitata Rafts, New Zealand	Reynella Station, Australia
Ride World Wide, Patagonia	Rivers Fiji, Fiji
Salani Surf Resort, Samoa	Savaii Surfaris, Samoa
Shangri-La River Expeditions, Tibet	Shearwater Adventures, Zimbabwe
Southern Sea Ventures, Australia	Southern Sea Ventures, Fiji
Southern Sea Ventures, Norway	Surtrek, Ecuador
Taka Dive, Australia	Team Gorky, Russia
Tiger Tops Karnali, India	Tyax Heliskiing, Canada
Ultimate Descents, New Zealand	Ultimate Descent, Nepal
Uncharted Africa Safaris, Botswana	Walindi Resort, Papua New Guinea
Wilderness Safaris, Botswana	Wilderness Safaris, Namibia
Wild Rivers, USA	Wilderness Safaris, South Africa
Wildwater Adventures, Australia	Willis's Walkabouts, Australia
World Expeditions, Australia	World Expeditions, Nepal
Yacu Amu, Ecuador	

Note: Countries indicate location of tours audited, not necessarily company headquarters. Updated from Buckley (2007a).

Figure 3.1 plots price per person per day in US$ against tour duration in days or weeks, using a log–log scale. Most of the major adventure activities can be distinguished broadly along these two product dimensions, but there is some overlap, especially near the centre of each scale. Figure 3.2 shows the mean price per day, ±1 standard deviation, for the nine activities where five or more products were audited. The various water-based activities such as whitewater rafting and kayaking (including longer river journeys), sea kayaking, and surfing have similar prices per day. Diving is somewhat more expensive, because of the need for specialist equipment including compressors. Heliboarding/skiing is significantly more expensive, because helicopters are used effectively full-time. The price difference between the

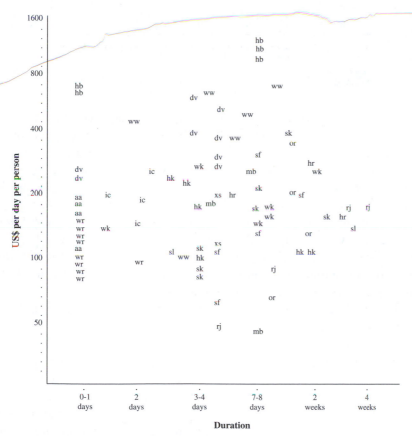

Codes: aa, aerial adventures; dv, diving; hb, heliboarding/skiing; hk, hiking; hr, horse riding; ic, ice climbing; mb, mountain biking; or, off-road driving; rj, river journeys; sf, surfing; sk, seakayaking; wk, whitewater kayaking; wr, whitewater rafting; ww, wildlife watching; xs, cross-country skiing. Data from Buckley (2007a)

FIGURE 3.1 *Prices and durations for adventure tourism products audited.*

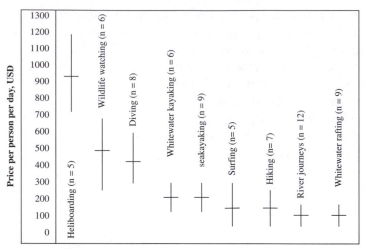

Note: Error bars show one standard deviation either side of the mean price per day for the activity concerned. From Buckley (2007a).

FIGURE 3.2 *Prices per day, means and standard deviations.*

heliboard tours ($n = 5$) and the various raft, kayak and surf tours ($n = 33$) is significant at $p < 0.01$ (Buckley, 2007a). This applies even though some of the heliboard tours are introductory one-day trips at the lower end of the market and some of the raft and kayak tours are top-end trips involving helicopter access or expedition boat support. Interestingly, the wildlife watching tours are also expensive (Figure 3.2): much more so, for example, than the hiking tours. This is because most of these particular tours involve small groups with highly skilled guides and trackers viewing large and potentially dangerous animals in relatively remote areas, with specialised transport and upmarket accommodation. These are the types of wildlife-watching experiences which are marketed as adventure tourism.

Remoteness and prior skill requirements for each major activity are summarised in Figure 3.3. Remoteness is characterised by difficulty of access. Prior skill requirements provide an indirect measure of risk. For these parameters, the differences between individual products within each activity subsector generally outweigh the differences between subsectors, so the distinction between subsectors is weak. The same subsector may include tours which offer first ascents, descents or traverses under dangerous and difficult conditions; and tours which include a day's training for complete novices in comparative safety.

Group size and client-to-guide ratios are summarised in Table 3.2. Group sizes listed are for an entire tour run by the same company at the same place on the same day for clients who have purchased the same

| Activity | Prior Skills | | | | | | | Remoteness, Access | | | | | | |
Note: prior skills and remoteness refer to commercial tours available, not private trips	World class	Highly skilled	Advanced/certified	Basic skill	Beginner instructions	Learn on tour	Nil needed- passenger	Local, near town	Developed, rural park	Backcountry	Developing, road	Hike, fly or boat in	Rarely visited	Uninhabited
River expeditions	*	*	*	*	*	*				*	*	*	*	
Whitewater kayaking	*	*	*	*	*			*	*	*	*	*	*	*
Whitewater rafting		*	*	*	*	*	*	*	*	*	*	*	*	*
Seakayaking			*	*	*	*			*	*	*	*	*	*
Sailing			*	*	*	*	*	*	*	*	*	*	*	*
Expedition cruises							*						*	*
Diving	*	*	*	*	*			*	*	*	*	*	*	*
Surfing	*	*	*	*	*			*	*	*	*	*	*	*
Heliski/snowboard	*	*	*							*	*	*	*	*
Cross-country skiing		*	*	*	*					*	*	*	*	*
Ice climbing		*	*	*	*				*	*	*	*	*	*
Mountaineering		*	*	*	*					*	*	*	*	*
Hiking and bushwalking			*	*	*					*	*	*		
Horse riding		*	*	*	*			*	*	*	*			
Mountain biking		*	*	*	*				*	*	*			
Off-road safaris			*	*	*	*	*		*		*	*	*	
Wildlife watching	*	*	*	*	*	*	*			*	*	*	*	
Ballooning								*	*		*			
Skydiving		*					†*		†*				*	*
Scenic/heli flights								*	*		*			
Bungy jumping								*	*					

† tandem jumps
From Buckley (2007a)

FIGURE 3.3 *Skill requirements and remoteness.*

product. The clients may be divided into subsidiary groups for operational purposes. Thus, group size for a rafting trip includes all the rafts travelling together, and group size for a heliski trip includes all the subgroups shuttled by the same machines in the same area.

Two thirds of these tours take 6–20 clients at a time. Only 13% take 5 clients or fewer, and 22% or so take 21 clients or more. The small-group tours are generally: those that need little equipment, such as hiking; those where equipment limits group size, such as helicopter tours; or those with prior skill requirements, such as whitewater kayaking. The large-group tours are: either those which can readily replicate smaller units to form a large group, such as rafting; or those where equipment necessarily has a large passenger capacity, such as expedition cruise vessels. For the data in Table 3.2, the number of tour products with group size over 20 is significantly higher for rafting than for kayaking, river expeditions and sea kayaking (Buckley, 2007a).

Client-to-guide ratios are determined principally by risk, difficulty, and skill requirements. Some trips take one or more guides for each client, as well as

Table 3.2	Group Sizes and Client-to-Guide Ratios							
Activity		**Group Size**				**Client-to-Guide Ratio**			
(*n* > 5 only)	*n*	1–5	6–20	21–50	>50	<1	2–4	5–9	>10
Whitewater rafting	17	1	2	14	0	0	2	15	0
Whitewater kayaking	9	1	5	3	0	0	8	1	0
River expeditions	10	1	4	5	0	3	2	5	0
Sea kayaking	8	1	7	0	0	0	3	4	1
Diving	9	1	6	1	1	0	3	2	4
Surfing	5	0	5	0	0	0	0	2	3
Heliski/board	5	0	3	2	0	0	3	1	1
Wildlife watching	6	0	6	0	0	0	5	0	1
Total	69	5	38	25	1	3	26	30	11

From Buckley (2007a).

a support crew. For trips with less demanding skill requirements where the main function of the guide is to manage logistics, there may only be one guide per 20 or 30 clients; though such trips may perhaps barely qualify as adventure tourism. For a wide range of activities and trips, the characteristic client-to-guide ratio is between 5:1 and 7:1; either because this represents the capacity of an individual vehicle, helicopter or boat, or because this is about as many people as a single guide can keep an eye on at any one moment. Client-to-guide ratios are significantly higher for rafting than kayaking (Buckley, 2007a).

The results presented above indicate that most adventure tourism activities have a recognisable commercial signature as measured by duration and price per person per day. Some, however, show a bimodal pattern. Heliski operations in the Himalayas and the Canadian Rockies, for example, are all designed around a 1-week all-inclusive package, irrespective of operator; but those in New Zealand are sold as single-day trips.

The main bulk of the adventure market consists of high-volume, low-difficulty products for unskilled clients. The leading edge, in contrast, consists of low-volume, high-cost products which require prior skills, involve significant individual risk for clients, and operate in more remote and inhospitable areas (Buckley, 2004a). Even the most skilled and remote commercial tours, however, are overshadowed by adventure recreation exploits and one-off expeditions. Between these extremes there is an enormous diversity in the design, duration, places, and prices for different adventure tours. Even so, however, there are identifiable patterns in price and duration, and in group size and client-to-guide ratio, for different adventure activities.

The results presented here consider each of the main product characteristics independently. This is an exploratory approach necessitated by the relatively small sample sizes. Skill requirements, group size, client-to-guide ratio, access and remoteness, duration, equipment, and accommodation may all be interrelated and all can affect the price per person per day. These interrelationships may be apparent for individual tour products, but such data are somewhat anecdotal. To test the relationships between product characteristics in a statistically reliable sense will require a larger set of data from specific activity subsectors, so as to apply standard multivariate analytical techniques.

Marketing

The range of different adventure tourism products is now so wide that there are options to suit almost all sectors of the global tourism market: young or old, rich or poor, skilled or not. As a result, a wide range of different marketing techniques are required and are in fact in use, for different types of products (Table 3.3). Most of the actual marketing approaches used in adventure tourism are much the same as in the rest of the tourism sectors (Holloway, 2004; Fyall and Garrod, 2005; Goeldner and Brent Ritchie, 2005; Cooper et al., 2008), but there are several features of particular interest, as follows:

1. Adventure tourism is a highly heterogeneous sector, incorporating a range of very different activities which appeal to very different markets. For activities requiring particular skills or qualifications, such as SCUBA diving, marketing strategies tend to focus on media and messages that are specific to that activity subsector.

2. Since many commercial adventure tour operators now offer a portfolio of different activities, there is also a degree of cross-marketing between different specialist activities; and there are approaches which aim to market the company first, the particular activity second.

3. Many other products are also sold using an adventure theme: equipment and clothing; food and tobacco; magazines and DVDs; television programmes and nightclub entertainment; and boats, cars, and property. As a result, there is often cross-marketing between adventure tourism and these other sectors.

Table 3.3 Marketing Methods for Adventure Tours

Components of strategy
- Identifying market sector: wealth, proximity, size, skills, or qualifications
- Prices, packages, product features cf competitors
- Communication with potential customers
- Booking, payment, delivery, evaluation

Features of product
- Type of activity or activities
- Geographic location
- Company reputation and reliability
- Scale of operations
- Seasonality
- Components included
- Upmarket or down-market positioning, exclusivity, market or accessibility
- Mark-up and ability to support sales commissions

Advertising approaches
- Retail shopfronts at adventure destinations
- Mainstream agents, brochures, trade shows, packagers
- Electronic agents (Expedia®, etc.)
- Mail-outs, email lists
- Websites, online enquiry, and booking options
- Editorial and endorsements including magazines, newspapers, TV
- Paid advertisements in specialist recreational or lifestyle magazines
- Co-sponsored advertising, e.g. regional or destination tour brochures or maps
- Distribution of flyers at adventure destinations
- Syndicated marketing, e.g. trade associations, branded collections
- Cross-marketing, e.g. with equipment, clothing, events, clubs
- Social media, e.g. travel blog and post sites, social utilities
- Competitions, telemarketing, etc.

Features of markets
- Geographic location, access
- Relative wealth
- Skills, qualifications, fitness
- Comfort and safety requirements
- Degree of exclusivity
- Lead time for booking decisions
- Prior bookings with same company

Table 3.3	Marketing Methods for Adventure Tours—cont'd

Booking, payment, follow-up
- Shopfront retail or via agents
- Mailed forms, bank transfers
- Online booking and payment
- Pre- and post-tour communications and follow-up
- Evaluating satisfaction, soliciting repeat bookings

Attracting attention to a website
- Search engines
- Links from other sites
- Postings, list servers, and blogs
- Email lists
- Print media, advertisements, and editorial
- Commercial directories, trade associations
- Social networking sites, especially YouTube®, Facebook®

Summarised and adapted from Buckley (2009a).

4. Within the clientele for each particular adventure activity, there is an enormous socioeconomic range from very cash-rich, time-poor to very cash-poor, time-rich. Different companies therefore devise different products to cater to clients with different demands, expectations, and abilities to pay for them; and these different products need different marketing approaches.

At one extreme, many of the more down-market adventure tourism products, which operate out of well-known adventure tourism destinations are marketed principally by distributing low-key printed leaflets in places frequented by backpackers. Such places may include particular hostels, cafes, bars or clubs, and transport hubs. This is the same mechanism, in fact, which has long been used to market backpacker accommodation in tourist gateway towns. Such products may also be marketed through backpacker magazines and internet sites. Since most of these are high-volume, low-skill, low-priced products, the key to a successful marketing strategy is to reach a large number of potential clients, cheaply.

At the upper extreme of the market, in contrast, the key strategy is to reach potential clients who have the ability to pay for the products on offer, so that sales staff do not waste time in responding to enquiries from people who will be unable to afford the product concerned. In addition, exclusivity is one of the characteristics used to help sell such products. There are thus several efficient marketing strategies for the most upmarket adventure tours. The first is for marketing campaigns simply to target wealthy frequent travellers in general, e.g. via upmarket travel and lifestyle magazines, or the top tiers of airline frequent-flier programmes. The second is to target adventure tourists who are already experienced in the activity concerned, but at a slightly lower level, and try to sell them more expensive products. The prime market for expensive exploratory heliski tours, for example, is the existing clientele of fixed-site, lodge-based heliski operations. And the third approach is to target the clients of competing companies, and try to persuade them to shift allegiance. Repeat business and word-of-mouth referrals from past clients may also be critical.

One of the key considerations in marketing many types of adventure tourism activities is that all but the most basic commercial tour products are only accessible to clients with prior skills in the adventure recreation activity concerned. The adventure tourism industry as a whole, however, also relies on high-volume, low-priced products which do not require any prior skills. One of the keys to structuring successful products is firstly to match the skills of the clients to the difficulty of the activity, and secondly to make up for deficiencies in client skills by using highly skilled guides.

The most recent development in electronic marketing of commercial adventure tourism products is the deliberate use of web logs or blogs, and social networking utilities. Sites such as Facebook® allow companies to establish a corporate profile, and a number of adventure tour operators have done so. Blogs need more active attention. According to Buckley (2009a, p. 70): 'With the advent of travel blogs and online travel recommendation and review sites, electronic marketing has gained an additional layer of complexity. It is no longer enough to maintain an attractive website. Tourism operations must now monitor websites worldwide to maximise the number of positive reports and recommendations, and minimise, remove or counteract any negative press or complaints. Successful operations are typically cross-listed in the websites of: regional and national tourism marketing organisations; activity-specific travel review agencies and magazines; specialist websites for high-yield clients such as yoga retreats or honeymoon planners; and generalised electronic travel booking agencies such as Expedia®. They continually search for opportunities to have favourable reviews posted in online versions of travel magazines, and when they are successful they also feature these links and reports in their own websites. They submit their own comments to semi-formalised travel blog sites such as Lonely Planet's Thorn Tree® site. The aim is to generate continuing positive feedback: the more websites contain favourable comment, the more likely that other websites will also include favourable comments. Some specialist ecotourism operators have become highly skilled at this approach.'

ACKNOWLEDGEMENTS

Parts of this chapter have been published previously in the Elsevier journal *Tourism Management* (Buckley, 2007a).

CASE STUDY 3.1: Adventure Travel Trade Association

The Adventure Travel Trade Association (2009), ATTA, is an offshoot of the former US-based Adventure Travel Society (ATS), started by Jerry Mallett in the 1980s. The Adventure Travel Trade Association runs a large annual adventure travel trade show in either the USA or Canada, advertised as the Adventure Travel World Summit (2009). It also publishes an annual *Adventure Industry Research Roundup*. Adventure Travel Trade Association currently has around 380 members, including tour operators, tourism promotion agencies, equipment and clothing suppliers, travel agents, and travel magazines.

CASE STUDY 3.2: The Adventure Collection

The Adventure Collection is a self-applied syndicated brand name adopted by a group of tourism companies based in North America and operating worldwide, which aim or claim to provide particularly high-standard products in the adventure tourism sector, broadly defined. Each offers slightly different products, so syndicate members are not generally in direct competition, though there is some overlap. Current members of the Adventure Collection (2009) are listed below.

Company	Base	Field	Main Activities
Backroads	USA	World	Hiking, biking
Bushtracks	USA	Africa	Air safaris
Canadian Mountain Holidays*	Canada	Canada	Heliski and hike
Geographic Expeditions	USA	World	Small groups, NFP[†]
Lindblad Expeditions*	USA	Oceans	Expedition cruises
Micato Safaris	USA	Africa	Luxury game ranch
Natural Habitat Adventures*	USA	World	Wildlife watching
NOLS, National Outdoor Leadership School*	USA	World	Outdoor education
O.A.R.S.*	USA	USA	River rafting
Off the Beaten Path	USA	World	Parks, nature

*At least one product audited by Buckley (2006a).
[†]NFP, not-for-profit.

CASE STUDY 3.3: Wild Women on Top

Historic first ascents of mountains such as Mt Everest have lead in turn to commercial-guided ascents where, for a steep price, relatively unskilled tour clients can make the same ascent. Similarly, the so-called Seven Summits, i.e. the ascent of the highest peak in each of seven continents, is now a commercial tour product as well as a personal goal for individual mountaineers (Hales, 2006). Since several of these peaks involve major expeditions with months or years of preparation, the Seven Summits cannot be offered as a single uninterrupted tour, but only as a multi-part tour programme run over an extended period. Since there are many different adventure companies offering guided ascents of each of the individual peaks, the problem from a marketing perspective is how to keep the client with the same operator for the entire Seven Summits. One particularly interesting approach has been adopted by a Sydney-based fitness and adventure company, Wild Women on Top (2009), which focussed initially on fitness training for young mothers and went on to offer its clients the opportunity to climb the Seven Summits, with four completed to date.

From a marketing perspective, there are several interesting features of this particular company and product. Firstly, the owner and chief guide gained a prior reputation in competitive aerobics and later as a fitness instructor and then established the adventure tourism operation by offering a staged series of successively more difficult hikes and climbs to her fitness clients. Secondly, whilst many tour operators offer some of their tours solely to female clients, they generally also offer identical tours to mixed groups. By offering its products only to women, this particular company has made a deliberate decision to pursue a market segment which is large, growing and under-catered for by other operators. In addition, by targeting young mothers specifically, the company takes advantage of widespread social concerns over post-pregnancy body shape in order to attract clients into fitness programmes, and then uses that client base to market first social low-key outdoor hikes, and subsequently more difficult, adventurous and expensive tour products. Essentially, instead of offering a selection of different products at a similar level, the company has created its own pyramid of products (Chapter 1) at a miniature scale, aiming for client loyalty and repeat business.

Unlike the fitness and smaller-scale outdoor hiking and climbing trips which are lead by company guides directly, Wild Women on Top is not in fact equipped to manage the logistics of a major international mountain ascent directly. What it does is to assemble a group of clients, supervise their training and equipment purchases, and subcontract the in-country logistics and guiding for the actual mountain ascents to specialist operators which do in fact conduct such ascents routinely. For these on-ground climbing companies, assembling a group of clients is generally an expensive exercise which involves time, money and effort: firstly in marketing, and secondly in negotiating with potential clients to ensure that they are both physically and financially capable of undertaking the climb. If a company such as Wild Women on Top can bring them a ready-made group of fit, paid-up and motivated clients, that justifies a significant discount on the price of the actual climbing component.

LOOKING BACK

1. The book on *Adventure Tourism* by Buckley (2006a) contains descriptions of individual commercial tourism products in various adventure activity subsectors. Choose one of these subsectors and identify a further six products within that subsector, either from your own experience, the academic literature, or the tour operators' own marketing materials (e.g. websites). Can you compile information for

all the categories of information provided in the 2006 book, or only some, and if so which? How reliable do you think the information you have compiled is likely to be, and why?

2. This chapter provides a graph of price per day against length of tour for a set of products as described in the 2006 book. Which types of tour activity are widely separated by these measures, and which overlap, and why? What other useful parameters can you identify to describe commercial adventure tourism products?

3. The data on adventure tour products provided in the first part of this chapter are derived from on-site audits published by Buckley (2006a). These are limited in number. Information on a much broader set of products, though with lower reliability and fewer parameters, is available on tour operator website and other marketing materials. Data on price and itinerary are likely to be most reliable. Select any one adventure activity, identify at least 100 individual products, and plot a graph of price per day against number of days. How do your results compare with those reported by Buckley (2007a)? Can you identify upmarket and down-market subsectors? What differences are there in the ways these products are pitched?

PART 2

Operational Management

CHAPTER 4

Risk Management

Lion walking past open safari vehicle at night, about 1 metre from camera

KEY ISSUES

- risk as a component of adventure activities
- managing risk as a key aspect of commercial adventure tourism
- assessing and avoiding commercial risks
- identifying and managing legal risks
- health and medical considerations
- operational issues and practices
- managing physical risks
- social components to risk management

CONTENTS

CHAPTER SUMMARY

Psychological studies of participants in various forms of adventure tourism and recreation routinely reveal that they consider risk as an integral part of the activity. Tourism researchers regularly include risk as one of the defining components of adventure tourism. A major distinguishing component of commercial adventure tours, relative to mainstream urban tourism, is the active attention to measuring, managing, and minimising risks. Some of these risk management steps can be taken at the scale of the company or operation as a whole, before any individual tour starts; but once any individual tour gets under way, most risk management measures rely heavily on the guide or leader.

At a broad scale, risk management measures can usefully be divided into six groups: commercial, legal, medical, operational, physical, and social. Commercial risks include both those common to all types of tourism and some which are specific to adventure tourism. The same applies to legal risks, where the adventure sector has a particular focus on the use of disclaimers to transfer risk to individual clients, as a key risk management measure. Similarly, some health and medical aspects are the same as for any type of travel, whereas others are specific to particular adventure activities. One of the key issues for commercial adventure tourism operators is to screen clients to ensure that they have adequate health, fitness, and skills to undertake the particular activity concerned. In addition, adventure tour operators are likely to be particularly concerned to ensure that clients carry their own comprehensive travel insurance, which includes both medical and medical evacuation cover.

One of the fundamental roles of a tour guide, in all but the shortest, simplest, and cheapest tours, is to manage operational logistics, such as equipment checks and group check-ins, and this is part of overall risk management approaches. During the actual adventure activity, the role of guides is critical in all aspects of safety, as they shepherd clients who will generally be less skilled and less fit than themselves. What they can achieve on tour, however, does also depend on the design of the tour, the provision of adequate equipment, and the selection and pre-trip training of the clients. The adventure recreation and outdoor education literature routinely consider guide skills in two categories, generally known as hard and soft skills respectively. The hard skills are the physical capabilities to carry out the adventure activity concerned themselves. The soft skills are the social and interpersonal abilities to teach and train a group of clients and promote group harmony and team behaviour, so as to ensure client safety and satisfaction. Both are important to risk management.

RESEARCH REVIEW

Introduction

Most of the published academic literature relevant to risk management in adventure tourism falls into three main categories: psychological literature about participants' perceptions of risk; medical literature about accident statistics in different activities; and legal literature about disclaimers, lawsuits, and liability-limiting statutes. There seems to have been rather little academic attention to the actual management of risk by commercial adventure tour operators, though there are one or two publications on the roles of guides which do include this aspect.

Psychology

Most research on the psychology of risk during outdoor adventure sports and recreation has focussed on private individuals and recreational groups, rather than on guided commercial tours, (Cater, 2006b; Page et al., 2005). There are a few exceptions: Arnould and Price (1993), for example, included comments from guides on commercial rafting tours, relating to the client's experience of excitement. The psychology of participants in potentially risky adventure recreation activities has now been studied for several decades. Examples include: Cheron and Ritchie (1982); Ewert (1985, 1989); Ewert and Hollenhurst (1989, 1997); Crawford et al. (1991); McIntyre (1992); Walle (1997); Jack and Ronan (1998); McIntyre and Roggenbuck (1998); Holyfield (1999); Schrader and Wann (1999); Slanger and Rudestam (1997); Fluker and Turner (2000); Cater (2006b); and Tran and Ralston (2006). Examples from specific adventure activities are listed in Table 4.1.

Medical

Accident and injury statistics for various adventure tourism activities have been compared, principally in New Zealand, by: Bentley and Page (2001, 2008); Bentley et al. (2000, 2001a, 2000b, 2000c, 2003, 2006, 2008); Ewert and Jamieson (2003); and Page et al. (2005). These statistics are commonly cited per million participant hours, which is a reasonable basis for comparison but does not consider that some adventure activities are generally short and intense, others more extended. In New Zealand, for example, reported injury rates range from 3000 to over 7000 per million participant hours (pmph) for quad biking, fishing, caving, and cycle tours; an order of magnitude lower (125–718 pmph) for diving, rafting, and horse-riding; and only 14 pmph, over two orders of magnitude lower, for kayaking. Some caution, however, is required in interpreting these figures. Many accident and medical insurance policies exclude adventure activities, so these may be under-reported. Since riding a bicycle on a road does not fall within this exclusion, cycling injuries may be reported more fully. The number of injuries from caving or fishing may be known, but the total number of hours spent on these activities is almost certainly under-reported. All-Terrain Vehicle rides and horse rides may commonly be quite brief, perhaps an hour or so in duration, whereas rafting trips may take several days, of which only short periods

Table 4.1	Participant Attitudes and Perceptions in Particular Adventure Activities

Activity	Examples
Climbing	Jakus and Shaw (1996), Feher et al. (1998)
Mountaineering	Bratton et al. (1979), Ewert (1985, 1994), Breivik (1996), Delle Fave et al. (2003), Pomfret (2006), Berger and Greenspan (2008)
Mountain biking	Hollenhorst et al. (1995)
Hiking	Martin and Priest (1986), Borrie and Roggenbuck (2001), Chhetri et al. (2004), Manning (2004)
Skiing, snowboarding	Gilbert and Hudson (2000), Heino (2000), Anderson (2000), Vaske et al. (2007)
Surfing	Farmer (1992), Dolnicar and Fluker (2003)
Rafting	Knopf et al. (1983), Hall and McArthur (1991), Brookes (2001), Arnould and Price (1993)
Skydiving	Lipscombe (1999), Costa and Chalip (2007)
Snowmobiling	Gyimothy and Mykletun (2004)

involve significant risk. Finally, kayaking presumably includes flatwater kayaking and sea kayaking as well as whitewater kayaking, and these are very different activities with very different risks.

At a global scale, more detailed medical and accident data are available for diving, skiing, and mountaineering than for other adventure activities. Data on diving accidents have been examined by Wilks (1999), Wilks and Davis (2000), Wilks et al. (2006), Trevett et al. (2001), Taylor et al. (2003), and Laden et al. (2007). Snow sports injuries have been studied by, for instance, Garrick and Kurland (1971), Requa et al. (1977), Aitkens (1990), Prall et al. (1995), Johnson et al. (1997), Deibert et al. (1998), Goulet et al. (1999), Tarazi et al. (1999), Machold et al. (2000, 2002), Macnab et al. (2002), Ronning et al. (2000, 2001), Yamakawa et al. (2001), Federiuk et al. (2002), Levy et al. (2002), Matsumoto et al. (2002), and Hagel et al. (2004). Mountaineering incidents and accidents, ranging from altitude sickness to fatalities, have been reported by authors such as Williamson (1999), Malcolm (2001), and Boggild et al. (2007). There is also limited information for wildlife watching (Moscardo et al., 2006), whitewater rafting (Schoen and Stano, 2002), surfing (Nathanson et al., 2002), and surf swimming (Morgan, 2006). There may also be increased risk of infections or injury from adventure travel to areas with poor hygiene, or civil or military conflict (Ezzedine et al., 2007; Ospina, 2006). Issues involved in management of risk have been considered, in various countries and circumstances, by authors such as Coxon (2006), Morgan and Fluker (2006), Wilks et al. (2006), Cioccio and Michael (2007), and Xiaoli (2007). Ways in which risk aspects of adventure tourism are presented in marketing materials and mass media have been considered by Walle (1997), Cater (2006b), and King and Beeton (2006).

BIG PICTURE

The role of risk

As noted in Chapter 1, adventure tourism may be defined in many different ways and may include many different activities. Some of these definitions, but not all, consider risk as a key criterion. Similarly, many adventure activities, though not all, do in fact involve a significantly higher element of risk than mainstream urban tourism. The aim of the tour operator is to make the clients feel that they can safely and successfully engage in a high-risk activity, so as to increase the excitement and consequent satisfaction which the clients experience; but at the same time, to manage the activity as closely and carefully as possible so that actual risk to clients, guides, and the company is as low as possible. The touchstone is that undertaking any particular adventure activity as a client of a commercial adventure tour operator should be significantly safer than undertaking the same activity in the same place, but independently.

Risk is one of the areas of adventure tourism research which has attracted a certain degree of academic attention, but the focus has been principally on the perceptions of participants, as outlined in the Research Review. In this chapter, however, the focus is on risk management from the perspective of the commercial adventure tour operator.

Commercial

As with any kind of business, there are a number of standard commercial risks which must be addressed as part of the basics of business management. These include, for example, measures to make sure that marketing reaches potential clients, that sales efforts are effective, that contracts are properly completed and payments are properly processed, and so on. There is also a category of commercial risks related more specifically to the tourism sector, such as downturns in the travel market overall, drops in visitor numbers to particular countries because of exchange rates or terrorism, and changes in demand for particular places or activities because of changing travel fashions. To be successful, any adventure tourism business must attempt to forecast such changes as far as possible and respond quickly so as to cut losses if downturns occur unexpectedly. This also means that it is important to adopt a business structure which allows costs to be cut quickly if need be, e.g. by avoiding a large equipment inventory or a large permanent staff on-site. This is one important reason why many adventure tourism operators, for example, hire guides only on short-term contracts.

There are also two particular categories of commercial risks which, whilst by no means restricted to the adventure tourism subsector, seem to be particularly prevalent. These are the hostile takeover and the copycat operator. Hostile takeovers can, of course, occur in any industry sector. There have been examples in adventure tourism where local partners in developing nations, or Indigenous groups in developed nations, have used their particular legal status to squeeze out the founders of a business, who because of expatriate or non-Indigenous status may be at a legal disadvantage. Two well-known examples are David Allardice's Ultimate Descents in Nepal (Buckley, 2006a) and the original whale watch operators in Kaikoura, New Zealand, who were apparently squeezed out by a politically powerful Maori-owned operator (Buckley, 2003a, pp. 215–217).

Copycat businesses can also occur in many different industry sectors, but may be particularly prevalent in adventure tourism because there is rarely any protection for new business ideas or intellectual property. Most new adventure tourism operations, especially in areas with no previous history of adventure tourism, face a significant start-up period before they turn a profit. They must continue to invest in marketing efforts so as to build up sales, before they reach the point where improved demand allows them to increase prices and recoup costs. If another operator starts to offer a nearly identical product at just that point, without incurring the same initial investment costs, they can take advantage of the original operator's marketing efforts to undercut the original operator's prices. Just as the original entrepreneur has established sufficient demand to raise prices and improve profits, copycat competitors can undercut those prices and force a price war, imposing an additional capital drain on the originator.

There are various potential measures to combat this problem, but none of them is easy. It is difficult, for example, for a new start-up business to demand that its marketing and distribution agents sell its particular product exclusively and refuse to market competing products. It is rare that an ecotour involves new technology which a tour operator can patent; and even if it does, a patent may mean little if the owner does not have the resources to enforce it. If a tour operates on private land, the tour operator may be able to negotiate exclusive access arrangements with the landowner, but this may be costly. If a tour operates on public land or water, such as a national park, the management agency may operate under legislation that requires it to offer all commercial opportunities equitably, e.g. by open tender. This applies particularly if the activity concerned is also available to private recreational visitors and there are no specific safety or intellectual-property issues to be considered. In practice, despite any such requirements, many protected area management agencies do in fact grant operating licences for particular activities or sites only to a limited number of commercial operators, for a variety of reasons (see Chapter 6). For any new ecotourism business, this issue is certainly something worth considering carefully.

In developing nations, arrangements for operating commercial ecotours within protected areas or other public lands may be rather more flexible or laissez-faire – either for cultural or political reasons, or simply because of lack of resources. A new ecotourism business may work hard to design a quality product and establish a market, only to find itself undercut, or worse, by powerful locals. If the original entrepreneur happens to be an expatriate, they may even find that sharp practice by local copycat operators receives local political support, at least covertly. This may happen even if the expatriate operator has invested enormous personal time, effort, and resources into establishing a business that provides local employment and benefits local communities. Well-known examples include John Gray's Sea Canoe in Thailand (Buckley, 2003a) and David Allardice's Ultimate Descents in Nepal (Buckley, 2006a). In Gray's case, businessmen from Bangkok copied his boats, his itineraries, and his company name, ignored the minimal-impact measures adopted by Gray's own company, and eventually, shot and wounded his Thai manager. In Allardice's case, the local silent partner staged a hostile takeover of the company once it had become successful. Both Gray's and Allardice's businesses have in fact survived and prospered, but only after several years of difficult times. Even where no sharp practice is involved, new start-up ecotourism operations still need to consider the likelihood that their products will be copied. According to Knowles and Allardice (1992), for example, the first commercial rafting trip in Nepal was run by Himalayan River Expeditions in 1976, but a number of other operators soon began to offer competing trips. In such circumstances, the question of who started first soon becomes commercially irrelevant. What matters is the ability to reach customers, especially overseas; to establish and maintain a reputation for higher safety standards and a better quality of service; and to continue pioneering new trips and itineraries, or adding new features to existing trips, to offer something that competitors do not.

Legal

There are many unavoidable legal aspects to running a successful adventure tourism business. Perhaps the most fundamental is that the operator will generally need a series of different permits and licences in order to be allowed to operate legally. Some of these relate to business operations generally, in the jurisdiction concerned – for example, company registration or registration for particular types of tax. Some relate to ancillary components such as transport – for example, the requirement for a guide to have an appropriate commercial licence if they are also going to drive a company bus, minibus, or four-wheel-drive vehicle which transports commercial clients. Some relate to the area of operation, such as permits to carry out commercial activities in national parks or other public lands. And some relate to the particular activity undertaken, such as requirements for guides to have diving instructors' certification or first-aid qualifications.

The second aspect of legal risk management is to ensure that contractual arrangements with commercial partners, suppliers, etc., are appropriate, with protection for the tour operator where required and penalty, enforcement, and compensation clauses if the other party to the contract fails to deliver or to deliver on time. The degree of detail required depends very much on the country concerned. In some countries, a handshake between friends is the most binding agreement available; in some, any supposedly contractual arrangement is continually renegotiable depending on the shifting political power of the parties involved; and in some, enforcement of contract through the courts is routine, and precise legal wordings become critical.

There are many adventure activities where guides need particular qualifications in order to be able to lead commercial clients. These qualifications may either be required by law; or they may be treated as part of normal industry practice, and hence essential for the company to obtain appropriate insurance or at least to rely on it should the need arise. For example, a number of developed nations have guiding and instruction standards for a wide variety of outdoor recreation activities, and national or regional bodies which are responsible for testing and certification. Even if these qualifications are not a legal requirement for guides to lead commercial clients in the activity concerned, if they are in fact widely adopted, then any operator who does not follow suit is taking on an additional risk. In some countries, there are guiding associations, either national or regional, and membership of the relevant association may constitute sufficient evidence of guide competence. For an adventure tourism operator who takes clients from developed nations to engage in adventure activities in developing nations, qualifications which apply in the country of origin are at least as important as those in the destination country, since that is where any possible lawsuits are most likely to originate.

Similar considerations apply for insurance. Most commercial adventure tourism operators rely heavily on waivers and disclaimers, as noted below; but even so, they must carry insurance to cover circumstances when disclaimers prove irrelevant or ineffective. In many jurisdictions, national parks agencies require such insurance as a mandatory criterion for obtaining an operating permit, and they may specify the minimum degree of cover, the type of insurance, and that the insurance also indemnifies the land management agency. Similarly, agents or international tour retailers who sell a particular adventure tour in another country may require that the tour operator hold insurance in the agent's country as well as the final destination country. There are many different types of insurance, and an adventure tour operator may need to hold several insurances simultaneously. For example, it may need one set of insurances for its motor vehicles, one set for loss or damage to specialist equipment, one set to provide medical cover for its staff, and one to cover any potential legal judgements against the company as a result of injury or compensation lawsuits.

Most adventure tourism operators will generally also insist that each individual client carry his or her own insurance, typically a travel insurance which includes medical cover and medical evacuation cover. Such insurances, however, commonly exclude potentially risky activities such as many of those involved in adventure tourism. This is currently a significant problem for the adventure tourism industry, since operators may insist on clients signing disclaimers which make the client, rather than the operator, liable for any loss or injury; whilst at the same time the client's own insurance may specifically exclude any claims associated with an adventure activity. This is one reason why accident statistics for many adventure activities are inaccurate, since in order to be covered by insurance, anyone requiring medical treatment may not reveal exactly how any injury was actually caused.

Legal waivers and disclaimers are a core component of any commercial adventure tour operator's risk management strategy. These are legal documents which each client is required to sign, which specify essentially that the client recognises that they are undertaking a dangerous activity, accepts all responsibility for any possible adverse outcomes, and in addition absolves the tour operator from any liability. Some of these disclaimers even purport to indemnify the tour operator for the operators' legal costs in the event of any dispute relating to the disclaimer. Perhaps surprisingly, even though the issues faced by most adventure tour operators are quite similar, every company seems to have somewhat different wording to its disclaimer, and the differences are not associated only with differences in the activity. Insurance for adventure activities has come to be seen as a specialist field of insurance law, with its own particular statutes in different jurisdictions, and its own particular precedents, including those relating to interpretation of waiver and disclaimer documents. In many jurisdictions, for example, disclaimers may be invalidated if they are signed under circumstances where the client is no longer free to decide whether or not to purchase the tour – for example, when they are already on the tour bus heading to the activity. This difficulty can be overcome if the tour operator provides every client with a draft copy of the disclaimer in advance, for example, as part of their online or shopfront booking procedures, so that clients are aware of the wording of the document well before they actually have to sign the hard copy. Ultimately, these disclaimers will not necessarily prevent an adventure tour operator from being sued; but they may contribute considerably to a legal outcome favourable to the tour operator, in the event that any such lawsuit proceeds to court.

One of the standard components of most disclaimers is a medical clause, where the clients certify that they are medically fit and capable of undertaking the activity concerned and do not have any known medical condition which might predispose them to illness or injury as part of that activity. Such clauses may also require the client to disclose any allergies, medications, etc. The balance between a client's privacy and right to assess their own abilities, on the one hand, and the tour operator's requirement to assure themselves of the client's capabilities, on the other, remains a contentious area in adventure risk management.

Subject to legal constraints such as those related to medical procedures as above, it is generally a practical requirement of most insurance policies that an adventure tour operator and its staff follow accepted good practices within the particular subsector of the industry concerned. This becomes an issue if any dispute arises which may trigger a lawsuit and/or an insurance claim. If it is standard practice in the particular sector concerned for operators to carry particular safety equipment, for example, then any operator who fails to have such equipment is more likely to be held liable for any adverse consequences of such failure. Likewise, if an accident occurs because of lack of supervision and the particular company concerned has a much lower guide-to-client ratio than standard practice in the sector, it is more likely that it will be found liable. There are a number of actual lawsuits where these principles have been tested in practice. In the well-known case following a Swiss canyoning disaster, for example, the fact that one company went ahead with the day's tour whereas most others had cancelled was taken strongly into account in assessing the company's liability towards its clients.

Medical

As noted briefly in the preceding section, the management of medical, health, and safety risk is a particularly difficult area for many adventure tourism operators. Indeed, the same applies for university academics leading adventure tourism field courses for students. The first consideration is to assess potential participants, well in advance, for their capability to undertake the particular trip planned. Depending on the place, conditions, and activities, such screening may involve criteria such as age, strength, and general health; fitness; any pre-existing medical conditions, either anatomical, physiological, or psychological; and in some cases, demonstrable skills and experience in a particular activity. For example, for a tour operator to take a client on a commercial whitewater trip down a river with potentially dangerous rapids, they may specify a minimum age limit and require the ability to swim a certain distance. In addition, if the client wants to paddle a kayak rather than sit as a passenger in a raft, the company may require demonstrated experience in rivers of similar difficulty.

In many countries and jurisdictions, nobody except a qualified medical practitioner is permitted to administer any form of medical treatment other than first aid. In some countries, for example, it is a criminal offence to give another person drugs prescribed for oneself, even in an emergency situation where it appears that the person concerned would otherwise die. In some other jurisdictions, however, there are so-called Good Samaritan clauses in relevant legislation which provide exemptions in the case of emergency. In general, guides who used to carry relatively comprehensive medical kits now carry only first-aid facilities. Instead, the tour operator will advise each client to seek their own individual medical advice before the trip. Unless every client's doctor happens to be a specialist in international travel and adventure medicine, however, this approach also has its limitations.

The second component of medical risk management, therefore, is that the tour operator must ensure that every individual client has made their own personal medical preparations to an appropriate standard. This may include: the purchase of appropriate medical insurance; vaccinations and inoculations for the country and area concerned and any other areas crossed in transit; appropriate prophylactic medication for any diseases where vaccinations are not available, such as malaria; an adequate supply, including a backup supply, of any medications which the client routinely relies upon; and an adequate personal first-aid kit, including prescription medications such as antibiotics, which may be needed during the trip concerned. From the commercial tour operators' perspectives, their own guides could probably provide detailed advice as to precisely what medicines the clients should bring; but unless a guide happens to be a qualified doctor, they are not permitted to do so. The approach which I follow myself in advising student field courses is to specify clearly that I am not authorised to give medical advice and they are required to consult their own doctor before the trip; but simply to provide the students, purely as a matter of information, with a list of items that I myself intend to take.

For any commercial adventure tourism operation, particularly those in relatively remote areas, it is generally critical that at least one guide has appropriate first-aid skills and experience. In many jurisdictions this can be recognised through various forms of first-aid qualification, such as those offered by various life-saving organisations. In some countries, various organisations also offer training in wilderness medicine, advanced first aid, and qualifications as a paramedic or emergency medical technician.

Last but by no means least in the panoply of medical risk management measures, every adventure tour needs an emergency medical evacuation plan. Depending on the activity and site, this may be as simple as telephoning an ambulance, or putting the client in a car and driving them to hospital; or it may be as difficult as activating an Emergency Position Indicating Radio Beacon (EPIRB) to call in an emergency services rescue aircraft to winch an injured client to safety. In some areas, such as remote polar, desert or mountainous regions, the only possibility of rescue is a separate rescue expedition. The key consideration is that whilst insurance may cover the cost of such an evacuation, it is up to the company and guide to know what to do and to have the communications ability to put the evacuation plan into action.

Operational

The most basic, often boring, but essential role of an adventure tour guide is to manage operational logistics, both routine and emergency (Table 4.2). In a routine sense, this may include: specifying the initial meeting point, date, and time unambiguously and ensuring that all clients are aware of it; arranging transfers, if requested, from the clients' various points of origin to that meeting place; arranging group check-ins, including collecting and redistributing passports and air tickets; and so on. Except for single-person tour operations, these aspects will generally be covered by office staff, but guides need to be aware of details and able to take follow-up action if necessary. It is commonplace that adventure tour operators will provide a personal gear list to each client well in advance of the tour concerned, and it is generally up to the guides to check that the clients actually have the items

Table 4.2	Guides' Roles in Risk Management

Logistics
- Itineraries
- Group vouchers
- Group check-in
- Passports
- Allocating rooms
- Time management

Training
- Hard activity skills
- Safety skills and practices
- Outdoor skills, e.g. camping

General safety
- Briefings on all aspects of safety
- Safety equipment: helmets, lifejackets, gloves, climbing gear, etc.
- Avoiding disease and pathogens: waterborne, insect-borne, etc.
- Avoiding dangerous animals: snakes, ticks, bears, lions, etc.
- Avoiding dangerous plants: poison ivy, stinging trees, etc.
- Avoiding dangerous marine life: sharks, jellyfish, stonefish, etc.
- Avoiding dangerous aquatic life: crocodiles, piranha, etc.
- Safe travel skills: avoiding slips, trips, falls, etc.
- Cultural safety skills: how to behave appropriately in different societies.
- Safe activity skills: very detailed and specific to individual activities

Client supervision
- Watching for exhaustion, discouragement
- Watching for sunstroke, overheating, hypothermia
- Watching for incipient illness, minor injury
- Watching for unfriendly interactions between clients
- Checking clients have adequate skills for conditions
- Deciding when clients need to rest, camp, eat, drink, etc.

First aid and medical
- Arranging medical evacuation procedures
- Checking for client allergies, medications, disabilities
- Re-stocking and carrying first-aid or wilderness medical kits

Social
- Forestalling any arguments amongst clients
- Accommodating differences in client skills and interests
- Catalysing and encouraging appropriate group ethics

prescribed. Guides may also need to provide an opportunity for clients to purchase any missing items at the last minute; or alternatively, to bring spare items themselves. These simple actions may have major consequences in managing risk.

It is important for guides to provide clients, particularly those who may not have much previous experience in the area concerned, with adequate advice and information so that every client knows what is planned each day and can make adequate preparations. Such advice may include, for example: how to carry out a particular adventure activity; how to set up camp efficiently in a wilderness area; and a variety of health and safety procedures. In addition to advice and information, guides may need to provide hands-on training and demonstrations for any of these components. They need to watch each of the clients to make sure that they are capable, encourage them to help each other where relevant, and be ready to halt an activity if anyone is endangering themselves or the group. Finally, in tours with multiple guides, it is the responsibility of the lead guide to watch, manage, and delegate tasks to the other guides, as well as deal with clients directly.

For operational risk management during emergency situations, there are at least four key components. The first is for the company to ensure that each tour group is provided with appropriate equipment. For high-altitude tours, for example, the group may carry a Gamow Bag, effectively a portable recompression chamber. The second is to make sure that the guides, and if necessary the clients, are trained in proper use of emergency equipment. Avalanche transceivers for off-piste backcountry skiing or heliskiing provide an example. The third is to make sure that guides, and, if necessary, clients have adequate communication capabilities. Examples include: standard non-verbal signals used by divers or whitewater rafters; whistles and signal codes for marine or whitewater; and radios or satellite telephones for communications from remote areas. If there is more than one guide with a group, they will generally also need short-range communications by either mobile phone or radio. Finally, operational risk management plans for emergencies must include an evacuation strategy and appropriate insurance. These issues were discussed in previous sections.

Physical

In the academic literature of tourism, recreation, and leisure studies, the main focus of risk management has been on physical safety during the adventure activity itself. From a risk management perspective, there are many steps to this. The first is to design the adventure tourism product carefully so as to minimise the physical risk whilst still providing the excitement which the clients crave. Clearly, the detailed options depend on the particular product concerned; but for almost any place and activity, there will be ways to improve safety through small details of product design. The second step, as discussed in relation to medical risk management, is to screen clients to ensure that they are in fact physically capable of carrying out the activity on offer. At the same time, the tour operator needs to ensure that the equipment used is appropriate to the activity, of suitable design and well maintained – whether it belongs to the company or the clients.

One key aspect of physical safety is to ensure that there are enough guides, relative to the number of clients. Appropriate client-to-guide ratios vary greatly with the type of activity and the details of terrain and equipment, as analysed further in Chapter 3. For different types of tours, there may be more guides than clients or many more clients than guides. For many types of commercial adventure tours, client-to-guide ratios seem to range from about 4:1 to about 12:1 (Buckley, 2007a), but these ratios do not necessarily apply across all types of activities.

Clearly, suitably skilled guides are a key component of physical risk management. This includes both the hard skills to carry out the relevant activities themselves and the soft skills to help clients do likewise. In addition, the lead guide needs the information, the judgement, and the authority to be able to cancel or abort a particular tour if he or she considers it necessary on safety grounds. This is not simply a question of the guides deciding whether conditions are safe for themselves. They also need to be able to decide whether conditions are safe for the particular clients on the tour concerned. In addition, the company needs to have legal, financial, and client-information procedures in place in advance, so that clients know that tours may be cancelled for safety reasons, and so that the company is easily able to process refunds or credits where necessary. For long or multi-day tours, there is always the possibility that the trip may have to be aborted part-way through, so the tour operator and the lead guide must maintain a continually updated escape or retreat strategy in case it should be needed. This involves a thorough knowledge of local geography, including escape routes and possible sources of assistance, and good route-finding ability, whether by GPS or map and compass, so that the group always knows where it is.

For most adventure activities, there are well-tested safety procedures which all clients need to know, and it is part of the guide's job to provide safety briefings and, if necessary, safety training and tests for all clients. Participants on game-watching safaris, for example, must know not to stand up in an open-topped safari vehicle in the presence of potentially dangerous wildlife. Divers need to know how to control buoyancy, how to ascend safely, and how to buddy-breathe if someone's air fails. Whitewater rafting clients need to know how to swim safely through a whitewater rapid and how to be rescued by a safety kayak. Heliskiers must be able to get safely in and out of a helicopter and know how to use avalanche transceivers. Both rock- and ice-climbing clients may need instruction in proper use of ropes and safety equipment. Every adventure activity has a similar set of safety considerations.

In addition to specific safety procedures, clients are less likely to get into trouble if they are skilled at the activity concerned, i.e. if they already know how to dive or kayak, ski, or climb or ride a horse or a mountain bike. Part of an adventure guide's role is to make an informal assessment of each client's ability both at the beginning of each trip and continually as it proceeds and to provide some tactful additional training as it may be required. This requires a combination of soft and hard skills. The guide must first demonstrate, but without showing off, that he or she is more competent than the client at the activity concerned and hence capable of providing training. In addition, unless the tour product has been sold specifically as an instruction session, guides must be very tactful in providing instruction in such a way that the clients concerned maintain face in front of other clients. This is part of an overall skill which is critical for good adventure guiding, but which needs tact and experience to develop: namely, the ability to shepherd clients unobtrusively but safely through a particular activity. This includes the ability to continually reassess each client's capabilities and condition and to judge when it is time to call for a halt or break so that clients can rest, replenish their blood sugar levels, or recover their enthusiasm.

Social

Managing interactions amongst clients, and between clients and guides, is also an important contribution to group safety. Clients who are angry with each other, who are competing with each other, or who refuse to work together or talk to each other may endanger the safety of the whole group. One of the skills of a good adventure guide is thus to pay constant attention to harmony within the group and to provide opportunities for clients with different levels of skills or interests. Guides may need to start and maintain social conversations so as to introduce the clients to each other and encourage them to befriend each other. They also need to catalyse the development of group ethics in regard to safety, minimal-impact camping practices, and so on. All these aspects are important not only for risk management, but also for client satisfaction. The same also applies for more overt soft skills such as training and interpretation by guides. It is this constant set of social interactions, perhaps more than the physical activities involved, which can make adventure guiding a tiring experience. This aspect has been referred to as 'emotional labour' (Sharpe, 2005) and the overall practices of leading an activity for client satisfaction as 'choreography' (Beedie, 2003; Pomfret, 2006).

CASE STUDY 4.1: Copycat Competition: John Gray's Sea Canoe, Thailand

One of the best-known examples of a copycat problem is that experienced by John Gray's Sea Canoe in Thailand (Buckley, 2003a, pp. 39–60). John Gray, an American expatriate and long-term Thai resident, discovered a set of limestone islands shaped like vertical tubes, accessible only through narrow intertidal passages. He designed and manufactured special boats to navigate through these tunnels and established a successful tourism business taking people to see the interiors of these islands. He put an enormous amount of time and effort into marketing these tours internationally, and he went to considerable lengths to employ local staff. The success of his business attracted the attention of unscrupulous entrepreneurs who took advantage of his discoveries and his marketing and copied his tour itineraries, equipment, and company name. These copycats overcrowded the hollow islands and access passages, causing environmental damage, significant safety risks, and loss of customer satisfaction. In addition, Gray ran afoul of a local mafia, which attacked his Thai manager in a drive-by shooting. Gray, his manager, and his business have all survived and continue to prosper, principally by diversifying into other places and products. The Sea Canoe story, however, continues to provide a salutary example of how a well-intentioned, well-designed, and well-run company can be pirated by copycats.

CASE STUDY 4.2: Hostile Takeover: David Allardice's Ultimate Descents, Nepal

An example of a hostile takeover is provided by David Allardice's Ultimate Descents in Nepal (Buckley, 2006a, pp. 52–56). As Nepal became a popular low-cost destination for trekking tourists in the 1970s and 1980s, a number of expatriate guides and visitors noticed the whitewater rafting and kayaking potential of many of the Himalayan rivers and began to explore them. Nepal became internationally famous for its whitewater and a number of commercial raft tours were established. Australian-based trekking company Australian Himalayan Expeditions, which later became the multi-activity worldwide adventure company World Expeditions, ran one of the first commercial descents of the Sun Khosi.

New Zealander David Allardice, an expert kayaker and co-author of the *Whitewater Guide to Nepal* (Knowles and Allardice, 1992) established a Kathmandu-based company called Ultimate Descents, which quickly established an excellent reputation for service and safety. Presumably as a local legislative requirement, the company had a local partner, a Nepali national. As the rafting sector grew, copycat companies sprang up in the same way as for the Thai sea canoe operations; and as in Thailand, innumerable touts and small companies also began advertising these tours even though they did not have their own operations. Of course, these secondary sales are by no means restricted

Continued

to developing nations: exactly the same happens for coral-reef tours in Cairns, Australia.

In the case of Ultimate Descents Nepal, however, an additional problem arose. The Nepali partner carried out a hostile takeover of the company under Nepali law. The details have not been made public, but clearly it was not an amicable transaction. The company owed its success and indeed its existence to Allardice's expertise, international contacts and marketing, and sales and managerial effort over many

years and indeed decades, and it appears that he lost this without recompense. The company name and logo were owned internationally by Allardice, so there was a period of market confusion where clients booking under the same name, but from different countries, could end up with different operators once they arrived in Nepal. Allardice has now established a new company, still trading internationally as Ultimate Descents, and is once again successful; but for several years his business suffered significantly.

CASE STUDY 4.3: Safety Evacuation: Qamdo Gorges Raft Expedition, Tibet

Campsite, Qamdo Gorge of Mekong, Tibet, shortly before aborting descent

The first attempted descent of the Qamdo Gorges in the Tibetan section of the Mekong River was made in 2005 as a commercial adventure expedition tour by a combined group of US, Japanese, Chinese, and Australian whitewater rafters and kayakers. The operational details of on-river safety are described by Buckley (2006a, pp. 41–45). In addition, however, a larger-scale risk eventuated when the tour group, already behind its planned schedule because of unexpected portages, came to a sheer-walled rock gorge

with no riverside access or view. Because of this gorge, it was impossible to judge how difficult the next section of river might be and it would have been impossible to retreat once the rafts entered the gorge. There was no known access to the river for at least another 100 km downstream, where a road bridge crossed high above the river. The entry to the gorge was through a severe rapid, runnable by kayaks but not rafts, and in other sections of the same river downstream, as indeed in other rivers worldwide, such gorges were known to contain significantly more severe rapids than the more open valleys where the group had already been forced to portage. Even portaging involved significant risks from near-continuous rockfalls from the valley sides into the river. A scouting party was sent downstream, but returned after 2 days with the news that the only track left the river and climbed a mountain valley. Since the tracks themselves were narrow, ancient Tibetan walking routes built up or carved out of rock, there was no opportunity to reach the river off-track. Under these circumstances, the only safe course for the group was to abort the descent and leave the river, and after some discussion, this was the course followed. It took the group 6 days to reach a road, enlisting assistance from small villages en route to carry all the dismantled equipment. The gorge has since been run by a group of expert kayakers (Winn, 2009) and the decision to abort the raft descent in 2005 fully vindicated.

CASE STUDY 4.4: Client-Supplied Equipment, Arctic Sea Kayaking Tour, Canada

Collapsible kayaks, Baffin Island, Canadian High Arctic

This case study is drawn from a multi-day fly-in fly-out sea kayak tour in the Canadian High Arctic. All equipment, including collapsible sea kayaks, was flown in to the tour staging point along with guides and clients. No equipment was stored on site and there was no easy opportunity to supply additional boats or other gear once the group reached the staging point. The sea kayaks, still folded up, were then transported in a sea-going speedboat to the start of the paddling section of the tour.

Most of the tour clients were using two-seater collapsible sea kayaks supplied by the tour operator, but one client had brought his own single-seater. When the boats were assembled, however, concern was expressed as to whether this boat was in good enough repair to survive the expected swell conditions, and if so to keep up with the larger and faster double kayaks. The two guides were paddling single-seater boats, but these were in good condition with the skin stretched tightly over the frame to create a strong though flexible hull. In the client's kayak, the skin was slack, severely reducing streamlining, speed, and strength. Most critically, the design relies on the tensile strength of the skin and the compression strength of the thin, lightweight aluminium tubes which make up the frame. If the skin is slack, the hull can bend severely as it crosses ocean swells, snapping the frame and sinking the sea kayak. In view of this risk, the client concerned agreed with the lead guide that he should immediately return with the shuttle boat and kayak only in calmer waters near the initial staging point.

LOOKING BACK

1. Consider any one activity subsector of the adventure tourism industry and list the various types of risk potentially faced by an enterprise offering that activity as a commercial product. Which of these risks are common to all forms of business, which to all types of tourism, which to adventure tourism generally, which to this particular activity, and which to the specific geographic area? What steps can the tour operator take to manage each of these risks?

2. Some authors argue that actual risk is an essential component of adventure tourism, whereas others argue that the aim is to give

clients the perception of risk without actually exposing them to any. Using examples, explain which view you think is more accurate.

3. If you were considering whether to insure an adventure tourism operator, how would you decide what risks to cover, what level of cover to require, and what premium to charge? Consider a specific example and identify what data you would need.

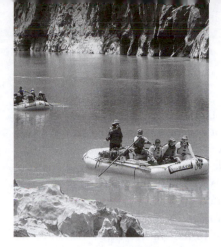

Last Descent, Great Bend of Yangtze
River, China

CHAPTER 5

Communications Management

KEY ISSUES

- communications as a key component of adventure tour products
- amongst staff: decisions
- staff to clients: instructions
- clients to staff: enquiries
- amongst clients: social
- routine communications: operations, hygiene, etc.
- emergency communications: safety
- communication modes: verbal, formal signals, informal
- cross-cultural communications: misunderstandings, e.g. of informal signs
- language barriers: social and safety issues

CONTENTS

CHAPTER SUMMARY

Communications between and amongst staff and clients are a critical component of commercial adventure tourism products. There is a useful division between routine and non-routine communications and a hierarchy from more to less urgent and critical. Detailed data are available from participant observations from 366 days of operations in 59 non-motorised water-borne adventure tours. In this particular tourism subsector, routine discussions amongst staff are relatively few but far-reaching. Staff instructions to clients are structured and are key to safe operations and satisfied clients. Client communications to staff include questions and clarifications which can be critical. Most communication amongst clients is conversational, social glue amongst strangers in an unfamiliar setting. Communications outside this pattern are largely associated with emergencies or emotional occasions. Workplace communications in adventure tourism deserve further research attention.

RESEARCH REVIEW

Analyses of communications in tourism have been concentrated in specific fields: service quality (Tsang and Ap, 2007); interpretation (Chen et al., 2006; Reisinger and Steiner, 2006); marketing (Pitt et al., 2007; Wu et al., 2008); and between tourists and home (Pearce and Foster, 2007; Swarbrooke et al., 2003; White and White, 2007). There seems to be little analysis, however, of communications within actual commercial tourism products, essentially a form of workplace communication (Xiao and Smith, 2006a, 2006b). This contrasts strongly with other industries and professions, where such analyses are carried out routinely to a very high degree of detail, addressing specific issues such as age (McCann and Giles, 2007), gender (Domagalski and Steelman, 2007), emotion (Miller, 2007), and language (Waldvogel, 2007).

In particular, there does not appear to be any previous analysis of communications in adventure tourism. Relevant research texts such as Buckley (2006a), Fennell and Dowling (2003), McCool and Moisey (2001), Manning (1999), Ryan (2003), Swarbrooke et al. (2003), Pigram and Jenkins (2006), and Weaver (2001) make little or no mention of this topic. Authors such as Beedie (2003), Borrie and Roggenbuck (2001), Delle Fave et al. (2003), Fluker and Turner (2000), Gyimothy and Mykletun (2004), Loeffler (2004), Pomfret (2006), and Sharpe (2005) mention various aspects of communications in passing, principally in relation to guiding in mountain and river tours, but none have treated it as a topic worthy of attention in its own right.

BIG PICTURE

Introduction

Communications are an essential component of commercial adventure tourism products, without which these products cannot operate. That is, communication is as critical as place, people, infrastructure, and equipment. As outlined above, however, there is as yet very little published literature on communications in adventure tourism. In this chapter, therefore, I describe communications in one particular subsector of the adventure tourism industry, namely, non-motorised water-based adventure tours. The detailed content of the communications examined is specific to that subsector, but the broad issues apply more generally. The subsector examined here consists of tours travelling in rafts, kayaks, or canoes, propelled only by paddles or oars, on rivers, lakes, and oceans. This is an archetypal activity component within the commercial adventure tourism sector (Buckley, 2006a). The 59 tours studied range from a day to a month in duration, from tropical to High Arctic latitudes, from beginner to expert clients, and from $50 to over $5000 in price (Table 5.1).

The methodological approach adopted was participant observation, as described by Spradley (1980) and De Walt and de Walt (2002). According to the latter (2002, p. vii), 'Participant observation is accepted almost universally as the central and defining method of research in cultural anthropology but in the twentieth century has become a common feature of qualitative research in a number of disciplines'. I travelled with each of these tours as an active participant, in some cases as a commercial client and in others as a member of staff. I was not identified as a researcher. Effectively, this was an ethnographic approach (Finlay, 2002a, 2002b; Hertz, 1996, 1997) but with an additional complexity. I took part fully in the life of each tour group for the length of each tour, but each tour formed only a small part of the life of each of the participants.

Each tour group consists of two different subgroups, the guides and the clients, respectively, who assemble only for the tour and then disperse again. Some of the clients are experienced, that is, they take part in numerous tours of the same general type and thus have an intermittent 'river life' distinct from their 'home life' but with a degree of continuity over time. Other clients are inexperienced: they take one tour as an adventure holiday, and it forms an isolated experience in their life with no other basis for direct comparison. Likewise, some of the guides run the same tour repeatedly all season or indeed year after year: for that period at least, tour guiding provides their living, the tour experience is a central component of their life, and if other guides work the same tour, they form

Table 5.1	Tours Used for Participant Observations				
Country	**Place**	**Tour Operator**	**Duration**	**Type**	**Audits**
Expeditions					
China	Lancang Jiang	Shangri-la River Expeditions	Multi-day	Raft/kayak	1
China	Yangbi River	Earth Science Expeditions	Multi-day	Raft/kayak	1
Tibet	Qamdo Gorge, Mekong	SSEA and ESE (jointly)	Multi-day	Raft/kayak	1
Tibet	Salween	Last Descents	Multi-day	Raft/kayak	1
Nepal	Karnali, Sun Khosi, others	Allardice's Ultimate Descents	Multi-day	Raft/kayak	4
India	Kameng	TLR Nepal, HOA, Windhorse	Multi-day	Raft/kayak	1
Brazil	Jatapu River	Carlos Colares	Multi-day	Dugout	1
Australia	.Drysdale River	Operation Raleigh, USNOLS	Multi-day	Canoes	2
USA	Grand Canyon	Expeditions Inc., OARS	Multi-day	Kayak, raft	2
Kayak tours					
Chile	Rios Futaleufu, Fuy	Expediciones Chile	Multi-day	Kayak	2
Argentina	Rio Manso	Expediciones Chile	Multi-day	Kayak	1
Costa Rica	Reventazon, others	Endless River Adventures	Multi-day	Kayak	1
Zimbabwe	Upper Zambezi	Shearwater, others	Multi-day	Kayak	1
New Zealand	Karamea River	Ultimate Descents NZ	Multi-day	Raft/kayak	1
Australia	Franklin River	World Expeditions	Multi-day	Raft/kayak	1
USA	Cataract Canyon	Various	Multi-day	Raft/kayak	1
USA	Lochsa River	Various	Single-day	Kayak	2
USA	Payette North Fork	Various	Single-day	Kayak	1
USA	White Salmon River	Various	Single-day	Kayak	1
USA	Westwater Canyon	Various	Single-day	Raft/kayak	3
Raft tours					
Ecuador	Rios Toachi, Blanco	Yacu Amu Rafting	Multi-day	Raft	1
Uganda	White Nile	Adrift	Single-day	Raft	1
Zimbabwe	Zambezi River	Shearwater Adventures	Single-day	Raft	1
New Zealand	Kawarau River	Queenstown Rafting, others	Single-day	Raft	2
New Zealand	Rangitata River	Rangitata Rafts	Single-day	Raft	1
New Zealand	Shotover River	Queenstown Rafting, others	Single-day	Raft	2
New Zealand	Buller River	UD NZ, Buller River Rafting	Single-day	Raft	2
Australia	Nymboida River	World Expeditions, others	Multi-day	Raft	3
Australia	Gwydir River	Wildwater Adventures, others	Single-day	Raft	1
Australia	Tully River	R'n'R, Raging Thunder	Single-day	Raft	2
USA	Green River	Various	Multi-day	Raft	1
USA	San Juan River	Wild Rivers Expeditions	Single-day	Raft	1
USA	Flathead River	Glacier Raft Co, others	Single-day	Raft	1

Table 5.1	Tours Used for Participant Observations—cont'd				
Country	Place	Tour Operator	Duration	Type	Audits
Sea kayaking					
Australia	Hinchinbrook Island	Southern Sea Ventures	Multi-day	Sea kayak	1
New Zealand	Abel Tasman	Ocean River, Natural High	Multi-day	Sea kayak	2
Alaska	Admiralty Island	Kayak Express	Multi-day	Sea kayak	1
Alaska	Prince William Sound	USNOLS	Multi-day	Sea kayak	1
Canada	Baffin Island	Blackfeather	Multi-day	Sea kayak	1
USA	San Juan Islands	Sea Quest Kayaks	Multi-day	Sea kayak	1
Norway	Svalbard	SSV and Aurora Expeditions	Multi-day	Sea kayak	1
Samoa	Upolu Coastline	Ecotour Samoa	Single-day	Sea kayak	1
Thailand	Phangna Bay	John Gray's Sea Canoe	Single-day	Sea kayak	1

a well-established social workgroup. Other guides work only intermittently or occasionally, or work on different tours each time and each season, making their living principally from other professions. Even amongst these part-time guides, however, there is a brotherhood and sisterhood of shared skill and experience. There are two key features of the guide subgroup. The first is a sense of difference from the client subgroup, based on outdoor ability and lifestyle choice. The second is an implicit internal ranking or pecking order based on the skill and experience of individual guides, the whitewater rivers and individual rapids they have run or the oceans on which they have paddled their sea kayaks.

For those tours in which I took part as part of the staff, generally as a safety kayaker, my position was defined within the guide subgroup. As a once-off and generally volunteer addition to the staff, my role and status within the guide group were very minor. I had no authority to make decisions or instruct clients, but only to help them as requested by the raft guides or instructed by the trip leader. My experience in a number of other water-borne tours conferred a certain initial cachet, which would quickly have been lost if I had performed poorly in my role as safety kayaker. That is, I was a marginal member of the guide subgroup, accepted on probation, under test, and subject to continual observation and assessment. If the clients were sufficiently observant to be aware of the dynamics within the guide subgroup, this ambiguous status would be discernible.

For those tours in which I took part as a client, my position was defined within the client subgroup. For both guides and clients, I would appear as a relatively experienced though not particularly skilled kayaker. In the more difficult whitewater rivers I would appear as someone who needed to be watched and looked after, in comparison to more skilled kayakers. In less difficult rivers or ocean kayaking trips I would appear as someone who could help in looking after and teaching less skilled and experienced clients. To the other clients, I appeared as a relatively experienced client, but not a guide. To the guides, it would be clear that I had some previous experience as a safety kayaker and some knowledge of guiding, which once again provided a somewhat ambiguous status.

In living through these tours as a participant I necessarily observed and took part in public communications between and amongst staff and clients, on a wide range of topics. It is these observations that form the basis for this analysis. I took part in conversations and communications as occasion demanded, referring to previous trips as relevant, but generally without attempting to influence or direct conversations or to record them.

These communications may be considered in four main categories. First is the overall conversational context where the same patterns are repeated consistently. Second are routine but critical operational communications, notably those related to risk and safety, health and hygiene, and client satisfaction. Third are emergency communications, occurring when at least one participant was at potential risk of immediate injury or death; and fourth are communications which though not emergencies, nonetheless involved strong emotional overtones for the participants for a variety of reasons.

Communication patterns and structure

For the overall conversational context, this chapter first considers the general patterns and topics of communication amongst the staff and amongst the clients independently and between the staff and the clients. The staff on these tours are generally expert raft or kayak guides, but for simplicity they are referred to here simply as staff unless circumstances require otherwise. I examine the main topics raised and the types of tours and the timing within the tour when those topics were generally mentioned. The principal aim of this component, therefore, is to provide a context of conversational communication, as a backdrop or norm against which to compare the more targeted or instructional communications in the other three categories.

The principal forms of communication and conversation are summarised in Table 5.2, with approximate measures of relative frequencies. The relative frequencies are comparisons between the four possible combinations of staff and client communication: amongst staff, staff to client, client to staff, and amongst clients. They do not indicate the relative proportions of time allocated to each of the topics either by staff or by clients, that is, they do not indicate comparisons between topics, but only within them.

Table 5.2	Major Subjects of Routine Communications

		Relative Frequency for Particular Subject			
Subject	**Examples**	**Guide to Guide**	**Guide to Client[1]**	**Client to Guide[1]**	**Client to Client**
Relevant to tour					
Safety	Throw rope, avoid danger	* *	* * *	*	*
Logistics	Lift boat, carry gear	* * *	* *	*	*
Logistics, planned	Campsites, stops, day's journey, cooking	* * *	*	* *	* *
Equipment	Expected weather, clothing needs, tents, tarps	*	* *	* * *	* *
Hygiene	Washing, fires, human waste	* *	* * *	*	* *
Hygiene	Do not drop litter, butts	*	* * *	*	* *
Hygiene	Wash hands, filter water, toilet practice	*	* * *	* *	* *
Observation	Wildlife, rapid	*	* * *	* *	* *
Relationships, on-tour	Existing or new	*[†]	*	*	* *
Not about tour					
Social	General chatter	*	*	*	* * *
Politics	Current events	*	*	*	* *
Interests	Outside the tour	*	* *	*	* * *
Relationships, outside tour	Status, opinions	*	*	* *	* *
Employment	Type of work	*	* *	*	* *
Travel	Other than this tour	* * *	*	*	* * *

[1]*Communications guide to client mostly instructions; client to guide mostly questions.*
[†]*Refers to public discussion only; much more out of clients' hearing.*
* = rate, * * = medium, * * * = common.

The patterns shown in Table 5.2 are relatively constant across a wide range of different paddle-powered tours, whether short or long, beginner or expert, and whether or not the staff and clients share the same language. Essentially, there are some aspects of the trip where staff need to make decisions on a day-by-day basis and which they therefore discuss amongst themselves. Most of the other aspects are so routine that no discussion is required. There are some aspects where the staff have to tell the clients what to do, either very specific and immediate instructions or more general operating procedures. These are also the issues where the clients most commonly have questions for the staff, usually requesting repetition or clarification of instructions. These topics are also covered to some degree in conversation amongst clients, most commonly where one client asks advice or information from another client instead of a staff member. These patterns have immediate parallels in other subsectors of the tourism and hospitality industries.

The majority of client-to-client conversation on most tours, in contrast, is of a more general social nature, as the clients get to know one another. During the more relaxed sections of the tour, when no instructions are being given and no strenuous activities are underway, similar social interactions occur between staff and clients. Much of this is simply social glue, for mutual entertainment and group cohesion, with no intention by the participants concerned to maintain contact once the tour ends. A proportion, however, is aimed at least potentially at the establishment of more lasting friendships or relationships which may continue beyond the tour itself. In addition, many commercial tours include some participants who already have relationships or friendships of various kinds, and much of their conversation is a continuation of ongoing social interactions unrelated to the tour itself.

Each of these categories of communication can be important to the proper operation of a tour. If communications are considered in a hierarchy according to their potential significance for the structure and safety of the overall tour, however, the highest-level communications are generally all amongst staff. It is communications amongst staff which determine whether or not to run a particular river or paddle a particular route at all, on a particular date and with a particular group. It is these communications which determine: whether or not to abort any particular trip in the face of unexpected difficulties or dangers; which particular camping areas to use, in the case of multi-day trips with a choice of overnight campsites; whether to run or portage particular rapids, and if so by what route; whether a sick or injured participant can carry on or needs emergency evacuation; and even what to eat each day, if there is a choice. Communications amongst staff may also include urgent information or signals, for example, drawing attention to a hazard or a client in difficulties, or pointing out the preferred route through a rapid or a preferred landing site on a lee shore.

Some of the communications between staff and clients are also critical to the safe and successful operation of the tour, though generally less far-reaching than those amongst staff. Some examples are given later in this chapter. In this particular subsector, staff also need to inform clients about many other aspects of the tour, though with a lower degree of urgency. In single-day trips this information is relatively rudimentary and is typically delivered either whilst driving to the river or at the same time as the initial safety briefing. In multi-day trips, where there is more information to convey, it is commonly reserved for a briefing at the first day's campsite, either on arrival or after the clients have eaten. Such briefings typically include information on: toilet practices; hygiene around the cooking and eating areas; tents and camping practices; and cleaning, washing, litter control, and other environmental management issues. On many tours of this type, some of the clients have little or no outdoor or camping experience and ask for these instructions to be repeated several times over. The majority of communications between staff and clients, particularly for single-day tours or in the early parts of multi-day tours, relate to detailed technical issues of this type. Towards the later part of a tour, however, even on single-day trips, communications between staff and clients become more conversational, as they learn about each others' lifestyles and sometimes seek to establish closer friendships.

Many tours of this type include at least a few clients who have previous experience on the water, and once the other clients discover this they will begin to use them as a subsidiary source of technical information, to avoid the need to continually question the staff. Most conversation amongst clients, however, is of a more general social nature, as noted above.

Routine operational communications on risk and safety

Most tours of this type include an initial safety briefing, and in all save expert-only trips, this is commonly combined with basic paddling instructions for those clients unfamiliar with the craft concerned. At particularly risky points in the tour there may be additional more specific safety briefings. For example, in a whitewater river trip the group may pull to the side of the river to inspect a rapid before running it and staff may use the opportunity to point out particular hazards and give specific instructions in case a raft overturns or a client falls out. Similarly, in a sea kayak tour the staff may call for the kayaks to raft-up, i.e. to assemble alongside each other and stop paddling, so as to give specific instructions for manoeuvres such as landing on a beach through surf. In whitewater paddle-raft trips, each raft commonly has a staff guide responsible for steering the boat, and during whitewater sections the staff may issue a near-continuous stream of commands to the clients, who are helping to propel and/or balance the boat.

Safety issues are of particular concern in developing nations, where not all tour operators meet the same standards as would be expected in developed countries. A good example is provided by an incident which occurred on a 1-day paddle-raft tour on a high-volume, warm-water river with a series of moderate and difficult rapids. The clients were inexperienced, and there were five rafts but only one safety kayaker. The group portaged the upper half of the most difficult rapid and ran the lower half. The rapid ended in a large wave above a wide circulating pool, neither of them deadly but sufficient to flip the rafts and spill the clients into the pool, where they were swept in circles, some dropped their paddles, and several were gasping rather desperately for breath. Despite this, the guides followed each other down the rapid without allowing time for previous rafts to be rescued. As it happened, every single raft flipped, and the 1 safety kayaker had to rescue 19 individual clients, some of them severely distressed, and a number of paddles. This situation occurred partly because the staff were not only overconfident and incautious, but also because they had no communication system so each guide made an independent unilateral decision to start their run, with no overall safety strategy.

In contrast to the case summarised above, there are many examples of good safety communications between staff and clients. One such incident occurred during a multi-day sea kayak tour in the High Arctic, with expedition cruise support, i.e. day kayaking from an expedition cruise ship. There was 1 guide and 1 experienced client in single kayaks and 10 clients in 5 double kayaks. The guide produced a small brand-new waterproof GPS unit and after checking that the more experienced client knew how to use it, handed it over with a request to track the group's course in case fog blocked the line of sight to the ship. As it turned out, this precaution provided unnecessary, but it provides a good example of forethought for group safety, making use of client skills, and setting up safety systems quietly without alarming less experienced clients.

Routine operational communications on health and hygiene

Raft and kayak tours travelling through national parks in developed nations are generally required to bring and use portable toilets and to carry all human waste out of the park for later disposal. One of the staff generally has the job of locating a suitably private site to install the toilet at each camp. Clients are rarely familiar with these systems and need clear instructions, which necessarily involve some human physiological references which would not normally be adopted during polite conservation in an urban setting. Outside protected areas, especially in developing nations, tours may dig group pit toilets at campsites or advise clients to dig individual catholes. Wherever there is a group toilet, there is generally a protocol to signify whether or not the toilet is occupied, and hand washing systems to maintain hygiene. These are likely to be unfamiliar to inexperienced clients and must be communicated clearly at the start of the tour.

There are similar but slightly different hand washing systems for anyone assisting in food preparation, and for all staff and clients before eating. There are systems for washing and sterilising crockery and cutlery and for separating and storing different categories of garbage. None of these are complicated, but they are new to many clients and they need to be followed quite precisely from the very beginning of the tour. Different staff adopt different approaches and terminologies for conveying the same information, generally involving a balance between embarrassment and unambiguousness. Clients are often uncertain over these procedures and discuss them amongst each other for clarification, explanation, or reassurance.

Many of these protocols were first developed by commercial raft tours on the Colorado Grand Canyon, a 2-week trip on a very heavily used, high-volume river through an arid-zone national park with few campsites. The terrestrial environment of the riverbanks has low-nutrient sandy soils and receives little rainfall, whereas the river has a high flow volume and is relatively rich in nutrients. To minimise impacts in this environment, rafters are told to urinate into the river rather than on land. This commonly causes some confusion amongst the clients and requires careful explanation. A similar issue arises in some sections of the Low Arctic used for multi-day sea kayak tours, where campsites are very limited and the ocean has high biological productivity so that organic detritus is rapidly consumed by marine organisms. Disposing of human waste in the ocean is thus preferable on environmental, hygienic, aesthetic, and safety grounds. There is a relatively straightforward technique for this, involving the use of flat rocks which are plentiful along the shoreline, and there is a certain knack to throwing these rocks into the ocean without mishap. Staff have to explain both the rationale and the technique to the clients. Once again, this is an important topic of communication, but one which can create some embarrassment on the first day of a trip, particularly if clients have little previous outdoor experience. There are other commercial operators in the same region who require their clients to make use of natural substitutes for toilet paper, in order to minimise impacts, and this can generate intense debate amongst participants as to the relative merits of different materials. These tours are routine retail products, and these topics of communication are a necessary part of every tour, critical to maintaining the operating areas in a hygienic condition for future trips, whilst simultaneously maintaining the health of the participants on the current trip.

In contrast to the examples above, many raft tours in developing nations operate on high-volume rivers in agricultural landscapes where human waste is of less concern since rivers already carry residues from livestock. Non-biodegradable litter, such as plastic bags and cigarette butts, however, has both ecological and aesthetic impacts. An example of poor communication on these issues occurred in a multi-day raft tour on a high-volume river in western Nepal. It was a large group with several eight-passenger rafts, and about half the clients and guides were smokers. The staff gave no instructions regarding proper disposal of cigarette butts, and both clients and staff simply dropped their butts onto the sandy beaches where the group was camping. This created a significant litter impact and an aesthetic impact for the non-smoking members of the group. The non-smoking clients picked up the cigarette butts every morning, in a pointed form of non-verbal communication, but neither the smokers nor the staff paid attention. This occurred even though the company policy was not to leave litter of any kind, and both staff and clients were expatriates familiar with anti-littering laws in their own countries. This case study therefore represents a failure and indeed lack of communication on a relevant topic.

A very different outcome occurred on another such tour, a multi-day expeditionary raft tour on a difficult cold-water, high-volume river in China. Cigarette butts were also the key item of litter in this case. The participants were drawn from several different countries, with different groups speaking various dialects of English, Japanese, and Chinese. None of the English-speakers smoked, but most of the Chinese- and Japanese-speakers did. The Japanese participants each had small containers, such as old 35-mm slide-film canisters, in which they stored cigarette butts until they could empty them into the group rubbish container. Initially, all the Chinese participants threw their cigarette butts into the river or onto the ground. Once they noticed the Japanese example, however, the Chinese began to follow the same practice without any verbal communication. This provides a good example of peer-to-peer communication amongst clients, solely by example.

Routine operational communications on sights and scenery

In many tours it is commonplace for staff to draw clients' attention to particularly spectacular or unusual scenery or wildlife and in some cases for clients to do likewise. Such communications are generally unremarkable. Occasionally, however, raft and kayak tours see sights sufficiently unusual to cause them concern, provoking non-routine communications. On a multi-day, cool-water ocean sea kayak trip with inexperienced clients in Abel Tasman National Park, New Zealand, the guides lead the group without prior warning to a particular point where seals approached and began to follow the kayaks. The guides lead the group through a narrow channel into a shallow tidal pool, and one of the seals followed them in and began to display acrobatic swimming prowess. The clients were amazed and impressed. Staff communication to the clients focussed largely on telling the kayaks to stay close together and paddle gently and slowly, and client communication to staff consisted mainly of thanks after the occasion. Similar events occur in a number of other sea kayak tours in various countries, with different marine mammals. In some cases, there are legal restrictions on approach distances, and guides must communicate these to clients. One example occurred on the final day of a multi-day, cold-water ocean sea kayak tour, with inexperienced clients, in the San Juan Islands, USA. The guides lead the group into a particular bay where there was a pod of orcas or killer whales. The area is a marine park and powerboats are not permitted into this bay. Some of the orcas swam very close and in a few cases underneath the sea kayaks, occasionally emitting bubbles which caused the kayaks to shake in the water. The clients were not only greatly excited and impressed, but also somewhat afraid. Their principal communications were questions to staff regarding safety, and the guides' principal communications were in the form of reassurance.

Emergency communications

The preceding sections all refer to communications which are routine in the sense that they are either repeated, necessary, or likely every time the tour concerned is run. In addition to routine operational communications of this type, however, many tours may involve non-routine emergency communications in circumstances where life or limb are at immediate risk, despite prior safety briefings. Such communications are critical for the safety of tour participants. One such incident occurred during a 12-day whitewater raft tour on a difficult cold-water river in Tasmania, Australia. The rafts and kayaks had regrouped in a small pool immediately above a runnable but potentially deadly rapid. A kayaking client miscalculated water flow and was washed under a raft, pinned against a rock, and had to bail out. The guides were in small paddle rafts, one on each side of the river, and as the client floated to the surface, the guide on the far side of the river threw a safety line. The client, miscalculating relative risks, ignored the line and tried to swim to the near bank. The guide very quickly retrieved his safety line, and both guides threw lines which crossed on the water immediately below the client, just as he was approaching the lip of the rapid. He grabbed one and was pulled to safety. No comments were made except by the lead guide, who said quietly: 'I hope you realise what a neat piece of bagging [i.e. rope throwing] that was.' This was a very effective communication, leading the client to pay greater attention to safety on the rest of the tour, but without causing undue embarrassment or alarm.

Another such incident occurred at the most difficult rapid on a 5-day raft and kayak tour on a medium-volume, cold-water river in the South Island of New Zealand. The rafters portaged this rapid but the kayakers ran it. The first kayaker, underestimating water speed, was nearly dragged backwards into a lethal 'rock strainer', a hole between rocks where the current would wash a human body and trap it under water. After a rather risky self-rescue, he stood by with a safety line for the remaining kayakers. One of these was indeed swept backwards into the rock strainer, but a thrown safety line rescued her just in time. Only one word was said or needed: 'Thanks'. This was an unusual client-to-client communication, compressing a wealth of content into a very brief utterance.

A more unusual set of emergency communications occurred on a 12-day expeditionary trip with both rafts and kayaks on a high-volume, cool-water river in China, with numerous large and difficult rapids. At the most dangerous of these, most of the kayakers portaged the rapid. One client kayaker ran the rapid successfully and waited below for safety, whilst one of the rafts attempted a run with one guide and one raft client. The raft was thrown high in the air and capsized, and the occupants were thrown clear and washed down the rapid. The guide washed through in a more dangerous position, and the kayaker first pulled him into calmer water, and turned to go back for the raft client. The guide, however, gasped: 'No! Get me to the bank!' The kayaker yelled at the raft client: 'Are you okay?' He replied calmly, so the kayaker took the guide to the bank before returning. This thus provides an example of clear communications in a critical situation, where a client was not only rescuing a member of staff, but rescuing a guide before a client. This particular rafting client was unusually calm in a dangerous situation. Indeed, he said quietly to the kayaker as they reached the bank: 'You told me that if I fell out in this rapid, I would be under water for at least nine seconds – and actually it was 18, I was counting.'

A key aspect of the example above is that everyone involved was fluent in the same language. Where this is not the case, it creates additional difficulties. One such incident occurred on a multi-day expeditionary descent of a remote river in Tibet, which included Japanese and Chinese as well as English-speaking participants. All communications had to be translated by the few multi-lingual members of each language subgroup. Two Chinese clients fell out of a raft at the top of a rapid and were rescued by a safety kayaker following standard procedure, i.e. to hold onto a handle at the end of the kayak whilst it towed them to a safe part of the river. They were not familiar with kayak rescue, however, and at first were unable to understand the kayaker's instructions, so the rescue was slow. Fortunately, this particular instance was a routine river rescue, not life-threatening, but it illustrates the critical role of rapid comprehension in emergency communications. If the rapid had been more serious this could have put both the clients and the kayaker at significant risk. The procedure had been explained during an earlier safety briefing, but clearly had not been understood. A Chinese-language article subsequently published about the tour by one of the Chinese participants concerned confirmed this.

Emotional communications

Not all non-routine communications relate to emergencies. Some of the tours in which I took part involved non-routine communications with a strong emotional component of some type, positive or negative, which affected the tour and client satisfaction but was not part of normal operations. Some of the routine communications outlined in the preceding section also produced an emotional outcome, such as clients excited by seals or orcas, but the communications themselves were routine and unemotional. Clearly, the distinction between routine and non-routine communications is not hard and fast, but it is still a valuable one.

One such incident occurred on a small and high-priced sea kayak tour in the High Arctic, without boat support but in an area frequented by high-speed Inuit fishing boats. The group, consisting of two guide kayaks plus two double client kayaks, was crossing an inlet in calm conditions. One of the client kayaks paddled ahead, and instead of simply sending the second guide to catch up with them, the lead guide fired a marine flare to halt them, even though they were in fact already waiting at a small iceberg. The group paddled together to shore, which was not far away, and the lead guide then berated the clients, to the considerable surprise of the rest of the group. No-one was at risk, and there was no urgency at the time of the communication. The clients would accept the guide's authority to give instructions and to make judgements on their behalf, overriding their own judgements if necessary, regarding safe practices for the group. For example, the guide could have instructed all clients to remain close together during the crossing or could have called out when the client kayak first began to pull ahead. If the guide felt it necessary, he could also have issued a calm admonishment to the clients concerned, after the event. An emotional and threatening communication, however, was not perceived as appropriate by any of the clients. This particular communication does not provide a good model for tour staff to follow!

Failure of communications between clients is illustrated by an incident which occurred on the first day of a multi-day ocean sea kayak tour in the High Arctic. The group had encountered narwhal, which were the principal attraction and advertising icon for the tour. Most of the staff and clients were content to watch the narwhal from land, where they had halted during the day's paddling. One double kayak with two clients, who had not known each other before the tour, paddled out to see the narwhal at close range. By paddling quietly when the particular narwhal concerned was submerged, they were able to approach it quite closely. One of the clients, however, became increasingly nervous, asking numerous questions of the other client. When the narwhal, a young male, became visible surfacing right beside the kayak, this client panicked and suddenly began to paddle backwards, scaring the narwhal into a crash dive. Since a close view of this type was exactly what the other client was trying to achieve, this introduced a certain degree of tension in their subsequent communications, albeit amused and resigned rather than annoyed.

Two incidents from rafting tours in developing nations illustrate the differences in attitude between experienced and inexperienced clients. The first of these took place during the first post-monsoon run of an often-rafted warm-water, high-volume river in Nepal. The group found first a dead buffalo and then a dead human being floating in large eddies. This produced a babble of excited and concerned conversation between the clients, which the staff played down. The clients were inexperienced, largely backpackers. They were not familiar with the country, the culture, or monsoon rainfall. Few if any had previously seen a human corpse. A rather different reaction to a human corpse occurred in the second case, a multi-day expeditionary raft and kayak tour on a difficult, cold-water, high-volume river in Tibet. On the second morning of the trip, at the first overnight campsite, one of the client kayakers found a dead body on the opposite bank of the river, completely rotted away to a skeleton, but still wearing clothes. Some local villagers passed it by without comment. The group had already seen vultures tearing up a puppy on the way to the river. The clients in this case were experienced travellers who were familiar with modern cultures in a variety of developing nations. They treated the skeleton more as a photo opportunity than a cause for concern, with conversation focussing somewhat sardonically on cross-cultural differences.

Finally, it is worth noting that not all communications are serious and not all emotions negative. Multi-day ocean sea kayak tours in the low Arctic may often see black bear on the shoreline; and indeed, must generally take precautions against equipment damage by bear at overnight campsites. Many of these shorelines are also dotted with large solitary dark rocks, however, which can easily be mistaken for black bear at a distance. On one such tour, the clients were competing to spot new bears, and the first person to see one would call out 'bear!' and point. If the object identified proved on closer inspection to be a rock, however, the other clients would call out 'rock bear!', accompanied by ribald commentary on the original client's powers of observation. This kept everyone amused for several days.

Key characteristics for different communication categories

The key characteristics for each of these major categories of communications are summarised in Table 5.3. These are extracted from the case studies above, which themselves are selected to illustrate the various categories. As outlined in Table 5.3, the case studies indicate that to achieve a satisfactory outcome, different characteristics of communication are critical for different categories of communication.

For routine safety briefings the key is to carry out the briefing in good time, to allow adequate discussion and feedback, and to make sure that information is conveyed across any barriers of language and culture. Such barriers can occur within a single co-linguistic group, e.g. if members differ in skill, experience, and attitude to risk. Indeed, such communication barriers seem to have been important contributing factors in a number of fatal incidents during rafting and canyoning tours (Cater, 2006a). For routine hygiene briefings the key issues are firstly, how guides can convey simple but

Table 5.3	Key Characteristics of Communication Case Studies		
Issue	**Between**	**Outcome**	**Features**
Safety	Staff, staff	Poor	Last-moment, hasty, unclear, no discussion, no feedback
Safety	Staff, client	Good	Timely, fully discussed, feedback
Safety	Staff, clients	Good	Timely, fully discussed, used leadership structure, multiple languages/cultures
Hygiene	Staff, clients	Good	Embarrassment, unfamiliarity
Hygiene	Staff, clients	Good	Embarrassment, unfamiliarity, technical instructions
Hygiene	Staff, clients	Poor	No instructions, no discussion, multiple languages/cultures
Hygiene	Clients, clients	Good	Non-verbal, multiple languages/cultures
Sights	Staff, clients	Good	Surprise, low-key management
Sights	Staff, clients	Good	Low-key management, reassurance
Emergency	Staff, clients	Good	Minimal, after event
Emergency	Client, client	Good	Minimal, after event
Emergency	Clients, staff	Good	Clear, critical, during event
Emergency	Clients, staff	Poor	During event, multiple languages/cultures
Emotional	Staff, clients	Poor	Inadequate pre-event; angry and confused after event
Emotional	Client, client	Poor	Inadequate pre-event; scared and confused during event
Emotional	Client, client	Neutral	Surprise, disgust, during event
Emotional	Client, client	Good	Interest, during event
Emotional	Client, client	Good	Amusement, during event

unfamiliar technical instructions to clients, sometimes across cultures, without causing undue embarrassment; and secondly, the importance of guides providing an example or role model, e.g. in food preparation. These aspects have recently been shown to be critical in other forms of guide–client communications, namely, those relating to minimal-impact practices (Buckley and Littlefair, 2007). For routine presentation of particular sights and scenery, the key issues are low-key management of client behaviour so as to maximise the experience through an element of surprise and provision of reassurance if clients are concerned.

In cases of emergency, the key issue is that communications must be clear, unambiguous, and to the point. In some cases, the actual emergency communication may take place without words, during the emergency event itself, through the throwing of safety ropes. Often, it is a key factor that all involved are experienced and able to make rapid and accurate judgements of risk; and also that they all speak the same language and are able to understand instantly. Where participants are unfamiliar with rescue practices, or unable to communicate quickly because of language barriers, risks are increased considerably. Also important for any emergency communication is that it should link well to prior safety briefings. If participants have received a safety briefing which includes emergency responses, they are more likely to understand emergency communications even despite language barriers or lack of prior practical experience.

For the communications labelled in Table 5.3 as emotional, the connecting factors are firstly that they all took place in response to particular unexpected and non-routine events which did not actually involve immediate risk to participants; and secondly that at least one of the participants involved experienced a significant emotional change at the time of the communication. There seems to be two general patterns. The first is simply that prior experience influences how an event is perceived. The second is that participants may have widely differing perceptions of particular events, because of inadequate prior communication and may experience emotional reactions to unexpected behaviours by other participants.

Discussion

Most commercial raft, kayak, and sea kayak tours involve coordinated action, including unfamiliar procedures, between groups of people who have not met each other previously, in circumstances which may involve risks to life and limb. Under such circumstances, communications become critical for human safety, health and hygiene, environmental management, and client satisfaction. In adventure tourism, interpretation of the natural environment and/or cultural experiences (the key form of communication in ecotourism) is only a small part of the overall matrix of communications. Instead, communications relating to safety and operational issues are paramount.

Most adventure tours are temporary assemblages of strangers whose communications are heavily mediated by the needs and opportunities of the tour experience itself. In particular, adventure tours involve a strong asymmetry of experience between clients and guides. For clients the experience is one of excitement and novelty; for the staff, control, and routine. For both staff and clients, however, there are typically short periods of stress, when communications become critical; interspersed with long periods when communication is more conversational. These patterns would also seem to apply in other sectors of the tourism and hospitality industries. In a hotel, coach tour or ski resort, for example, there are routine workplace communications amongst staff, general conversation amongst clients, and operational instructions and questions between staff and clients.

A total of 366 person-days of direct observation on 59 commercial tour products, as reported above, indicate that there are common patterns of communication between staff and clients, amongst staff, and amongst clients. There are relatively standard patterns of routine communications, which help to establish smooth operational structures and teamwork, partly through technical advice and partly through social bonding. Overlaid on these routine patterns, which make up the majority of communications on tours of this type, are a variety of non-routine communications which occur during emergencies, emotional outbursts, frightening events, unusual sightings, internal critiques or criticisms within the tour group, or circumstances which may lead to embarrassment.

Broadly speaking, from a safety and operational perspective there is a hierarchy of communications. Those which are most far-reaching and critical are commonly amongst staff. Many of the instructions from staff to clients, and to a lesser extent questions from clients to staff, are also of high importance for safety and operations, though generally not so far-reaching as communications amongst staff. The majority of communications amongst clients fulfil a mainly social function, but a proportion is also used to reinforce or occasionally to question information provided by staff.

For this subset of the tourism industry, communication is indeed a critical component. Communications amongst staff, from staff to clients and clients to staff, and even amongst clients can all be essential for safety, for hygiene, for operational decisions and actions, and for client satisfaction. If the staff and clients could not communicate, these tours could not operate:

communication is as critical component of the tour as equipment or staff, but one which has received far less attention to date.

As one example, these adventure tours illustrate the critical role of language compatibility. It is possible to run single-day raft tours for inexperienced clients who do not speak the staff language, but only if the staff learn some simple instructions in the clients' language. Indeed, this is commonplace for raft trips with Japanese clients on Australian and New Zealand rivers. Similarly, it is possible for individual experienced international clients to take part in multi-day tours where all the staff and other clients speak only the domestic language, but only if the staff can also communicate key instructions and information in the language of the international client. On multi-day tours in difficult and potentially dangerous circumstances, groups comprising members from several different nations without any single language well understood by all face considerably increased risks and difficulties even if they can all communicate to some degree through multiple translations.

It seems likely that the findings presented here would also apply for most forms of adventure tourism and indeed for most types of tours more generally. It is possible to check into a hotel in a foreign country without a word being said, but this is because the sequence of actions needed by host and guest is generally known to both. When there are cross-cultural mismatches in information or expectations, complete communication breakdowns can occur. It appears, therefore, that communication is indeed an important aspect of adventure tourism management and one which deserves more attention than it has received to date.

LOOKING BACK

1. This chapter has illustrated the roles of social, routine, and emergency communications in one particular adventure tourism subsector, namely, paddle-powered raft and kayak tours. Provide some examples or incidents, real or imagined, for each of these categories of communications, in a different activity subsector such as mountaineering, horse-riding, or driving tours – or any other such sector you wish to nominate.

2. This chapter suggests that there is a hierarchy of communications, with those between guides being most critical and those amongst clients least critical. Do you think this is correct or not, and for what

reasons? Give examples from any of your own experiences in adventure tours or outdoor recreation.

3. There is an extensive academic and industrial literature on workplace communications, including issues such as safety, worker rights, sexual harassment, crisis communication, and so on. Considering the outdoors itself as a workplace for commercial adventure tourism enterprises, how would those aspects of industrial workplace communications law and practice apply?

Charter boat and local dugouts, Indonesia

CHAPTER 6

Land Management: Access and Amenity

KEY ISSUES

Access

- land tenure: public, private, community
- permissions, conditions, monitoring
- insurance, indemnities, fees
- conflicts between different user groups

Amenity migration

- links to outdoor recreation and commercial adventure tourism
- social conflicts, economic opportunities

CHAPTER SUMMARY

Access

Adventure tourism is heavily dependent on terrain. Tour operators need access to areas of land or water where particular adventure activities can be carried out at a skill level appropriate for their clients, under conditions and costs which allow them to assemble marketable commercial products. Most adventure tour enterprises do not own the areas concerned, but must obtain permission to use them from landholders or land management agencies. These may expect some financial return and will generally impose conditions to limit impacts and potential liabilities. In heavily used areas, particularly in publicly owned lands popular for outdoor recreation, conflicts between different user groups are commonplace, and land management agencies use a variety of tools to provide for different adventure activities. In more remote and rarely used areas, physical aspects of access such as infrastructure and emergency evacuation opportunities become critical.

Amenity

In many developed nations, and increasingly also in the wealthier developing countries, there are counter-urbanisation trends where individuals are taking advantage of improved communication technologies to live in rural rather than metropolitan areas. The main driver for such trends is lifestyle amenity, and adventure recreation is a major contributing factor. Amenity migration is leading to significant changes in land use practices and rural societies in many areas, and in some cases this also brings social conflicts.

RESEARCH REVIEW

Access

Restrictions on access to protected areas for adventure tourism activities form part of the standard suite of visitor management tools used by parks agencies, described by authors such as Hammit and Cole (1997), Pigram and Sundell (1997), Pigram and Jenkins (1999), Butler and Boyd (2000), Eagles and McCool (2002), Hendee and Dawson (2002), Page and Dowling (2002), Buckley et al. (2003a), Lockwood et al. (2006), and Buckley (1998b, 2009a, pp. 229–268). The issues have also been reviewed and discussed by, e.g. Brown (1989), Jim (1989), Cole and Hendee (1990), Heberlein et al. (1996), Manning et al. (1996), McCool and Stankey (2001), and Manning (2004). Zoning approaches have been considered by Leung and Marion (1999a), McIntyre et al. (2001), and Lusseau and Higham (2004).

Techniques which rely on limiting numbers, e.g. through carrying-capacity approaches, have been critiqued by Lindberg et al. (1997), Buckley (1999a), McCool and Lime (2001), and McCool and Stankey (2001), and illustrated by Symmonds et al. (2000). McCool and Lime (2001), for example, describe the carrying-capacity approach as 'a seductive fiction, a social trap, or a policy myth'. Approaches which rely on education have been described by Mallick and Driessen (2003) and tested by Medio et al. (1997) and Littlefair (2004). The role of marketing and demarketing is considered by Beeton and Benfield (2002) in Australia and by Kastenholz (2004) in Portugal.

The actual behaviour of small tourism operators in UK national parks has been examined by Dewhurst and Thomas (2003). Responses to various charges and regulations by recreational anglers in Yellowstone National Park, USA have been compared by Kerkvliet and Nowell (2000). Relations between tour operators and regulatory agencies were examined recently by Russell et al. (2008).

Monitoring is an essential component of any strategy to manage commercial tourism operations in protected areas, whether it relies on rangers (Gray and Kalpers, 2005), researchers, or community involvement (Freeman, 2004). The role and use of monitoring data have been reviewed recently by Moore et al. (2003), Buckley and King (2003), Pullin et al. (2004), Danielsen et al. (2005a, 2005b), Hadwen et al. (2007, 2008), and Buckley et al. (2008b). Pullin et al. (2004), for example, found that in the UK 'the majority of conservation actions remain experience-based', with little use of scientific evidence. Individual case studies are summarised in Table 6.1.

Amenity migration

Amenity migration in North America and Europe has been analysed extensively. Recent reviews and major regional case studies include Price et al. (1997); Boyle and Halfacree (1998); Duane (1999, 2004); Shumway and Otterstrom (2001); Stewart (2002); Johnson and Rasker (1995); Johnson et al. (2003); Johnson (2004); Moss (2004, 2005); and Hunter et al. (2004). In addition to lifestyle preferences of individual people, such reviews have considered issues such as jobs and wages, living costs, taxes, retirement, mailbox economies, footloose businesses, technologies, tourism, turnover, community change, infrastructure, and resource impacts. Key areas in North America include: the Sierras in California; the Rocky Mountain states of Wyoming, Idaho, and Montana; and the Kootenay and Okanogan corridors in south-eastern British Columbia, Canada. In Europe the issues are phrased somewhat differently (Glorioso, 1999; Dijst et al., 2005; Gordijn and De Vries, 2004; Prados, 2005). Amenity migration has also been described in Australia (Bell, 2001; Buckley et al., 2006b), and there are localised case studies from Zimbabwe (Tonderayi, 1999) and the Philippines (Moss and Glorioso, 1999; Moss, 2004). In Australia, the most-studied aspect is so-called sea-change migration, where people buy property on the coast

Table 6.1	Case Studies, Monitoring Tourism in Parks	
Country	**Region or Feature**	**Reference**
Kenya	All parks	Olindo et al. (1991)
Canada	Bow Valley, Banff	Ritchie (1998)
USA	Wilderness	McCool and Stankey (2001)
USA	Campsites, trails	Cole (1981, 2004); Leung and Marion (1999b, 1999c, 1999d)
USA	New Jersey West	Burger et al. (1995)
Cayman Is	Stingray tourism	Shackley (1998a)
Europe	Protected areas	Simpson (1996)
China	Tianmushan National Park	Li (2004)
Australia	Western Australia parks	Dowling and Sharp (1997)
Australia	WA whale sharks	Davis et al. (1997)
Australia	Michaelmas Cay, Qld	Muir (1993)
Australia	N-NSW rafting	Buultjens and Davis (2001)
Australia	Tasmania WHAs	Bennett et al. (2003)
Australia	Australian Alps	Pickering et al. (2007); Hadwen et al. (2007, 2008)
New Zealand	National	McIntyre et al. (2001)
New Zealand	Dolphins	Lusseau and Higham (2004)
Sub Antarctic	Islands	Hall and Wouters (1994)
Global	World Heritage Areas	Shackley (1998b)
Global	Caves	Cigna (1993)
Global	Coasts	Carlson and Godfrey (1989)

(Burnley and Murphy, 2004). There is also a smaller but still significant 'tree-change' or 'green change' pattern (Buckley et al., 2006b) analogous to migration to the mountain regions of North America.

BIG PICTURE

Introduction

From the perspective of an adventure tourism entrepreneur, the key aspects of management are those associated with running a successful business. As outlined in previous chapters, these include aspects such as: managing product design and marketing; managing staff, structures, finances, and operational logistics; managing risk and communications; and managing environmental impacts. One key issue is access to appropriate areas and terrain for the particular products and activities on offer.

From the perspective of the owner or manager of land or water where adventure tours take place, adventure tourism management has a somewhat different meaning, namely, controlling which particular adventure tourism enterprises should operate there, what products they can offer, what precautions they must take and guarantees they must provide, and where exactly they can and cannot go. At a broader scale still, local and regional government planning agencies may need to take into account the effects of adventure tourism on large-scale changes in land use patterns, property markets and subdivisions, infrastructure requirements, and community composition and concerns. Although the primary focus of this volume is on the commercial adventure tourism sector, tour operators need to be aware of these broader-scale issues. In many cases, operators may need to negotiate with landowners, land management agencies, and planning bodies in order to gain permission to carry out a particular commercial activity in a preferred area. This chapter, therefore, examines adventure tourism management from these alternative perspectives.

Access

Most outdoor adventure activities rely on particular types of terrain. Skiers and snowboarders need slopes with snow; whitewater rafters and kayakers need rivers of particular sizes and gradients; surfers need waves whilst sea kayakers prefer calm oceans; and so on. The individuals or organisations who own or manage these areas, or control access to them, may thus need to decide whether or not they will allow commercial tour operators to carry out particular activities on their land or water; and if so, under what conditions. In considering this question they may be concerned about risks, both physical and legal; about impacts, whether economic or environmental; and about returns, in the shape of fees, rent or revenue sharing. They may also be concerned about the practicalities of local control, management, and monitoring – essentially, if they let someone onto their land under a particular set of conditions, how will they know that these conditions are being met, and what will they do if they are not? These issues have been reviewed recently by Buckley (2009a) with particular reference to ecotourism, and much of that analysis applies equally to adventure tourism.

For public land management agencies, the overall land management framework is commonly set in: the legislation which establishes the agency; other statutory instruments and regulations; and management plans and policies for individual areas. Subject to these, however, on-ground managers of individual sites or areas may still have considerable discretion as to what activities they permit and under what conditions. Protected area management agencies, in particular, may set conditions relating to: the time of year or the time of day when an activity is permitted or prohibited; the precise locations and access points; the maximum group size and the maximum total number on site at any one time; specific items of equipment which are either required or forbidden; and so on. They may also set conditions relating to the adventure tourism enterprise rather than the adventure activity: for example, conditions relating to business, safety, medical or environmental certification of the company or its guides; or requirements for particular types of insurance or indemnity. Similar considerations apply for other land management agencies, though they may be less concerned over environmental issues. These public land management agencies may also prescribe standard fees and charges for all visitors, for particular activities, or for commercial tourism operations in the areas under their control.

Private landholders face the same issues, but commonly have not considered them in such detail, or established any standard systems to address them. They may either run the tourism business themselves, or grant exclusive access to a single commercial tour operator whom they know personally. In some countries, adventure tours may also operate on land held under communal or community titles of various types. The community may either lease the entire portion of land to a tour operator, as for a number of the wildlife tourism operators in Botswana or Namibia; or they may lease a particular site for a more intensive and localised adventure tourism activity, such as off-road driving. Depending on the country and the type of community title, the conditions of such leases may either be provided for at a national level; or negotiated individually; or some combination of the two.

Two recent analyses of the same community leases for wildlife tourism in northern Botswana, for example (Mbaiwa, 2008; Massyn, 2008), emphasised different aspects and reached rather different conclusions. One analysis, noting that the actual wildlife tourism enterprises were relatively upmarket and catered principally to wealthy international visitors, concluded that these particular developments were 'tourism enclaves' and argued that this necessarily represents exploitation of the community landholders. The other analysis, noting that community members received substantial financial returns from rental payments and profit-sharing arrangements and also received preferential access to employment throughout the entire property, concluded that the community members were in fact shrewd negotiators who had taken advantage of the tour operators' goodwill and ethical concerns to reach a bargain which in fact gave them very substantial benefits.

For large-scale land management organisations such as national parks or forestry agencies, one of the key issues in the management of adventure tourism is to minimise conflicts between different users. This includes conflicts between different activities, and conflicts between private and commercial groups. Such conflicts fall into two broad categories: those within the same activity and those between different activities. The first category is typically related to crowding, where many people want to undertake the same activity at the same time and place. Many land management agencies, for example, have had to introduce complex advance booking systems to control crowding on hiking trails, raftable rivers, designated camping areas, and cliffs routinely used by rock climbers. The second category, conflicts between different activities, commonly arises from asymmetry of impacts, where one set of users disturbs another. Hunters, for example, typically disturb wildlife watchers, birdwatchers, and photo-safari clients. River rafters, not to mention jet-boaters, may disturb recreational riverbank anglers. In general, users with motorised equipment such as vehicles, powerboats, or aircraft tend to disturb those without; users with livestock or wheeled equipment, such as horse riders and mountain bikers, may disturb those without, notably hikers; and users who disturb wildlife, such as trail runners or joggers, may disturb those who want to watch wildlife. There is now an extensive literature analysing such conflicts, and land managers have various ways to separate different user groups in either time or space.

The most common management approach to reduce conflicts is through spatial separation of activities through zoning and permit conditions. In the national parks of the Rocky Mountains and the Pacific Northwest in the USA, for example, horse riding is permitted only on certain tracks. Since frequent use by horses greatly reduces the amenity of a track for hikers, because of droppings, damage, and danger, this effectively means that these designated tracks are used only for horse riding and the remainder only for hiking.

On the south coast of Upolu, the main eastern island of Samoa in the Pacific, there are several commercial surf tourism lodges which operate under locally negotiated arrangements with nearby communities. These lodges maintain communications with each other so as to avoid the crowding and conflict which can occur if too many surfers show up at the same break simultaneously. There is at least one other operator, however, who does not run a lodge and apparently does not communicate with those who do, and this can create conflicts which are difficult for either the local villagers or the long-established lodge operators to manage. Similar conflicts occur in the Maldives and in Indonesia's Mentawai Islands: between different surf charter boat tour operators; between boat-based tour operators and island-based lodges; and between commercial tour clients and independent surfers using boats hired locally. In the Maldives there are certain breaks which are considered exclusive to particular island lodges, but others which are not. In the Mentawai Islands, there has been long-standing conflict between particular tour operators who have established a regulatory mechanism endorsed by the provincial government, and other operators who apparently refuse to acknowledge it.

Amenity migration

At a larger scale, conflicts over adventure tourism and recreation can also occur between different socio-economic groups. A number of rural areas previously used only for agricultural production have subsequently become popular for outdoor recreation and then for amenity migration (Johnson et al., 2003; Johnson, 2004; Moss, 2006).

Amenity migration means moving to live somewhere you like, rather than where you can make the most money. Generally it is used to describe relatively wealthy urban residents who buy property in rural areas as a life-style choice, and change their source of income so as to allow them to enjoy the outdoor amenities of their new neighbourhood. It is one part of complex patterns of urban and counter-urban population shifts which have occurred in many developed countries, and between more and less developed countries, over past decades and indeed centuries.

Amenity migration is relevant to adventure tourism because outdoor recreational opportunities are one of the key attractions or amenities. There are many other factors which contribute to amenity migration, notably: improvements in rural access and communications; the growth of creative and knowledge economies; changing structures of business; and the increasing costs of metropolitan land and facilities. These, however, merely make amenity migration technically, socially, and financially feasible. It is the outdoor amenities themselves which provide the primary driver. And for most amenity migrants, it is a passion for a particular adventure recreation activity which finally triggers the move.

Different people enjoy different types of climate and recreation. Some want snow, skis, and steep slopes; some want lakes, boats, and fish; some want rainforest, hiking boots, and watchable wildlife. Most people want easy access for themselves through well-developed transport and communications infrastructure, but protection of nearby land tenure so their amenity values are not eroded. The preferred areas hence tend to be close to national parks and often close to gateway communities which already have infrastructure and available private land. People also want adequate fresh water and reasonably equable weather, whether tropical, temperate, or montane.

Amenity migrants fall into several rather different categories, and different types dominate in different geographic areas. The stereotypical amenity migrant is a wealthy professional in the finance or information industry, who can use modern communication technologies to maintain a highly paid metropolitan career from a remote rural location. In reality, however, this is only one category. There are also retirees, some wealthy and others less so, and many semi-retired people searching for new challenges and social opportunities through farm work or tourism. There are young families searching for areas with a small-town environment to raise children in an area perceived as low in crime. There are other younger in-migrants who move for a year or two only, taking local employment to pursue recreational opportunities. There are artists and writers seeking inspiration from nature. And there are political or cultural refugees, international or internal, who are simply escaping city society.

Amenity migration is commonly associated with increases in land prices in destination areas. Once these increases are assimilated by relevant government agencies, increases in local government rates and in state or national government land taxes also occur. Such increases may have various social effects, notably the 'rating out' of long-term or retired residents who can no longer afford the increased rates and land taxes and are hence forced to sell up and leave. If these departures offset the arrival of new amenity migrants, migration may not necessarily lead to net population growth, but rather to turnover and replacement of former rural residents by new amenity migrants. Such turnover is commonly accompanied by conflict, between family landholders with a long history of farming and new arrivals who bring different tastes and interests (Johnson et al., 2003).

In some counties in the American West, there are such acute differences in social expectations between long-term resident farming families and new amenity migrants that brochures have been written specifically to instruct new residents as to what they can and cannot expect and what they should and should not do. At the same time, however, recreational amenity migrants often bring new employment opportunities, particularly in the adventure tourism sector, which can be particularly valuable in rural regions where the increased mechanisation of agricultural production has reduced the number of jobs available.

Amenity migrants still want rural landscapes and still need to maintain their land. They may also keep their farms operational, either for tax advantages, for access to government assistance programs, as a basis for tourism businesses, or for personal lifestyle reasons. In addition, large-scale amenity migration may often involve significant subdivision of rural properties into acreage estates and lifestyle communities, as well as individual purchases of entire farm landholdings. Such subdivisions may simply feature residential opportunities in a rural landscape, or they may incorporate specific recreational opportunities such as access to ski fields, golf courses, or waterways for fishing or boating.

Conclusions

As the economic and social scale of adventure tourism worldwide continue to grow, these land management issues of access, conditions, conflicts, and amenity migration will become increasingly critical. The management approaches have been explored in most detail in North America and Europe, though within somewhat different frameworks, and to a lesser degree within Australia and New Zealand. In many developing nations, there are ongoing political conflicts between use of land for conservation and tourism and use for subsistence agriculture. In countries such as China and India, where populations and wealth are expanding rapidly and domestic adventure tourism is doing likewise, there are already large-scale land-use conflicts where outdoor recreation and adventure tourism are in competition with industrial land uses such as hydropower development. In addition, growing domestic tourism is leading to severe crowding in particular protected areas, with consequent environmental impacts (Buckley, 2009a). Environmental management measures are therefore examined in the next chapter.

CASE STUDY 6.1: Amenity Migration, Victorian High Country, Australia

Australia has only very small areas of alpine and subalpine terrain, principally in the Australian Alps in southern New South Wales and northeastern Victoria. Historically, these areas were first used for cattle grazing, which is contentious but still permitted in the Victorian High Country. The NSW sections were subsequently declared as national park, though also used for hydropower development. There are ski resorts in both States, but severe restrictions on residential property development. An area known as Dinner Plain, near the Mt Hothan ski resort in Victoria, has been subject to limited residential development. It is accessed via the gateway town of Bright. Figure 6.1 shows how land prices rose in Dinner Plain, relative to other sections of the Alpine Shire, as a result of residential sales to amenity migrants.

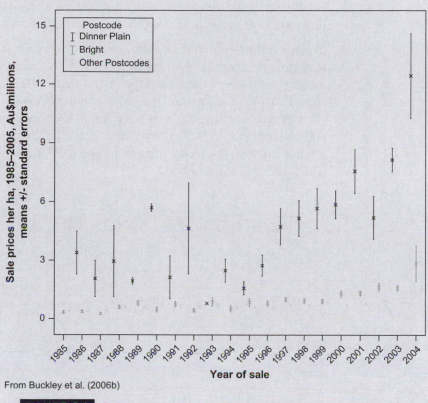

From Buckley et al. (2006b)

FIGURE 6.1 *Sale prices per ha, 1985–2005, Alpine Shire, Victorian Alps.*

LOOKING BACK

1. Identify any area which has experienced significant amenity migration associated with adventure tourism and adventure recreation opportunities. What types of commercial adventure tours are offered there currently? How significant is this sector, and related businesses such as equipment sales and gateway services, for the regional economy? How have property prices changed over recent decades, and how does the financial scale of the residential property market compare with that of the adventure activity sector?

2. If you were a private landholder approached by a commercial adventure tourism operator for permission to operate tours on your

land, what factors should you consider in reaching a decision, what conditions would you apply, and what returns would you expect? Illustrate your answers by considering a particular area and activity.

3. In some countries, public forestry agencies earn more, and contribute more to local economies, through adventure tourism than through logging and timber sales. What factors influence the relative value of these two uses, and how and why do they differ between countries? To what extent may the two users be compatible or incompatible? What political factors may influence whether or not public forestry agencies promote or oppose adventure tourism and recreation in the lands for which they are responsible?

Outside shower, & Beyond Phinda
Forest Lodge, South Africa

CHAPTER 7

Environmental Management

KEY ISSUES

- major components: long-haul travel, mainstream components, adventure activities

- adventure activities: airborne, aquatic, terrestrial

- motorised cf non-motorised activities

- impacts of different adventure activities

- impacts in different ecosystems and at different seasons

- equipment, technologies, and management to reduce impacts

- minimal-impact codes, guidelines, and interpretation

- how to teach minimal-impact behaviour in different activities and ecosystems

- adventure activities in protected areas, other public lands, and private lands

- impact assessment and permitting requirements

- adventure infrastructure: roads, tracks, parking areas, cables, ladders, airstrips, helipads, jetties, launching sites, marinas, pontoons

- events and competitions

CHAPTER SUMMARY

Adventure tourism creates environmental impacts through three main mechanisms: long-haul travel to remote destinations; pro rata use of mainstream tourism facilities; and the adventure activity itself. Different activities have very different types of impact. There are broad distinctions between airborne, aquatic, and terrestrial operations; and significant differences between motorised and non-motorised activities. The impacts of any specific activity also differ greatly between ecosystems and depend heavily on factors such as season, equipment, group size, and individual behaviour. Impacts have been studied extensively for some activities and areas, but barely at all for many others. For some, environmental management measures have been provided through codes of practice, though these are not often well followed. In some cases, new technologies have been developed or adopted specifically to reduce environmental impacts. This applies particularly to noise reduction and waste management.

RESEARCH REVIEW

The environmental impacts and management of various types of adventure tourism have been reviewed by a number of authors, including Mosisch and Arthington (2004), Warnken and Byrnes (2004), Newsome et al. (2004a), and Buckley (2004b). There are also a number of relevant reviews carried out under the heading of ecotourism (e.g. Cater and Cater, 2007; Weaver, 2008; Stronza and Durham, 2008; Buckley 2009a, pp. 117–174, 2009c).

There has been a particular focus on the impacts of adventure tourism on various species of wildlife. Buckley (2004c, 2004d) reviewed published literature on this topic up to 2003, and Buckley (2009a, Table 8.4) listed 45 such impact studies published since that date, and a further 27 on impacts associated specifically with habitat fragmentation. Species examined included various birds (24 studies), bears (7), large cats (3), large mammalian herbivores (5), primates (1), marsupials (8), marine mammals (4), and reptiles and amphibians (7) (Buckley, 2009a, Tables 8.4 and 8.5).

Impacts associated with the inadvertent dispersal of plant weeds by adventure tourists, and also of both plant and animal pathogens, have received attention from, e.g. Wikelski et al. (2004), Buckley et al. (2004a), Whinam et al. (2005), Amo et al. (2006), Pickering et al. (2007), and Newsome et al. (2008).

The environmental impacts of adventure tourism have been examined in much more detail for some activities and ecosystems than others. The impacts of skiing and ski resorts have been reviewed by Buckley et al. (2000) and Hadley and Wilson (2004). Local impacts of ski resorts were studied in Austria by Meyer (1993) and Illich and Haslett (1994); in Scotland by Watson and Moss (2004); in Australia by Mansergh and Scotts (1989), Broome (2001), and Sanecki et al. (2006); and in New Zealand by Fahey et al. (1999). The impacts of snowmobiles were studied by Neumann and Merriam (1972), Pesant (1987), and Vail and Heldt (2004).

The impacts of mountain biking have been considered by Weaver and Dale (1978), Goeft and Alder (2000), Symmonds et al. (2000), Thurston and Reader (2001), and Cessford (2002) and those of horse riding by Weaver and Dale (1978), Summer (1980, 1986), Whinam et al. (1994), Newsome et al. (2002), and Newsome et al. (2004a). The impacts of rock climbing were examined by Camp and Knight (1998) and Farris (1998); of off-road driving by Buckley (2004b); and of hiking and camping by Cole (2004) and Leung and Marion (1999b, 1999c, 1999d, 2004). The impacts of recreational boating have been analysed by Jaakson (1988), Roe and Benson (2001), Mosisch and Arthington (2004), Warnken and Byrnes (2004), and Burfeind and Stunz (2006).

Impacts on vegetation and soils were reviewed by Cole (2004); impacts on birds by Buckley (2004c); and impacts on other terrestrial wildlife by Beale and Monaghan (2004) and Buckley (2004d). Impacts on sharks and stingrays have been described at particular sites by Shackley (1998a), Lewis and Newsome (2003), and Newsome et al. (2004b).

Impacts of SCUBA diving have been examined in Florida and the Caribbean by Dixon et al. (1993), Talge (1993), Marion and Rogers (1994), Hawkins and Roberts (1992, 1993, 1999), Hawkins et al. (1999), Williams and Polunin (2000), Tratalos and Austin (2001), and Townsend (2003); in Greece by Petreas (2003); in the Red Sea by Riegl and Velimirov (1991), Hawkins and Roberts (1994), Jameson et al. (1999), and Zakai and Chadwick-Furman (2002); in South Africa by Schleyer and Tomalin (2000) and Walters and Samways (2001); in the Maldives by Allison (1996); in Australia by Davis and Tisdell (1995), Harriott et al. (1997), Rouphael and Inglis (2001), and Newsome et al. (2004b); in Indonesia by Musa (2003); and in Vanuatu by Howard (1999). Milazzo et al. (2005) examined the impacts of fish feeding by snorkellers.

With a few exceptions, such as Schaeffer et al. (1999), most of these diving impact studies were carried out in coral reef ecosystems. The main impacts reported were breakage of branching corals through direct contact, and swamping with sediment resuspended by divers' fins

(Neil, 1990; Rogers, 1990). Inexperienced divers, and photographers, apparently cause the greatest impacts. Corals can also be damaged by monofilament fishing lines (Asoh et al., 2004).

The impacts of tourism have also been studied for a number of marine mammal species (Bejder and Samuels, 2003; Higham and Lusseau, 2004) including: sperm whales (Gordon et al., 1992); humpback whales (Corkeron, 1995); grey whales (Watkins, 1986); beluga whales (Blane and Jaakson, 1994); dwarf minke whales (Birtles et al., 2002); Hector's dolphins (Bejder et al., 1999; Nichols et al., 2000); bottlenose dolphins (Janik and Thompson, 1996; Scarpaci et al., 2000; Constantine, 2000; Nowacek et al., 2001); other whale and dolphin species (Orams, 2004); manatees (Nowacek et al., 2004); and harp seals (Kovacs and Innes, 1990). Behavioural changes include: avoiding swimmers and/or boats; changes to surfacing patterns; and different vocalisation patterns. Miller et al. (2000) found that male humpback whales sing for longer if their songs are disturbed by low-frequency acoustic interference. Cox et al. (2006) examined the impacts of anthropogenic noise on various species of beaked whales; and Holt et al. (2009) found that when underwater noise levels increase, orcas call more loudly to compensate. Frohoff (2005) reviewed sources of stress in dolphins. Whale watching codes have been compiled and compared by Gjerdalen and Williams (2000), Carlson (2001), and Garrod and Fennell (2004), and compliance with such codes has been tested by Scarpaci and Dayanthi (2003), Mason (2007), and Wiley et al. (2008).

BIG PICTURE

Introduction

A wide variety of different regulations, technologies, management tools, and educational approaches are used in order to reduce the impacts of adventure tourism on the natural environment. These environmental impacts, and associated environmental management tools, may usefully be considered in three main categories. The first category is the impact of long-haul air travel to an adventure tourism destination. Except for group tours, these impacts typically differ between individual participants in the same commercial adventure tourism product, because they originate from different places and have different holiday itineraries. In the past, the environmental impacts of long-haul air travel received relatively little attention. Currently, they are the focus of significant scrutiny because of their contribution to global climate change and its consequent impacts. These are considered in the next chapter.

The second major category of environmental impacts consists of those which derive from components of an adventure tourism experience, that are essentially part of the mainstream tourism industry: such as hotel accommodation in gateway towns, short-haul air or road transport from a gateway town to a tour activity starting point, and so on. Adventure tourism contributes pro rata to the impacts of such mainstream tourism infrastructure, but the proportional contribution is generally rather small. These are considered below, but briefly.

The third category consists of the impacts of adventure activities themselves. These depend on the type of activity and on the terrain, ecosystem, season, equipment used, and the size and behaviour of groups. It is these impacts which form the main focus of this chapter.

Mainstream components of adventure tours

Many half-day or single-day adventure tours, particularly high-volume tours at the lower end of the adventure tourism pyramid shown in Fig. 13.1, operate directly from an urban tourist destination. The tour itself does not include any accommodation or transport, and it is the responsibility of individual participants to make their way to the tour's starting point. This applies, e.g., for short-duration marine tours, which can operate from a marina or a beach; or river jetboating tours, which operate directly from a dock; or balloon rides, which operate from a nominated take-off area. The tour operator may send a minibus to collect participants from urban hotels if needed, but otherwise it is up to each participant to arrive in their own vehicle and to make their own accommodation arrangements before and after the tour. For adventure tourism products of this type, the tour product itself may not include any components of the mainstream tourism industry. The adventure sector, however, still relies on those components; firstly because they support the infrastructure from which the tour operates, and secondly since the tour clients also make use of mainstream facilities during their holidays.

For longer-duration and more inclusive adventure tours, components of mainstream tourist transport and accommodation are packaged into the adventure tour product. The most common accommodation component is simply one or two nights' hotel accommodation before and after the adventure component. The most common transport components are shuttles from a gateway town or airport, to the starting point for the adventure activity. Such shuttles may be by road, e.g. in a tour bus; or by air, when the tour includes a charter or other special flight arrangements either by helicopter, floatplane, or to a local landing strip. Shuttles may even be by sea, using high-speed ferries to transfer passengers between ports or pick-up points in order to take part in a marine adventure tour.

Where an adventure tour makes use of mainstream tourist facilities either directly or indirectly, it contributes pro rata to the environmental impacts of the mainstream facilities. The proportional contribution, however, is relatively small, and environmental management approaches for the adventure component cannot be separated from those for the mainstream facilities as a whole. Environmental management in mainstream tourism accommodation and transport is generally considered under the heading of sustainable tourism (Stabler, 1997) and is beyond the scope of this book.

Adventure activities

The environmental impacts of adventure activities, and the environmental management tools and technologies to reduce and control those impacts, differ greatly between different adventure activities. As a result, relevant literature is relatively scattered. Much of the material available is commonly considered under the heading of recreation ecology (Liddle, 1997; Buckley, 2004e, 2005a; Raschi and Trampetti, 2008). The term is not well defined, and there are strong overlaps with the literature on specific activities, such as skiing, cruise ships, helicopter tours, the boating sector, and so on. The analysis of adventure tourism products by Buckley (2006a) includes a brief section on environmental management for each of the tour products presented.

At the broadest level, adventure activities produce very different environmental impacts according to whether they are carried out on land, on water, or in the air; and on whether or not they are motorised. The environmental impacts of any particular adventure tour product are also affected by when, where, and how it is operated, and it is these aspects which are under the greatest degree of control by the tour operator. There are more fundamental differences, however, associated with the type of tour, the type of terrain, and the type of equipment used. Measures used to manage the impacts of a backcountry horse riding tour, for example, are necessarily very different from those used in a polar expedition cruise or a heliskiing lodge. This is one of the major difficulties and shortcomings associated with eco-certification programmes: they focus on the relative attention paid to environmental management issues by different tour operators within the same type of tour, without considering that differences between tour types are far more fundamental in terms of the tourism industry's overall environmental impacts. This section, therefore, sets out briefly the major types of environmental impacts from different types of adventure activity, and the main management measures which may be used to address those impacts, with a brief commentary on the degree to which different adventure tourism operators may actually have adopted such measures in practice.

Airborne adventure tourism activities

The main environmental impacts of motorised airborne tours using helicopters, light aircraft, floatplanes, or motorised microlights are: noise; leaks and spills at backcountry refuelling sites if used; and atmospheric emissions from burning fuel in aircraft engines. Atmospheric emissions depend on the size and type of aircraft, the type of engine it uses, and its fuel consumption and efficiency. For level flight with the same load, a helicopter necessarily uses more fuel than a fixed-wing aircraft. Such comparison is rarely relevant, however, because helicopters are generally used where fixed-wings are unable to operate effectively: either because there is nowhere for them to land; because they need to make repeated short-haul shuttles; because they need to manoeuvre slowly in tight terrain; or because the flight journey is vertical rather than horizontal.

Small fixed-wing aircraft, including ski planes and floatplanes as well as those with conventional undercarriage, are used widely throughout the adventure tourism industry: not only for scenic flights and joyflights but more importantly, to shuttle clients in and out of small remote airstrips at the beginning and end of their adventure activity. The big-game wildlife watching lodges of sub-Saharan Africa, for example, rely extensively on light aircraft to shuttle clients between lodges. Some of the larger operators own their own aircraft specifically for that purpose. Wilderness Safaris in Botswana, for example, owns its own airline, Sefofane. Similar practices are followed by a number of small island resorts worldwide. Lady Elliot Island Resort in Australia and the local airline which brings its clients are co-owned. Many other adventure tour operators use charter flights, or scheduled flights on small regional airlines, to transport guides and clients to an adventure activity area. Sea kayaking operator Blackfeather, for example, uses a small local airline to shuttle trip participants to Pond Inlet on the northern end of Baffin Island, for its sea kayaking tours in the Canadian Arctic. Canoe tours in parts of Canada rely on floatplanes to land participants in one of the multitudinous small lakes in order to start their journey.

Other than fuel consumption and atmospheric emissions, there are three main potential environmental impacts from these light aircraft operations. The first category consists of the impacts from construction of airstrips; or in the case of floatplanes, the impacts of repeated landings on lakes, rivers, or bays. The main techniques to minimise the impacts of airstrips are: to make them no larger than necessary; to site them where least vegetation clearance is required and they will cause least disruption to wildlife feeding or migration; and to construct and maintain the strip so as to minimise soil erosion and runoff. In practice, there may be limited flexibility in locating airstrips, because of requirements for safe take-off and landing in relation to prevailing winds and terrain, and the need to find a space which is long and level enough for the aircraft concerned to land and take-off.

The second main potential impact is of local fuel leakage, either from drums stored in remote strips, or during actual refuelling operations. There are straightforward techniques to minimise either of these risks, such as bunding and sealing fuel storage areas and using drip trays whilst refuelling. Some helicopter-based operations, including some backcountry heliski operations, use fixed refuelling sites accessible by road: either during summer, as for the Canadian heliski lodges; or year-round, as for the New Zealand heliski operations. Others, however, use the helicopter itself to lift mobile refuelling tanks into the day's operational area, so as to provide a greater range from the operational base. In such cases, it is critical that the fuel tanks can withstand continual lifting and replacement without damage or leaks. This is of particular concern in areas where watercourses support endangered aquatic species or where they provide drinking water for local residents nearby. Himachal Helicopter Skiing in the Indian Himalayas, for example, uses heavy-duty semi-flexible plastic fuel containers for this purpose.

The third major environmental impact of motorised airborne adventure tours is noise and to a lesser extent visual disturbance, both to wildlife and to other human users of the area concerned. Noise disturbance to humans, for example, is the main reason why heliski operations are very tightly restricted in the European Alps. Noise is also the major impact of Canadian heliskiing operations on remaining populations of mountain caribou, and a continual point of contention between heliski operators and conservation groups. Helicopter sightseeing tours in Purnululu National Park in the Kimberley region of Western Australia cause very major disturbance to backcountry hikers and possibly also to a number of endangered bird species resident in the park. Noise has been the principal issue in long-running political debates in relation to aircraft overflights in national parks of the USA, most especially the Grand Canyon of the Colorado. In Australia, sightseeing tourists carried in unpowered gliders fly over Mount Warning National Park in order to approach the summit of Mount Warning, whereas powered aircraft do not. In Springbrook National Park, part of the Gondwana Rainforest World Heritage Area, helicopter sightseeing tours historically exploited a loophole in civil aviation regulations to bring tourists very close to a large waterfall, generating considerable noise disturbance both for wildlife and for tourists on foot, and generating significant controversy between the tour operators and the parks service. Sightseeing tours by powered microlight aircraft, flying at relatively low altitude with unshielded two-stroke engines, also cause significant noise impacts, e.g. to beachgoers in northern New South Wales in Australia. Helicopter tours operating out of Kaikoura in New Zealand apparently cause significant stress to surfacing sperm whales, which are the icon attraction for the tour.

Measures to minimise noise impact from motorised airborne tours may be considered in two main categories: technological modifications to the aircraft, and behavioural modifications to the way it is flown. Different individual makes of light plane and helicopter produce very different volumes and frequencies of noise. The type and design of engine used, and to a lesser extent the placement of the engine and the design of the engine compartment, are major factors influencing noise generation. For helicopters, blade slap may be equally significant. This is the noise created by the helicopter rotor under some flight conditions. It is blade slap which creates the characteristic sound of a helicopter in flight, distinguishing it from a fixed-wing aircraft. The effect is created when each individual blade passes through turbulent air created by the other blades, and occurs particularly during sharp turns and banks and during flight at high speed or under heavy load. Different helicopters produce blade slap under different flight conditions, and the pilot's ability to fly quietly depends on how the helicopter is being used. It also depends very much on the particular type of helicopter, with some being very much quieter or noisier than others. There is some scope to retrofit helicopters with so-called hush kits to reduce noise, but this is limited. The bottom line is that most helicopters are unavoidably noisy.

In comparison to these motorised airborne adventure activities, non-motorised aerial adventure tours have far less environmental impact. The main example is ballooning. This does produce a certain amount of noise when the gas burners are fired to reduce more hot air and generate more lift; and the visual appearance of a balloon at low altitude, or a rapidly moving shadow on the ground, may disturb wildlife. These impacts, however, are relatively limited and in any event far less than those of motorised aircraft. Where balloons fly across relatively remote terrain, as in some areas of Africa, there may also be some impacts on soils and vegetation if the recovery vehicle has to travel off-track. Such impacts, however, would generally be similar to those of wildlife watching safari vehicles. Similar considerations apply for ground-launched non-motorised adventure tourism activities, such as hang-gliding and paragliding, where the only significant impacts are likely to occur at regularly used take-off and landing points.

There is also a significant category of aerial adventure activities which are themselves non-motorised, but which require motorised aircraft to launch them. These include: gliders, which are towed into the air by light aircraft; skydiving and parachute jumping, which require specially fitted jump planes; and certain high-adrenalin activities which do not yet seem to be offered as commercial tours, such as bungy jumping from helicopters. For these activities, the environmental impacts combine those of the aircraft and those of any ground-based recovery operations.

Marine and aquatic adventure tourism activities

For water-based adventure tourism and recreation, there are broad divisions into motorised cf non-motorised, freshwater cf marine, and above-water cf below-water activities, each with its own environmental impacts and management approaches.

Where motorised ships and boats are used in commercial adventure tourism, environmental impacts depend on: the size and speed of the vessel; the size and type of the engine and propulsion systems; hull draught; surface coatings, particularly antifouling substances; techniques for treating and discharging sewage or blackwater, graywater, food scraps, and other rubbish; and for larger vessels, systems for fuel bunkering and refuelling, and systems for taking on and discharging ballast, particularly water ballast. Impacts may also be caused through oil spills, groundings, or collisions. Yachts and other sailboats also discharge sewage and also use antifouling paints.

Marine engines consume fuel and produce both atmospheric and water-borne emissions. In particular, the engine exhaust may deposit unburnt fuel residues on the water surface, and in areas heavily used for commercial or recreational boating, this can create significant surface pollution with petroleum residues. Oil spills associated with boat damage through groundings, collisions, etc., though less common, may be considerably more severe. Most larger vessels, which remain continuously in the water except during major maintenance, are coated with antifouling paints to reduce the build-up of marine organisms on the hull surface. Most of these coatings are based on organic compounds of copper or tin and can create a range of unintended ecological impacts on non-target marine organisms. Shallow-water sessile organisms, i.e. those which are fixed to the substrate and cannot swim away, are most severely affected. For example, there is a considerable literature on the effects of tributyl tin compounds, a common component in antifoulings, on various marine molluscs. As a result, antifoulings based on tributyl tin have been banned in some jurisdictions, and a range of alternative antifouling compounds has been developed.

In addition to these chemically mediated impacts, powerboats can create a variety of direct physical impacts on the natural environment. As well as the impacts of infrastructure, such as marinas and launching ramps, powerboats create erosion along riverbanks and turbulence and sediment disturbance in shallow lakes, seas, and estuaries, which may lead to the death of corals, seagrasses, etc. In shallow seas frequented by marine mammals, high-speed watercraft may cause direct injury to wildlife through boat strike and propeller wounds. A significant proportion of the remaining manatees in the shallow coastal waters of Florida, USA, for example, has been wounded by propeller chops. In many popular near-shore coastal areas, there are regulated speed restrictions on all watercraft in order to reduce such impacts, and also for reasons of human safety, but these restrictions are often ignored.

Even where boats do not actually collide with marine wildlife, they may still cause significant disturbance to marine wildlife species. Concerns over the impacts of whale watching and dolphin watching tours in many countries have led to the development of a wide variety of whale watching and dolphin watching codes and guidelines, some of them voluntary and some statutory. A number of such codes were reviewed by Garrod and Fennell (2004), who found considerable differences amongst them. The degree of compliance with such codes by commercial tour operators has been examined in several countries (Scarpaci and Dayanthi, 2003; Mason, 2007), and it appears that they are often flouted or ignored. Even so, however, they may still be effective in preventing an indiscriminate scrimmage of boats around individual animals.

Motorised boats also create noise. This applies particularly for those with two-stroke outboard motors, such as small runabouts, inflatables, and jet-skis. Noisiest of all are the airboats of the Florida wetlands, which use an unshielded car engine to drive an aircraft propeller mounted on a shallow flat-bottomed hull.

A variety of regulations and guidelines have been adopted in attempts to reduce other environmental impacts of boat-based adventure tours. For ocean-going vessels, discharge of wastes whilst at sea is regulated by MARPOL, an international convention intended to prevent marine pollution. Many vessels ignore MARPOL, and marine wildlife is still at significant risk from flotsam and jetsam, but the majority of this is probably from commercial freighters and perhaps large cruise ships, rather than the smaller boats involved in marine adventure tourism.

Within the coastal waters of individual nations, a wide variety of national legislation may apply to manage marine environmental impacts. In many marine protected areas, particularly those with shallow seas and heavy boat traffic, discharge of human waste may be restricted or prohibited. Tour boats operating in such areas must be equipped with holding tanks for toilet waste. Depending on local regulations, they may be required to pump this waste to an on-shore treatment plant, through pump-out facilities at a marina; or if they are equipped with a waste macerator, they may be permitted to discharge macerated waste whilst underway and well distant from swimming, snorkelling, and diving areas. Smaller day-use boats may have to carry chemical toilets, which can be removed from the boat, emptied, and cleaned at the end of each day.

Even if measures such as these are not mandated by regulation, boat-based tour operations in lakes, rivers, near-shore marine areas, and marine protected areas generally need to adopt minimal-impact practices so as to avoid deterioration in their tourist attractions. To provide technical information on environmental management measures available, and to encourage all operators to adopt them, marine adventure tour operators in particular areas have formed industry associations and in some cases adopted ecocertification programmes. Such associations are not necessarily concerned only with environmental management issues: they may have been formed principally to carry out political lobbying and commercial marketing activities. Once in existence, however, they may also take up an environmental education role.

The Association of Marine Park Tour Operators, AMPTO, in Australia's Great Barrier Reef, was originally formed to represent private sector tour operators in negotiations with the government management agency over issues such as zoning and user fees. Subsequently, however, it also took a role in negotiating a local ecocertification programme operated by the Great Barrier Reef Marine Park Authority, the High Standard Tourism Programme. Members of this programme receive preferential treatment in regard to permitting and licensing. Also well-known is the International Association of Antarctic Tour Operators, IAATO. One of the reasons that IAATO was formed was to fill the vacuum left by the lack of any local environmental regulation in the Antarctic, since the *Antarctic Treaty* does not create any organisation with statutory powers to regulate in Antarctic waters. Membership of IAATO is voluntary, however, and the US-based companies that run the largest and potentially highest-impact cruise ships into the Antarctic have refused to join it. Some individual nations, notably New Zealand, have legislated to provide minimum environmental standards for domestically registered vessels even if they are operating internationally, notably in the Antarctic. Since larger ships which are chartered to a range of different tour operators are more likely to be registered in so-called flag-of-convenience nations, however, such legislation currently has only limited effect.

Minimal-impact codes and guidelines are also available for a range of other boat-based adventure tours, including small boat operations (Rainbow et al., 2000), whitewater rafting and kayaking (Buckley, 1999b), and diving (Rainbow et al., 2002). Guidelines containing similar information and recommendations, but with examples and illustrations, have also been produced by UNWTO (2008).

The environmental impacts of diving as an activity, independently of the dive boat, have been studied in a number of locations and ecosystems, as summarised in Research Review for this chapter. Apart from deliberate effects on marine species, such as those caused by spear-fishing or shell collecting, there may be behavioural impacts on fish, caused by regular feeding; and physical impacts on corals, caused by contact, breakage, and siltation. Coral reefs which have been visited frequently by divers over an extended period commonly suffer significant damage, particularly if the divers are inexperienced and thus less able to control their buoyancy, and more likely to kick corals with their fins. These impacts can be reduced greatly through proper dive training and by minimal-impact briefings before each dive (Medio et al., 1997).

For some marine adventure tours, notably polar expedition cruises, some of the most ecologically significant environmental impacts actually occur during landings, when passengers may cause disturbance to hauled-out seals and sea lions or to roosting or nesting seabirds. Expedition cruise tours to the Antarctic Peninsula and sub-Antarctic islands, for example, land their passengers to look at various species of penguin, albatross, skua, and other seabirds, including nests and chicks. The IAATO code of practice specifies a minimum approach distance, especially for adult seabirds on the nest, but enthusiastic photographers do not always comply, and the same islands are also visited on occasion by larger-scale cruise ships which are not members of IAATO. If the parent birds leave the nest, then eggs or chicks are very rapidly taken by predatory or scavenging bird species (Giese 1996, Giese and Riddle, 1999). Generally, therefore, the parents will remain on the nest even if humans approach quite closely, but they exhibit symptoms of severe stress (Giese, 1998; Holmes et al., 2005). Some of these symptoms are behavioural, such as so-called beak clacking, and can be observed by guide or clients, if they know what to look for. Others are physiological, such as a raised heart rate or elevated levels of stress hormones in the blood, and can only be detected using relatively sophisticated biological research techniques (Giese et al., 1999). This research has shown that the minimum approach distance prescribed by IAATO, currently 5 m, is considerably too close for the birds' comfort and should be increased to at least 10 m or more.

On-ground environmental management approaches for such wildlife encounters are straightforward. Humans should approach nesting seabirds and other wildlife only in small groups, quietly and slowly, keeping low to the ground, staying far enough away so as not to provoke any symptoms of alarm and stress. Everyone should approach from the same side, so that the birds or animals are not encircled and have an easy escape route. Wildlife watchers should move as slowly and quietly on departing as they do on approaching; and each small group should move well away before another group approaches. For the relatively small expedition cruise boats, where passengers generally do pay attention to educational information provided by guides and experts and generally do follow their instructions, it is feasible to ensure that these protocols are generally followed. Impacts may still occur, however, if the same breeding colonies are visited repeatedly by a series of different tour vessels, so that they have little opportunity for recovery between visits; or if they are visited by large-scale cruise ships which try to put as many passengers as possible ashore during a limited time, and do not control their behaviour whilst on shore.

Terrestrial adventure tourism activities

Terrestrial adventure tours range from guided small-group backcountry hikes or cross-country skiing trips, to large groups of off-road vehicles or snowmobiles driven at speed without any concern for the environment. Other types of terrestrial adventure tour use human-powered but wheeled transport, such as mountain bikes; horses or other livestock; or specialist vehicles such as hovercraft or tundra buggies.

As with airborne and water-borne adventure tours, the environmental impacts of terrestrial adventure tours may be considered in four main categories: noise, atmospheric emissions, physical damage, and behavioural effects. Where motorised vehicles are used, even if they are modified or customised for a particular type of tour, the engines are relatively standard two-stroke or four-stroke models designed originally for motorbikes, 4WD vehicles or trucks, and heavy machinery, and this is reflected in the atmospheric emissions from such vehicles. Snowmobiles, for example, are a major source of air pollution in Yellowstone National Park, USA. Noise impacts range from human voices in non-motorised backcountry tours, to the sound of unsilenced two-stroke motors in tours using All-Terrain Vehicles. Noise and associated visual disturbance can have severe ecological impacts on wildlife as well as on other backcountry users. There are many different mechanisms to reduce noise. Some of these are technological, such as changing from two-stroke to four-stroke engines, or improving the design of mufflers and silencers. Others are behavioural, such as talking rather than shouting, and driving slowly at low revs rather than quickly at high revs (Buckley, 2000).

Physical impacts include those of boots, hooves, and wheels on soils and vegetation, both on unsealed tracks and off-track areas; and a contribution to wildlife roadkill, though this is due principally to high-speed traffic on sealed roads. Off-road vehicles driving on beaches may kill nesting birds and burrowing crabs (Buckley, 2004b), and oversnow vehicles may crush small mammals which burrow under the snow, or compact the snow so that they are forced onto the surface and vulnerable to predation (Sanecki et al., 2006). The effects of trampling and tyres in causing soil erosion and compaction, and damaging vegetation, have been studied extensively and were reviewed by Cole (2004) and Manning (2004). In areas dominated by grassy vegetation, and visited only occasionally and only by small groups, it has been suggested by some authors that the best approach to minimise overall impacts is for hikers to spread out widely, so that no two people travel exactly the same path. In almost all other circumstances, however, and especially in areas of heavy use on non-grassy vegetation, it appears that the best approach to minimise overall impacts is for everyone to follow the same track, so that soil and vegetation damage may be acute, but restricted in extent. Similar considerations occur for backcountry campsites.

The environmental impacts of off-road driving on soils and vegetation have also been examined in a range of different ecosystems, from forests to sand dunes (Priskin, 2004). Information available up to 2003 was reviewed by Buckley (2004b), and an update to 2008 is available in Buckley (2009a). Not surprisingly, impacts are higher for vehicles with higher tyre loadings, i.e. the weight carried per unit area of tyre surface touching the ground. They are also higher if vehicles are driven fast, erratically, or with frequent high-speed cornering or acceleration and deceleration. These concerns are all considered in relevant environmental management guidelines, such as those of Buckley (2000).

From the perspective of an adventure tour operator, there is a range of possible approaches to reduce environmental impacts of off-road tours. Most basic is the type and design of the tour and the selection of an appropriate site. Additional approaches include appropriate selection of tyres and vehicle fit-out, and driving with the skills needed to minimise impacts (Buckley, 2000). For an adventure tour which uses 4WD or off-road vehicles to watch wildlife, the vehicle can almost always be driven slowly and carefully so as to minimise impacts, at the same time enhancing rather than detracting from the client experience. In some cases, such as the tundra buggies used to watch polar bears in the Canadian Arctic, very large low-pressure tyres are used to raise the vehicle above the reach of the bears, and this also minimises impacts on soil and vegetation.

For other types of adventure tour using off-road vehicles, however, the selling point is the opportunity for clients to test their off-road driving skills in difficult terrain. Since this creates considerable environmental damage, the key concern is to operate only in areas which are already degraded and have low value for conservation, such as land which has already been cleared for other purposes. The most severe environmental management issues occur when high-impact activities are carried out in inappropriate areas. One example is provided by so-called random use zones for snowmobiles in public lands immediately adjacent to Jasper National Park in the Canadian Rockies, an area which should form part of the buffer zone for the park and part of the winter range of its wildlife. Because of its zoning, however, it can be used by snowmobilers aiming to test the limits of their machines, e.g. by running up steep snow slopes at maximum speed. This creates high-level engine noise and associated disturbance which extends far beyond the on-ground boundary and well into the National Park.

Similar environmental management issues occur in any area where relatively high-impact adventure activities are legally permitted in protected areas or other areas of high conservation value. Because of historical precedents, for example, certain outfitters are permitted to take riding horses and pack horses into national parks in parts of the Australian Alps and the Pacific Northwest in the USA. This creates impacts over and above those of hikers, because horses' hooves cut the soil more than hikers' boots, and because it is more difficult to control the transport of weed seeds and pathogen propagules via horses than via hikers. The problem is not with horse riding as an adventure activity, but with identifying appropriate areas where it does not create damage. Similar considerations apply for other adventure tourism activities such as mountain biking and adventure racing, both of which create significantly higher impacts than backcountry hiking. Methods to build minimal-impact tracks for mountain bikes are well established (Webber, 2004, 2007); but this is very different from allowing free access for high-speed biking on hiking tracks in national parks.

Terrestrial adventure tourism activities can also create significant impacts on wildlife, including endangered species. This includes both terrestrial mammals (Buckley, 2004d) and birds (Buckley, 2004c). Many different animal species can be disturbed by the presence of human activity – particularly by loud noises and machinery, but in many cases also simply by sighting a person, hearing human voices or footfalls, or seeing lights at night. Disturbance may cause an animal to move, exposing itself to higher risk of predation. It may cause animals to stop feeding and remain alert, and if this occurs repeatedly, it may affect the animal's ability to eat sufficient food: e.g. for migration, to overwinter in a cold climate, or to produce and feed offspring. Where birds are nesting, disturbance may reveal a hidden nest site to predators, or remove the protection of the parent birds for long enough that the eggs or chicks may be seized by scavengers. If the parent birds are alarmed suddenly and take off in panic, they may even crush their eggs themselves. Examples of all these types of impacts are reported in the recreation ecology literature (Buckley, 2005a). A list of the species and impacts studied most recently was provided by Buckley (2009a, pp. 161–163).

From an environmental management perspective, as outlined in Chapter 9, there is a fundamental difference between adventure tours where wildlife watching is the primary attraction, and guides and clients are therefore concerned to minimise their impacts on wildlife; and those where the primary activity involves the use of mechanised equipment, and clients may not even be aware that wildlife are in the vicinity. Participants in wildlife watching tours generally want to see and photograph the animals at close range. On the one hand, this means they are prepared to approach quietly; but on the other, it means they want to approach very close. Participants in mechanised adventure activities may not care whether they see wildlife, but may cause major impacts through carelessness or even deliberate harassment.

CASE STUDY 7.1: Turbo Diesel Light Plane

For many of the more remote and adventurous wildlife watching lodges in southern Africa, especially those in northern Namibia and northwestern Botswana, access for tourists is largely by light aircraft. For some lodges, such as Nxabega and Sandibe operated by &Beyond in the Okavango Delta, there is no wet-season road access at all, and air access is the only option. For others, such as Jack's Camp on the saltflats south of Maun or Wilderness Safaris' Skeleton Coast Lodge, access by four-wheel drive vehicle is possible, but neither quick nor comfortable, and generally inappropriate for the clientele concerned. The entire wildlife adventure tourism sector for this region thus depends on light planes, and these create environmental impacts through noise and atmospheric emissions.

In an attempt to reduce these impacts, during 2008 the Wilderness Safari's airline Sefofane successfully trialled a new diesel engine design in one of its Cessna 172 light aircraft. One reason for using this engine is that it runs on Jet A1 fuel, used by larger aircraft and hence widely available, rather than the Avgas used by most light aircraft, where it is more difficult to obtain a reliable supply of uncontaminated fuel. In addition, however, there are a number of significant environmental advantages to the turbo diesel engine. It uses 40% less fuel per unit time and also gives the aircraft a 10% higher cruising speed, with both factors decreasing fuel consumption per unit distance. It uses – and loses – far less oil, about one tenth that of the conventional aircraft engine which is standard in the Cessna 172. Its exhaust contains fewer particulates and much less carbon monoxide. Its fuel mixture is fully automated, improving safety by reducing the need for the pilot to make manual adjustments during flight manoeuvres.

Continued

And perhaps most importantly, it is much quieter than its predecessor, with the difference very clearly discernible both within the aircraft and on the ground as it flies overhead. The former makes it possible to converse rather than wearing earmuffs or headphones; the latter greatly reduces disturbance to wildlife and people alike. The turbo diesel engine is manufactured by Mercedes, and as of mid-2008 only one aircraft had been fitted with one. It is not clear whether the manufacturer and aircraft operators see a sufficient demand to produce these engines in quantity and retrofit existing aircraft, or whether it will remain solely an experimental trial for the time being.

LOOKING BACK

1. The book on *Adventure Tourism* (Buckley, 2006a) specifies environmental management practices for individual tour products from various adventure activity subsectors. Further information on impacts of some of these activities, but not all, is reviewed in Buckley (2003a, 2004e, 2009a). By comparing these case studies, can you rank the different adventure activities from low to high environmental impact?

2. In what ways, and for what reasons, do the environmental impacts of commercial adventure tours and competitive adventure sports events differ from those of individual adventure recreation? Should these differences affect the management of these three categories of use in areas of high conservation value such as national parks, and if so how?

3. It has been argued that adventure tours based on watching wildlife can provide political and financial support for conservation of the wildlife species concerned, which could outweigh the direct environmental impacts caused by the tours themselves. How could you test and quantify this claim?

Polar bear, Hudson Bay, Canada – at risk from climate change

CHAPTER 8

Climate Change

KEY ISSUES

- long-haul travel of domestic self-drive
- offsets and mitigation measures
- changes in tourist travel patterns
- direct impacts on natural resources
- indirect impacts through social factors, e.g. access
- adaptation by destinations, enterprises
- change in technology, product, market, location, season, advertising
- likely futures for adventure tourism under climate change

CONTENTS

CHAPTER SUMMARY

There are four main links between adventure tourism and climate change (Buckley, 2008b). (1) Adventure tourism contributes to greenhouse gas emissions through, e.g. long-haul travel to adventure destinations; use of vehicles and motorised boats and aircraft for adventure activities; and manufacture and transport of food and service items to supply tourists in remote locations. (2) Individual travel patterns, and hence the commercial adventure tourism sector, will be affected by changes in financial costs and social acceptability of travel, associated with climate change mitigation measures. (3) Climate change will modify the attractiveness of particular adventure tourism destinations in several ways. It will make their climates more or less comfortable for humans. It will change natural features such as coastlines, coral reefs, rivers, snow cover, and watchable wildlife. It will also affect access to natural areas, as extreme weather events become more commonplace and severe. (4) Finally, climate change will affect climates in tourists' countries of origin, so that differences in weather between home and holiday destinations may become more or less marked.

Adventure tour operators who offer a portfolio of adventure activities in different locations will be able to adapt by changing this portfolio. Urban destinations may be able to rely more heavily on artificial indoor climates, though with increased energy costs and greenhouse gas emissions. For single-site, single-activity enterprises, there will be opportunities to adapt through a variety of engineering or management measures. Most of these involve costs, and many can only be carried out in concert with other landholders or local government agencies.

RESEARCH REVIEW

The contributions of long-haul air travel to climate change have been considered at a conceptual level by a number of authors (Hoyer, 2000; Hall and Higham, 2005; Becken and Hay, 2007; Peeters, 2007; Becken, 2008; Buckley 2008b; Hall, 2008; UNWTO-UNEP-WMO, 2008; Verbeek and Bargeman, 2008; Broderick, 2009; Ceron and Dubois, 2009; Gössling et al., 2009; Peeters et al., 2009; Straadas, 2009). Calculations of carbon footprints for particular types of travel are relatively straightforward (Becken and Simmons, 2002; Simmons and Becken, 2004; Byrnes et al., submitted for publication; Byrnes and Warnken, 2006). Calculating the carbon footprint of a single commercial tour product, however, taking into account the different origins of each of its clients, is significantly more difficult (Folke et al., 2006). Weighing the net climate impacts of this long-haul travel against other social, economic, and environmental effects is more difficult still (Buckley, 2003c, 2009a, 2009c).

Hall (2008) documented the increasing attention given to the tourism sector within international negotiations on climate change. Becken (2008) explored the industry's potential role in mitigation; and Buckley (2008b) outlined the ways in which tourist destinations of various types are likely to be affected by climate change, the ways in which they may respond, and the research they will need to inform those responses. In particular, Hall (2008) listed much of the relevant literature currently available and compared the relative frequencies with which more detailed subtopics have been referred to.

BIG PICTURE

Introduction

From a tourism perspective, climate change is unlike most other human impacts on the natural environment, because the physical mechanism of impact operates both at a global scale and with time lags measured in decades or longer. Unlike impacts such as noise, sewage discharge, or loss of icon wildlife species, there is no local-scale link between the contributions which an individual tourism operation makes to greenhouse gas emissions and the consequences it experiences as a result of climate change. The ways in which different stakeholders at individual tourist destinations can respond to climate change, therefore, and the associated costs and benefits, are almost completely independent of the steps which the tourism industry, and its government regulators, might take to reduce the industry's net contribution to the problem. A few minor measures, such as increasing use of renewable energy sources, may be seen both as mitigation measures and as adaptations to increased costs and public concerns over energy from fossil fuels. Across the tourism industry as a whole, however, such overlaps are negligible in scale, and mitigation and adaptation can be addressed quite separately.

It is also worth noting that individuals and organisations, in tourism as in other sectors, do not simply adapt to climate change in a passive manner. They take active steps to respond to perceived risks and opportunities, and these responses are driven principally by their own interests rather than by any general concerns about humanity or the planet. When airlines propose carbon offset schemes, it is because they are concerned about loss of customers if carbon taxes increase airfares, not because they care about planting trees or about the well-being of impoverished communities which earn income from up-market international wildlife tourists. When ski resorts argued for many years that climate change was just a scientists' scare, this was simply to buy time to reposition themselves as mountain resort-residential developments where retail, real estate, and summer activities far outweigh the financial significance of lift tickets.

Analytical framework

The links between adventure tourism and climate change can be classified into a small set of logically distinct topics, as follows. The first topic includes the contributions of adventure tourism to climate change and ways to reduce these contributions. Topics such as carbon footprints, energy efficiencies, radiative forcing, and offset schemes fall under this general heading, as do proposals for carbon trading and for fuel, flight, or passenger taxes. These are largely the same as for any other subsector of the tourism industry.

The second topic relates to travel costs and consequences for travel patterns. Topics under this general heading include, e.g. mechanisms by which possible measures to mitigate climate change may modify travel costs; the scale of such changes relative to other factors affecting travel costs; the significance of travel costs, relative to traveller wealth and other factors, in influencing individual travel decisions; substitutabilities between different adventure activities, between different destinations, and between time and cash, for different tourists; and the net consequences for the global geography of travel and tourism. If travel patterns are influenced by individual concerns or social pressures related to climate change, these factors could also be considered under this heading.

The third issue is that climates are changing at home as well as in holiday destinations. Many adventure tourists travel annually to escape seasonal periods at home which provide poor opportunities for adventure recreation. If high-latitude winters become less severe, but low-latitude summers more so, travel patterns may change accordingly. From the perspective of the individual adventure tourist, what matters are differences in weather between home and holiday destination. From the perspective of the commercial adventure tourism industry, however, there is a distinction between push factors at points of origin and pull factors at tourism destinations.

The fourth area of concern involves changes in the attractiveness, safety, and comfort of different adventure tourist destinations, to tourists of different origins and characteristics. Different natural environments and human societies will be affected by and respond to climate change in a wide variety of different ways, and these effects and responses will modify each region's attractiveness as an adventure tourism destination. Responses by the commercial adventure tourism industry may be designed specifically to maintain or increase market share, but the industry operates within a broader context of responses made by resident communities independent of tourism interests.

This is a functional classification from a tourism industry perspective. Each of these four headings may involve a number of different economic, environmental, and engineering components. This chapter focuses on the fourth issue, impacts and responses at adventure tourist destinations.

A useful distinction may be drawn between: changes to climatic means; climatic variability; and artificial climates. At the crudest level, climate scientists predict that on average, some places will get warmer and some colder; that some will get wetter and some drier; that mean sea level will rise somewhat; and so on. Such changes may affect adventure tourism by modifying, e.g. the average number of days with skiable snow cover at various altitudes and latitudes; the configurations of coastal beaches and estuaries; and river flows and lake levels.

Each of these will also be influenced, however, and perhaps more immediately, by changes in climate variability. Both the natural environments and human communities are typically more susceptible to extreme weather events outside the range of routine variability. It is the major storms which change the shape of surf beaches and river rapids, and major heat waves which spark wildfires and bleach tropical corals. It is through such extreme events that climate change is likely to have its initial impacts on both the terrain and the infrastructure used for adventure tourism (Buckley, 2008b). Some of these impacts are only temporary. Rivers can recover from flooding and beaches from erosion, and forests and coral reefs can regrow after fires or bleaching, if climatic conditions return to their former state for long enough. Some, however, are irreversible. If the only remaining population of a globally endangered plant or animal species is unable to survive an extreme climatic event, it will become extinct; and this includes icon species which form the key attractions in some wildlife adventure tours. Since extreme climatic events are typically short-lived, it is sometimes possible to protect infrastructure through engineering means. If a tourism resource or attraction is lost even for a short period, however, this will still affect revenue for tour operators who rely on it.

Long-haul travel and offsets

Measures to manage the impacts of long-haul travel to adventure destinations are largely beyond the powers of either individual adventure tourists or most smaller-scale adventure tour operators. A number of airlines are claiming to reduce their carbon footprints by purchasing more fuel-efficient aircraft. Indeed, some have even applied for environmental awards on these grounds. In fact, however, it appears that they are simply rolling over their fleets, and more modern aircrafts have been designed with greater attention to fuel efficiency because of increases in fuel prices. The actual carbon footprint of an individual journey by an individual traveller depends more on factors such as the precise route and the proportion of empty seats, on that particular flight, than on the airline selected and the fuel efficiency of its aircraft.

A number of tour operators also offer their clients opportunities to purchase carbon offsets, but it seems unlikely that these are in fact effective. Individual tourists may decide to take fewer long-haul short-break holidays, including adventure tours, either for economic or social reasons. Countries which have a strong economic dependence on international inbound tourism, however, particularly those in the developing world, are already lobbying hard against any such reduction. There are now certification programmes for individual tour operators wishing to claim climate-friendly credentials, but these refer principally to the local operating practices of the enterprises, which are largely irrelevant in comparison to the impacts of their clients' long-haul travel.

Destination-scale responses

Adventure tourists currently visit a huge variety of different destinations, with a wide range of different climates, to undertake a great variety of different activities. If the conditions or attractions at a particular destination are modified by climate change, the easiest response by the commercial adventure tourism industry is simply to offer different products to different markets. If there is no longer enough natural snow to ski, ski resorts make artificial snow, as long as it freezes hard enough at night and there is enough water to spare. And if winter is shorter, winter ski resorts reposition themselves as all-season mountain resort-residential developments.

The second major approach is for the industry to take active measures to protect infrastructure against the effects of climate change. An island tourist resort, for example, may invest in protective seawalls to guard against the risks of more severe storms. Conservation of icon wildlife species may involve private as well as public reserves, with tourism interests in each. In regions where adventure tourism forms a significant component of the economy, industry associations and entrepreneurs may be represented directly in planning processes to protect critical infrastructure such as roads, power, and water supplies; and to establish and maintain emergency services and evacuation plans. Tourist lodges and resorts in areas without access to reliable municipal infrastructure may be able to upgrade their own, e.g. by building or enlarging local water supply dams, installing backup generators and fuel tanks, constructing cyclone shelters and similar emergency infrastructure, and designing and testing their own emergency evacuation plans. Island resorts with over-water bungalows can strengthen foundations and increase floor heights every time they upgrade or refurbish their accommodation. Most protective measures such as these are taken principally for extreme events and emergencies; but as noted previously, this is how the effects of climate change will first be felt (Buckley, 2007b).

The ski industry

One particular subsector of the tourism industry whose vulnerability to climate change has been apparent for some time is the ski industry, at least in some countries. Many of the ski resorts of North America and Europe, and even more so those of Australia and New Zealand, have a relatively short operating season and are financially vulnerable to poor snow conditions during critical holiday periods. Many of these resorts are at relatively low latitudes and altitudes, for several reasons. The first is to be close to major population centres and reduce the costs of access and infrastructure. The second is to give skiers as comfortable a climate as possible whilst still being able to ski. The third is that in some countries, these are the only skiable areas available. These areas are quite sensitive to a warmer climate in winter, which reduces the number of days with reliable snow cover at any given altitude, and also reduces the number of nights cold enough for snowmaking. They are also sensitive to any reduction in precipitation, since this reduces snowfall and also reduces water available for snowmaking. Not all ski fields are equally vulnerable. Those in Hokkaido in Japan, for example, experience much lower average temperatures than most of those in North America or Europe, and are hence much more resilient to climate change. Indeed, they may benefit from increased custom if their competitors in other continents suffer continual poor conditions. Similarly, the ski industries of Siberia, Northern Canada, Alaska, and Greenland may also receive a competitive boost, though there are limitations on skiable terrain.

The ski industry was the first subsector of the tourism industry to respond actively to climate change. Broadly speaking, the larger ski corporations such as those in North America took four successive steps. Initially, they denied strongly that the climate was changing at all. Presumably this was a delaying tactic to maintain the value of their mountain property as they moved to the next steps. The second step was to move from winter ski resorts, largely closed during summer, to year-round mountain resorts offering other activities in summer. The third step was to shift the core business model from a reliance on tourist activities and hotel-style accommodation, to a reliance on residential land and property sales and associated retail businesses. The fourth and most recent step is that these corporations are now lobbying governments for special consideration in the face of climate change, irrespective of local ecological impacts, e.g. for permission to extract more water for snowmaking from local rivers; to extend ski runs and infrastructure into new terrain or at higher altitudes; or to reshape their ski slopes more radically during summer so that they can spread snow more thinly during winter. The second and third of these steps, the transition to a four-season multi-activity business model based principally on property rather than activities, would probably have occurred in any event because of the changing corporate ownership structure within the ski industry and indeed the changing expectations of ski tourists; but these steps have also provided a very successful buffer against the economic impacts of climate change on a particularly vulnerable sector of the tourism industry.

Islands, coasts, marine

There is a very large coastal and island resort industry which is potentially vulnerable to rising sea levels and increased storm and flood risk (Buckley, 2008c), but which to date has done rather little to respond to that risk. Most of this sector is urban beach tourism, but it also includes coastal and island resorts and lodges catering to adventure sectors such as surfing, diving, and whale watching (see Chapter 10). There are a number of possible reasons as to why coastal destinations have been much slower than ski resorts to respond to climate change. Firstly, sea level rise is caused by melting polar ice and by thermal expansion of ocean water, and these are slower processes than the atmospheric warming which affects winter snow. Perhaps, therefore, ski resorts felt the effects of climate change before their coastal counterparts. Indeed, even though the most critical impacts of climate change on coastal communities and environments are through more severe and frequent storms and floods rather than increase in mean sea level, ocean weather patterns are too complex to differentiate the effects of climate change from those of shorter-term climatic oscillations at scales of decades.

The second possible reason, perhaps equally important, is that most ski resorts are owned and operated by individual corporations which face any financial risks directly and can respond quickly and coherently. Most coastal tourist communities, in contrast, are municipalities with numerous individual landholders who face different degrees of risk and a local government subject to complex political and financial constraints. This cannot be the only factor, because some ski resorts are municipalities and some coastal and island resorts are private corporations. It does, however, appear that in coastal areas there is extensive debate over the respective liabilities and responsibilities of private landholders, local governments, and higher-level governments. Some of this is legal, e.g. over current liabilities for past planning decisions. Some is economic, over current and future responsibilities to invest in protective engineering works, to meet the costs of repairing damage, or to pay compensation to those disadvantaged by changes in development control regulations. Some is political, combining all of the above. In addition, it appears that there have been misunderstandings and misperceptions over the particular impacts of climate change in coastal areas, with an erroneous focus on mean sea level rather than the combination of storms and flooding (Buckley, 2007b, 2008c).

The impacts of climate change on coral reef communities, critical for the dive tourism sector, have received significant attention because of a number of coral bleaching events. Whilst ecologically significant, these seem to have had rather little effect on the related tourism industries, despite widespread publicity. Even in destinations where the reefs are nominally the key attraction, most tourists spend relatively little of their time and money actually diving and snorkelling. Experienced divers spend more of their time at depth, where bleaching effects rarely reach; inexperienced divers and snorkellers have little standard of comparison. Many divers and snorkellers are more interested in fish than in corals, and many of the more colourful reef fish species thrive perfectly well on bleached reefs. Tourists continue to visit coral reefs damaged by pollution or heavy visitor pressure, and it seems that they also continue to visit reefs damaged by bleaching.

To date, however, climate-related coral damage has been relatively minor. It is possible that storms and rising sea levels may change the dynamics of reefs and reef islands quite significantly, and it is also possible that increased carbon dioxide concentrations will cause widespread ocean acidification, leading to replacement of calcareous corals by algae and other organisms which are less attractive for tourism (Hoegh-Guldberg et al., 2007). There have been periods in the geological past when vertical growth of coral reefs has been unable to keep pace with the rising sea levels, so-called reef drowning, and this may well happen again under anthropogenic climate change.

Deserts, grasslands, and forests

Many of the world's iconic wildlife watching adventure tourism destinations are grassland and forest ecosystems. Lions like savannas, tigers live in jungles. Rains in savannas and monsoon forests are commonly seasonal, and the availability of grass, the food which supports the herds and flocks, is entirely dependent on adequate rainfall every year. The great wildlife migrations of sub-Saharan Africa, for example, are driven by seasonal rainfall patterns. In dry savanna grassland ecosystems, the effects of climate change are likely to be felt initially through failure of the seasonal rains, leading to widespread starvation amongst herbivore populations and probably also to desertification through overgrazing. From an adventure tourism perspective, localised areas which have slightly higher rainfall or access to permanent watercourses will be buffered against change and may even benefit as wildlife from drier areas are forced to seek food and water. In the drier areas, herds are likely to thin out, and in the longer term some substitution of species is probable. Interactions with domestic livestock, however, and the politics of parks in the face of grazing pressure around the boundaries, are likely to be critical mediating factors.

Adventure tourism in deserts relies partly on wildlife, partly on scenery, and partly on activities such as off-road driving. The latter will be little affected by climate change, though the costs of maintaining a comfortable living environment for guests may well increase if temperatures rise and water becomes even more scarce. Impacts on wildlife watching opportunities are likely to be similar to those in less arid grasslands: the animal species may be adapted to drier conditions, but they are at least equally sensitive to any change in those conditions.

In forested areas, the chief risk from climate change is an increase in the frequency and intensity of wildfires, caused not so much by warming, as by more extended drought periods. This applies not only to the conifer forests of North America and the eucalypt forests of Australia, but also to tropical and subtropical rainforests, which have hitherto been too wet to carry fire except at the margins of agricultural clearance. From an adventure tourism perspective there are four considerations. The first is that a burnt forest is generally much less attractive to tourists than an unburnt one. The second is that the impacts of fire and the impacts of tourists may interact, and land management agencies may therefore close burnt areas to visitors, including commercial tours, to allow opportunities for recovery. The third is that tourist access to forest areas requires infrastructure, ranging from roads and tracks to lookout towers, treetop walks, and forest lodges. These represent significant capital investment, and if they are burnt it may take some time for them to be replaced. Finally, though at a longer time scale, any type of forest which is burnt more frequently than in the past may suffer ecological change, being replaced by a different type of vegetation. Where forest tourism relies on specific features of a forest ecosystem, whether individual giant trees or particular wildlife species, changes at ecosystem scale may effectively destroy the key tourist attractions.

Potential responses to such climate-related changes differ between fixed-site and mobile tour operators. For the latter, the principal response will simply be to modify the specific sites visited so as to maintain maximum wildlife watching opportunities. For fixed-site lodges such as those in and around national parks and private conservation reserves, there would seem to be three main options. The first is to gain exclusive access, if this is possible, to permanent water sources, e.g. by buying or leasing new land, by buying out competing water rights, by sinking bores to ground water if available, or by building surface dams where feasible. This, however, is only a partial solution since it does not provide feed. In some cases, the economics of tourism may allow operators to buy in supplementary feed to tide over sparse periods, as already happens in some parts of the world. If there are widespread regional reductions in rainfall and hence in the availability of fodder, however, this approach will also become increasingly difficult. Finally, in countries and areas where tourism competes politically with grazing for access to particular areas of land, it will become increasingly important for the tourism industry to maintain a strong political presence and demonstrate its significance to regional economies.

Conclusions

Climate change is a highly significant issue for the adventure tourism industry worldwide. It is less acute than wars, terrorism, and disease, but larger-scale and longer-lasting. Long-distance travel will almost certainly become more expensive, and we can anticipate some major changes to global travel patterns. For most countries, however, the social impacts of climate change through other sectors will far outweigh those through tourism. Even within the tourism industry itself, those companies which rely principally on packaging travel opportunities should easily be able to adapt without loss of business. Similarly, larger-scale tourist destinations which already offer a mix of natural and built attractions can adapt by changing this mix, and the key issue will be integration with other industry sectors and government services.

The subsectors of the tourism industry most affected by climate change will be smaller fixed-site operators or destinations, which rely heavily on a single natural attraction such as snow, reefs, or wildlife which happens to be particularly susceptible to climate change. Even in these cases, however, there are opportunities to reposition either the product or the target market segment so as to maintain revenue. The key in these cases will be forethought and innovation, to maintain a competitive position as corresponding adjustments occur worldwide.

The interactions of tourism and climate change do not occur in isolation. Climate change affects all countries and all sectors of human societies, and the responses of those sectors may affect, and be affected by, the responses of the tourism sector. There are other simultaneous large-scale changes to the global economy in addition to climate, and some of these will have differential influence on the tourism industry. Most notable, perhaps, is the very rapid increase in wealth in the highly populous nations of India and China.

Climate change is likely to become such a pervasive issue that it will need to be mainstreamed into all aspects of human societies, including all components of the tourism industry, and hence all types of tourism research. Already, many analyses in tourism economics refer routinely to various climate change scenarios in much the same way as they routinely specify discount rates. Future research in tourism planning, policy, and geography will no doubt refer to regional climate change patterns and predictions in a similar way.

In the short term, however, it would seem that if we were to pick a single top priority for research, it would be the social and environmental consequences of extreme weather events and the flow-on effects for tourism.

ACKNOWLEDGEMENTS

The conceptual framework for the four links between tourism and climate change is derived from Buckley (2008b).

CASE STUDY 8.1: Byron Bay, Australia

Interactions between tourism and climate change at an international beach tourism destination in Australia have been analysed in a political ecology framework by Buckley (2008c), who argued that:

'Local politics at Byron Bay on Australia's east coast have led to misunderstanding and misrepresentation of the likely effects of climate change on sea-level and coastal erosion. A voting bloc of self-proclaimed "green" members of the local government authority (LGA) has adopted policies and planning instruments that have affected tourism by: placing severe and irrational restrictions on development of residential and holiday accommodation; reducing the opportunities for holiday letting; increasing rates and costs for businesses that provide services to tourists; and creating community division and dissent, which drives away higher yield family tourists. This is occurring even though the LGA acknowledges the town's dependence on tourism. The key issue is that the LGA has prevented beachfront landowners from protecting their own properties against erosion, which the LGA now claims, incorrectly, to be due to climate change but which is in fact caused by a groyne built to protect facilities owned or managed by the LGA itself. Addressing this erosion is completely straightforward from a technical perspective, but is prevented by political power plays. Through this political mechanism, misperceptions of climate change have hence damaged the town's tourism industry and investment, which have moved to neighbouring local government areas."

Buckley, R.C., 2008c. Misperceptions of climate change damage coastal tourism: case study of Byron Bay, Australia. Tourism Review International 12 (1), 71–88.

CASE STUDY 8.2: Australian Ski Industry

The Australian ski industry is particularly vulnerable to climate change because it is in any event marginal in terms of snow quality, quantity, and length of season. Australia has no high mountains, and only a small area of the Australian Alps receives sufficient snow to support a commercial ski industry. In poor snow years, skiers travel to nearby New Zealand instead, further reducing custom at the Australian ski resorts. There has been considerable amenity migration to the nearest township areas with private freehold land available. The ski resorts' operating corporations currently argue that they can maintain their snow season by increased snow farming, snow grooming, and snowmaking. In fact, however, it appears that at least for the lower-altitude resorts: (a) the river systems from which they take water for snowmaking would not be able to supply the additional volumes needed; (b) the number of days cold enough for snowmaking will be insufficient to make enough snow; and (c) price increases associated with infrastructure, energy, and water will render them uncompetitive. The most likely scenario is thus that the higher-altitude resorts will continue to operate as ski fields, but the lower-altitude ones will attempt to change to summer activities and residential developments (Pickering and Buckley, in press).

LOOKING BACK

1. How is climate change and its associated effects likely to affect: (a) large global adventure tourism retailers; (b) recognised adventure tourism destinations; and (c) small single-activity adventure tourism providers at single locations? Illustrate with examples of places and activities.

2. If measures to mitigate climate change increase the cost of travel, how is that likely to affect the adventure tourism industry?

3. Pick any one adventure tourism activity and consider how its global geography is likely to be modified by climate change.

PART 3

Representative Subsectors

Lions strolling past tourist safari
vehicles in a private reserve

CHAPTER 9

Wildlife

KEY ISSUES

- captive, habituated, free-ranging

- positive, neutral, negative habituation

- icon species or overall diversity as key attractions

- birdwatching and marine wildlife as specialised subsectors

- risks to tourists from wildlife: predators, poisons, pathogens, etc.

- impacts of tourism on wildlife:

- behavioural, physiological, energetic, reproductive, communication

- population-scale effects, especially for endangered species

CHAPTER SUMMARY

Many commercial tourism products combine animals and adventure. In some of these tours, the key attraction is watching potentially dangerous animals at short range. Examples include: gorilla, grizzly bear, or buffalo on foot; lion at night from an open safari vehicle; tiger from elephant back; or sharks in an open-water dive. Most of these animals are at least partly protected in parks or private reserves and often habituated to tourism, and the tourists are tightly managed by guides.

In others, the key attraction is adventure travel in a remote area, with wildlife as an added bonus, e.g. narwhal from a sea kayak in the High Arctic, condor from horseback in Patagonia, caiman at night from a dugout canoe on the Amazon. The animals are visited only occasionally, are not habituated, may be hunted by local residents (or other tourists), and must often be stalked to be seen.

In others again, the key attraction is an adventure activity, with wildlife as a primary target, e.g. watching polar bear or sperm whale from a helicopter, hippo from a canoe, whales from a speedboat. The tourist activity itself may potentially create significant impacts on the wildlife concerned, considered either at the level of individual animal welfare, or conservation of species populations.

RESEARCH REVIEW

The most extensive academic analysis of the worldwide wildlife tourism subsector is that of Newsome et al. (2005). Additional reviews are available in Higginbottom (2004). A number of case studies have been presented by Buckley (2003a, 2006a, pp. 352–379). Various wildlife watching opportunities in North America are described by, e.g. Clayton and Mendelsohn (1993), Luzar et al. (1995, 1998), Boyd and Butler (1999), and Mangun and Mangun (2002). Information for Australia is available in, e.g. Bennett et al. (2000) and Rodger et al. (2007). Analyses centred around particular icon species include: e.g. Shackley (1995) for gorillas in Rwanda; Buckley (2003a, pp. 38–41) for gorillas in Uganda; Russell and Ankenman (1996) and Marshall et al. (2006) for orangutan in Borneo; Croft (2000) for kangaroos in Australia; Lemelin and Smale (2006) for polar bear in Canada; and many more.

Research in marine wildlife adventure tourism has focused largely on diving, especially on coral reefs; and on marine mammals and to a lesser extent sharks and rays, especially whale sharks and manta rays. Tourism based on various species of dolphins has been described in Europe (Berrow et al., 1996; Hughes, 2001); southern Africa (Karxzmarski et al., 1998); and Australia (Scarpaci and Dayanthi, 2003). Whale watching tours involving various seas and whale species have been examined by, e.g. Duffus (1996), Anderson et al. (1996), Findlay (1997), Beach and Weinrich (1989), Hoyt (2000), and Higham and Lusseau (2007). Shark diving is reviewed by Carwardine and Watterson (2002), and tourism products based on stingrays are described by Shackley (1998a) and Newsome et al. (2004b). Case studies in dive tourism were presented by Buckley (2006a, pp. 166–192). Impacts of tourism on terrestrial wildlife and birds were reviewed by Buckley (2004c); those on cetaceans by Higham and Lusseau (2004); and those on coral reefs by Cater and Cater (2007).

BIG PICTURE

Introduction

Adventure tourism and wildlife tourism are commonly treated as two separate subsets of the outdoor tourism industry. A significant subsector of the adventure tourism industry, however, involves animals in various ways, and a significant proportion of wildlife tourism products incorporate features which are otherwise characteristic of the adventure tourism sector. There is thus a significant overlap between wildlife and adventure tourism – whether from product, management, or marketing perspectives. In addition, some adventure tourism products may create impacts on wildlife even though the wildlife are not featured as part of the product, and even if the product does not involve consumptive activities such as fishing or hunting.

The analyses presented here are based on case studies of retail tour products audited or analysed by the author (Table 9.1). Most of these have been described in detail previously (Buckley, 2003a, 2006a), but in a different context. Others are included in this analysis for the first time, though they may have been reported previously by other authors. Criteria to consider particular wildlife tourism products as adventure tourism may include features such as risk, remoteness, or particular skills and activities (Buckley, 2007a). Each of these may be linked to animals in commercial tourism products. They provide a useful means to classify the collection of case studies.

Watching potentially dangerous wildlife

A number of wildlife tourism products involve close-range encounters with animal species which are large, strong, and/or dangerous enough to pose a very real threat to human life and under other circumstances might well do so. These commercial products rely on particular features of animal behaviour and tour design to minimise such risks, but in many cases the clients must still remain very alert and attentive, and the experience involves a significant adrenalin component, qualifying it as adventure tourism.

There are both terrestrial and marine tours in this category. Archetypal examples of the former include tours to watch Big Five and other large mammals in sub-Saharan Africa, and tours to watch bears in North America and Russia. Tours to look for tiger in India and southern Nepal, puma or jaguar in various parts of South America, and orangutan in Borneo also involve

| Table 9.1 | Animals in Adventure Tourism Products: Selected Case Studies |

Country	Place (Operator)	Wildlife	Adventure
South Africa	Phinda* (&B)	Big Five and more	Close encounters
South Africa	Madikwe* (&B)	Wild dog, sable	Close encounters
South Africa	Ngala* (&B)	Big Five and more	Close encounters
South Africa	Bongani*(&B)	Big Five and more	Close encounters
South Africa	Sabi Sabi*	Big Five and more	Close encounters
South Africa	Chitwa Chitwa*	Big Five and more	Close encounters
South Africa	Rocktail Bay* (WS)	Whale shark	Diving
Botswana	Sandibe (&B)*	Big Five, delta game	Close encounters
Botswana	Nxabega* (&B)	Big Five, delta game	Close encounters
Botswana	Jack's Camp*	Desert and migration	Close encounters
Botswana	Mombo* (WS)	Big Five, delta game	Close approach on foot
Botswana	Savuti (WS)	Big Five, delta game	Close approach
Botswana	Vumbura* (WS)	Big Five, sable	Close encounters
Namibia	Ongava* (WS)	Black and white rhino	Tracking on foot
Namibia	Desert Rhino* (WS)	Desert rhino	Tracking on foot
Namibia	Skeleton Coast* (WS)	Seal colonies	Approach on foot
Seychelles	North Island* (WS)	Rare birds, turtles	Close views on foot
Kenya	Kichwa Tembo* (&B)	Big Five and more	Close encounters
Tanzania	Grumeti* (&B)	Big Five and more	Close encounters
Tanzania	Kleins* (&B)	Big Five and more	Close encounters
Tanzania	Ngorongoro* (&B)	Big Five and more	Close encounters
Tanzania	Manyara* (&B)	Big Five and more	Close encounters
Zanzibar	Mnemba* (&B)	Reef fauna	Diving
Uganda	Mgahinga*	Mountain gorilla	Close views on foot
Uganda	Busingiro	Chimpanzee	Close encounters
Madagascar	Natural Habitat Adventures*	Lemurs, birds	Close views on foot
Nepal	Annapurna*	Thar	Hiking
Nepal	Bardia*	Tiger, rhino	Elephant safari
Nepal	Baghmara*	Rhino	Canoes
India	Baghwan* (Taj Safaris)	Tiger	Close encounters
India	Mahua Kothi* (Taj Safaris)	Tiger	Close encounters
Maldives	Delphis Diving*	Reef fauna	Diving
China	Last Descents*	Birds of prey	Whitewater
Russia	Explore Kamchatka*	Brown bear	Close encounters
Mongolia	Gobi Gurvansaikhan	Rare mammals	Off-road driving
Malaysia	Kuantan	Fireflies	Boat at night
Sarawak	Ulu Ai	Orangutan	Forest hike

| Table 9.1 | Animals in Adventure Tourism Products: Selected Case Studies—cont'd |

Country	Place (Operator)	Wildlife	Adventure
Thailand	John Gray's Sea Canoe*	Birds	Sea canoes
Indonesia	Togian Islands	Rare mammals	Forest hike
Indonesia	Komodo	Komodo dragon	Access
Indonesia	Tangkoko Dua Saudara	Rare birds, mammals	Forest hike
Fiji	Lalati*	Reef fauna	Diving
Philippines	El Nido	Birds, dugong	Diving
New Guinea	Walindi*	Reef fauna	Diving
Philippines	Suba Olango	Seabirds	Canoes
Australia	Earth Sanctuaries*	Rare marsupials	Hiking
Australia	Broome Observatory	Shorebirds	Hides, hikes
Australia	O'Reilly's*	Forest birds	Hiking
Australia	Binna Burra*	Forest birds	Hiking
Australia	Taka Dive*	Reef fauna	Diving
Australia	Quicksilver*	Reef fauna	Diving
Australia	King Dive*	Whale sharks	Snorkel
New Zealand	Penguin Reserve	Penguins	Hides, hikes
New Zealand	Waitomo*	Glow worms	Caving
Antarctica	Explorer Shipping*	Penguins, seals	Expedition cruise
Svalbard	Aurora Expeditions*	Polar bear, walrus	Sea kayak
Alaska	Prince William Sound* (NOLS)	Sea otter, bear	Sea kayak
Alaska	Denali National Park*	Bear, wolf	Hiking
Canada	St Lawrence River*	Beluga	Boats
Canada	Hudson Bay* (NHA)	Polar bear	Close encounters
Belize	Baboon Sanctuary	Howler monkeys	Close encounters
Belize	Cockscomb Basin	Ocelot, birds	Access
Costa Rica	Horizontes	Rare birds	Forest hike
Costa Rica	Monteverde	Quetzal	Forest hike
Costa Rica	Rara Avis	Rare birds	Forest hike
Panama	Wekso Ecolodge	Harpy eagle	Forest hike
Brazil	Una Ecopark	Rare monkeys	Canopy walk
Brazil	Cristalino	Birds, otter	Hike, canoe
Brazil	Pousada Caiman	Birds, mammals	Hike, horse ride
Brazil	Jatapu River*	Caiman, hoatzin	Canoe
Ecuador	Galapagos Islands*	Tortoise, birds, seals	Boat access
Ecuador	Podocarpus* (Surtrek)	Condor	Hiking
Peru	Tambopata*	Forest mammals	Hike, canoe

Data from Buckley (2003a, 2006a) and subsequent field research in 2007–2008.
*Audited in person.
&B, &Beyond; WS, Wilderness Safaris; NHA, Natural Habitat Adventures; NOLS, National Outdoor Leadership School.

species which are potentially dangerous, but opportunities for a very close approach are much more limited and the animals are more likely to run away. In marine environments, archetypal tours are those which involve diving to watch sharks at close range. Other dive tours focus on large rays, principally manta; on whales of various species; or on seals, sea lions, and their relatives.

For both marine and terrestrial species, there are some tours where the tour clients have no immediate physical protection from the animals, and safety relies on an understanding of animal behaviour, and the management of human behaviour so as to avoid provoking predatory, defensive, territorial, or competitive attacks by the animals. There are other tours where such behavioural approaches are not sufficient to guarantee safety, and the tour clients and guides must be physically isolated from the wildlife using reverse zoo techniques, where the humans are in a cage and the animals are outside it. There are both shark watching and bear watching tours, for example, which use these approaches.

The principal adventure-related features of some of these tours may be outlined as below. At a global scale, the most famous examples of large and potentially dangerous animals used as tourist attractions must surely be the Big Five of east and southern Africa. Though this term has now long since entered the lexicon of tourism marketing, it was originally used by big game hunters to refer to the five African animals which were the most dangerous to hunt. These are: elephant, rhino, buffalo, lion, and leopard. These species, however, are by no means the only large and potentially dangerous animals to be seen in the African savannahs. Most of the larger herbivores have potentially lethal hooves and horns, even though they do not often use them against humans. Hippo and crocodile are also responsible for a number of deaths every year; and for those sleeping outdoors, precautions against potential hyena attacks are necessarily routine.

The vast majority of independent travellers and large-scale African wildlife tours use fully enclosed vehicles, sometimes with an observation hole in the roof, and drive only during the day. In most national parks, these are regulatory requirements. A range of private tour operators, however, offer wildlife tours either in open vehicles, at night, on horseback, in hides, on foot or in canoes. In each of these cases, safety depends on behaviour rather than on physical protection. Such tours are led by expert guides who carry large-calibre rifles, but it is very rarely indeed that these are needed. In addition, there are many circumstances under which a rifle would be of little use. Tours of this type, therefore, rely on a very close understanding of the behaviour of the animals being watched.

Many also rely on an extended process of habituation during which the individual animals concerned learn to treat humans in open safari vehicles as a neutral part of the landscape, neither a threat nor an opportunity. The vehicles drive slowly when in sight of wildlife; the occupants stay still, silent, and sitting; and the guides watch the wildlife carefully to detect signs of agitation, and move the vehicles slowly away if need be. In private reserves where the animals have been habituated for a long period, tour options may include game drives at night in open vehicles, e.g. to watch lion and leopard. When travelling on foot, horseback, or by canoe, however, a guided group will avoid such potentially dangerous situations, generally travelling only during the middle of the day and avoiding areas where wildlife might hide or sleep.

A range of approaches are used for close-range bear watching in the northern hemisphere. Some guides are prepared to lead clients on foot to watch bears at close range. Elsewhere, for example, in parts of Alaska and Kamchatka, there are raised viewing platforms next to rivers where brown bears congregate to feed on salmon at particular times of year. These are open wooden structures and the bears almost certainly could, if they wished, climb or destroy them, but they have no reason to do so since fish are plentiful. Similarly, it is possible to watch brown bear at very close range from an inflatable dinghy in the Khutzeymateen Inlet in northern British Columbia, Canada, because the dinghy driver knows the individual bears well and keeps the boat at a sufficient distance that it could outspeed the bears if they should, in fact, turn aggressive. In searching for polar bear in and around Svalbard north of Norway, however, guides will typically keep inflatables at a greater distance since polar bears can swim extremely well and may indeed see humans as potential prey. In watching black bear from sea kayaks in Southern Alaska, in contrast, the minimum approach distance is set by the bears, which run away if the kayaks approach too closely. Finally, to watch polar bear at Churchill on Canada's Hudson Bay, where the bears are extremely hungry as they gather to wait for the sea ice to form, tourists must be physically protected from attack either inside giant tundra buggies where the windows are too high for bears to reach, or inside a caged lodge where bears are unable to push their way between the bars to get at the tourists inside.

To watch tiger in the Terai region of southern Nepal, a different approach is used. In Bardia National Park, for example, the tigers live in dense thickets and tall stands of elephant grass cut by creeks and marshes. To look for tigers in such terrain, the only realistic option is on elephant back, and this is indeed how tiger watching tours are run. To travel on foot through tiger country with very low visibility would be highly risky, and the chances of seeing a tiger safely would be small. No vehicle can negotiate all the different types of terrain except perhaps a very large amphibious all-terrain buggy, but such vehicles would drive off the tigers through engine noise, damage the vegetation with large tyres, and are in any event not available. The elephants have an additional advantage in their own keen senses, which combine with those of their mahouts and the wildlife guides to help locate and approach hidden tigers. The mahout sits on the elephant's neck, the tourists ride in a kind of shallow wooden box strapped to the elephant's back with a giant girth, and the guide stands in a special stirrup attached to the back of the box. The seating arrangements are far from comfortable and could easily be much improved, but they do give tourists a unique opportunity to see tigers in the wild. The experience is exciting for several reasons. Riding on elephant back, for one not previously accustomed to the experience, is exciting enough in itself. The tigers themselves, if one is fortunate enough to get a good view, are magnificent animals of stunning power and beauty. And finally, if a tiger is eluding the elephants and they try to encircle it, then the sensation of clinging to a flat wooden frame on top of a charging and trumpeting elephant, knowing that a tiger waits below if one falls off, is certainly adrenalin provoking.

It is not only bears and big cats which can provide an adventurous wildlife watching experience through the element of risk. The same also applies for a number of the larger primates, and indeed also for baboons and many of the smaller monkeys. Most powerful amongst the primates are of course the gorillas, notably the lowland gorilla of the Congo and the mountain gorilla of Uganda, Rwanda, and Burundi. The habituated mountain gorillas of Bwindi and Mgahinga National Parks in the Virunga Mountains are particularly well known, and the encounters have been described by a number of authors. Approach is made on foot, in a small group led by several experienced trackers who follow the gorillas' trail from the previous day in order to locate the troop. Once the gorillas are sighted, the group approaches very gradually under the guides' careful directions, and can then watch for up to 1 hour before retracing their steps. There is a set minimum approach distance, and if the gorillas move towards the tourists, the tourists must move back. No loud noises or flash photography are permitted. The adventure derives from scrambling through the forest for several hours; from the tense moments of first contact when the guides have to assess the gorillas' mood and behaviour; and of course, from the knowledge that the gorillas are extremely powerful and could easily attack their visitors if they chose so.

One of the critical reasons why close but tightly managed encounters such as those with the mountain gorillas or with Big Five and other wildlife in private reserves can take place safely is that the animals concerned have never learnt to associate humans with the presence of food. Where individual animals have learnt that they can obtain food from humans by begging or stealing it, interactions may rapidly become aggressive. This can often occur, for example, in unpatrolled national parks' picnic grounds where visitors may feed wildlife either intentionally or inadvertently. In Fraser Island National

Park, a World Heritage Area in Australia, for example, a dingo once stole a family size bar of chocolate from a picnic table where I was sitting and ran off before we could pursue it. In Lake Manyara National Park in Tanzania, I and two colleagues were once involved in a minor punch-up with a baboon which managed to hurl all our food and camera equipment into the dirt before retreating. Aggressive interactions may also be provoked by territorial behaviour. Many years ago I was attacked by a troop of monkeys which assembled suddenly when I climbed up onto a ruined building in a forest in northern Thailand, presumably because this was their own favourite vantage point.

There are other close-range wildlife interactions where the animals might potentially see the humans themselves as food. In addition to the various interactions with bears and big cats as outlined above, there are a number of places worldwide where one can watch large and potentially dangerous reptiles, but only from a safe or protected vantage point. Examples include: alligator in the southeastern States of the USA; saltwater crocodile in northern Australia, Papua New Guinea, and nearby areas; large crocodiles, known as muggers, in India; cayman in South America; and Komodo dragon in Indonesia. Some of these can be seen from bridges and riverbanks, some from national parks' boardwalks and lookouts, and some by boat. The so-called jumping crocodile tours in Australia's Northern Territory, where crocodiles leap partly out of the water to grab food dangled from a stick, have become a well-known tourist attraction in the region. Historically at least (Buckley, 2003a), there have been tours by dugout canoe on the upper tributaries of the Amazon River in Brazil, where one can catch the thin-snouted cayman by hand at night, using only a stick and a piece of string. This is definitely not something one would attempt with any of the broad-jawed crocodiles or alligators. Likewise, whilst it is possible to catch monitor lizards and pythons by hand if they are not too large, they do have extremely sharp teeth if one is not quite quick enough. Perhaps unsurprisingly, such activities are not generally offered as a component of commercial tours.

A number of commercial dive and snorkelling tours also involve relatively close-range encounters with large wildlife, in this case marine. Most controversial of these are cage dives, or in some cases even free dives, with large and potentially aggressive shark species. More common are dives with more docile shark species, such as the gray nurse or ragged-tooth shark. There are also dive and snorkel tours where one has a good chance to encounter stingrays, eagle rays, or manta rays in significant numbers; and there are various places where one can dive or snorkel with whale sharks at particular times of the year. In some areas, there are also opportunities to dive with a variety of whale species. Tonga, for example, is particularly known for its whale diving tours. In some of these cases, it is possible for divers or snorkellers to approach the marine animals quite closely either because the animals are resting, as in the case of ragged-tooth sharks in South Africa; or because they are so large that they essentially pay no attention at all to individual divers, as in the case of whales and whale sharks.

The tours outlined above all rely on finding particular wildlife species, often-known individuals, in a relatively well-defined location. The animals are wild, in the sense that they maintain their own territories, find their own food and mates, and fight or flee from each other as occasion demands. They are, however, all habituated to the presence of humans and do not expect either to be fed or shot at. They are not confined as in a zoo, but their whereabouts are followed or tracked day-to-day at least approximately, so that guides can take tourists to see them with a high degree of confidence.

Wilderness adventure travel through wildlife habitat

Wilderness travel in remote areas is one of the major categories of adventure tourism, and the remote areas traversed may often provide habitat for a variety of animal species which tour clients are keen to see. In contrast to the tour products outlined in the previous section, however, for these tours it is the place and the activity which form the primary focus, with the wildlife as an unpredictable bonus component. For example, one may be lucky enough to see a wolf, grizzly bear, or Dall sheep whilst hiking or rafting in wilderness areas of Alaska or northern Canada, but there is no guarantee of this. In addition, since these animals are hunted throughout much of their range, they are likely to run away at the first sign of humans, and close encounters are unlikely. Of course, it is still a good idea to carry capsicum spray, and in some national parks it is a mandatory requirement.

In this category of adventure tourism, the principal adventure component derives from remoteness rather than risk from the animals themselves. Whilst some of the animals seen may potentially be dangerous, such as polar bear or indeed brown or black bear, other animals species which do not pose any immediate threat to human safety may be an equally important component of the tourism experience. Visitors to Svalbard may be particularly keen to see polar bear, for example, but would also be glad to see reindeer, walrus, Arctic fox, snowy owl, and a wide variety of seabirds. Most tours of this type cannot guarantee that clients will see any particular species, so they tend to phrase their marketing materials in somewhat guarded terms. They might say, for example, that the group will look for a particular animal or that they hope to see it. A sea kayaking tour at the northern end of Baffin

Island in the Canadian Arctic, for example, is billed as 'In search of the narwhal' (Buckley, 2005b).

A very large number of tours worldwide fall into this general category. Hiking trips to Annapurna Base Camp in Nepal, for example, may expect to see Himalayan thar. Rafting tours in Tibet may, if they are very lucky, catch a glimpse of a snow leopard. River tours on the Amazon may see freshwater dolphin, macaw, or hoatzin. Off-road vehicle tours in central Australia would be disappointed if they did not see kangaroo and emu. Horseback tours in Patagonia would look out for puma, guanaco, and vicuna. Mountaineers in the Andes would look out for condor, and those in Scotland for golden eagle, whilst sea kayakers in southwestern Alaska would certainly expect to see bald eagle and black bear at appropriate seasons. The jungle lodges of tropical South America advertise the diversity of their bird and mammal fauna as a major attraction, without necessarily singling out any particular species. Hikers on Mt Kenya might hope to see hyrax or malachite sunbird, depending on their particular interests.

In the marine environment, the majority of dive tourists expect to see a variety of ocean wildlife, but in most cases they would still see diving itself as the primary activity and wildlife as a secondary attraction. The animals concerned range from sessile and sedentary creatures, such as corals and anemones, to giant pelagic creatures, such as the larger sharks, whale sharks, and whales. Most dive tours, however, search for particular fish species characteristic of the area concerned, whether these be scorpion fish or sea-horses, Maori wrasse or moray eels, blennies or butterfly fish. Turtles are also a strong attraction, and so are various crustaceans, from fairy shrimp to the larger lobsters. Even molluscs can be a significant attraction, as for example the triton shell or the red file clam.

Most commercial dive tours visit the same particular sites repeatedly, and some species and indeed individual marine animals can be seen routinely at the same place on every dive. With few exceptions, however, they are not habituated to human presence in the same way as some of the terrestrial wildlife, so dive tours of this type are more akin to wilderness travel than to close-range wildlife watching experiences. The exceptions typically involve particular places where divers routinely feed, and sometimes touch, individual fish or stingrays.

Adventure technologies for wildlife spotting

Most wildlife tours aim to watch animals with minimal disruption to normal behaviours, because it is precisely these routine activities that people want to see and photograph. A certain number of tours, however, provide opportunities to see particular species which might be otherwise be hard to find, but in ways which may indeed create significant impacts on their behaviour. Some of these use particular technologies, more generally associated with adventure tourism, to approach the animals concerned. The degree of potential disturbance can vary greatly from tour to tour. There is no clear distinction between low- and high-impact wildlife watching operations, but rather a gradual scale. In addition, different species and sometimes different individual animals may respond quite differently to the same type of disturbance. Thus, for example, many species of shorebird will take flight if approached by people on foot whilst the birds are feeding. Several species of seabird which nest on shore in the Galapagos Islands may still allow tourists on foot to approach quite closely, because they are habituated to a steady stream of visitors along marked and formed tracks. Seabirds nesting on sub-Antarctic islands, approached by shore parties from expedition cruise vessels, will generally also remain on their nests, but in that case it is because they are likely to lose their entire year's offspring if they abandon their eggs or chicks even briefly – and a year's clutch represents about the same proportion of total lifetime offspring for a skua or albatross, as a single child does for a human mother. Even though the adult birds may stay on the nest, however, they still show signs of severe stress when approached too closely by expedition tourists.

In a similar way, some tour operators use helicopters to take tourists to watch wildlife from the air. In New Zealand, for example, one can watch surfacing sperm whales off the coastal town of Kaikoura from a helicopter hovering a bare 100 metres overhead. The whales have to stay on the surface because they need to breathe in preparation for their next dive. The site where they surface lies over a deep submarine trench where sperm whales can catch giant squid, their preferred food. Apparently, however, whales which are approached by hovering helicopters spend less time on the surface, and dive more steeply, than those which are undisturbed.

Another helicopter-based wildlife viewing experience is provided by a local operator in Hudson Bay in northern Canada. At the time of year when polar bears are congregating to wait for the sea ice to form, a number of bears spend their time on a beach east of the town of Churchill. A local helicopter operator offers relatively low-level overflights along the beach, offering the tourists the opportunity to see the bears from above. Many of the bears, perhaps the older and more experienced ones, pay little or no attention to the helicopter, but some panic when they hear it and start to run, either along the beach or towards the back of the beach.

There are many other examples, some relatively low-key and others quite clearly high-impact. Searching for tiger on elephant back, as described earlier, would generally be considered a benign and environmentally friendly form of transport; but even so, some of the tigers may experience significant disturbance. There are quite clear and unambiguous guidelines or indeed regulations for the conduct of whale watching and dolphin watching boats, but these are often violated, and the animals do experience disturbance in consequence. A more severe disturbance is caused when people pursue individual animals or herds in motorised vehicles, as sometimes occurs, for example, by snowmobilers in caribou country. Disturbance to winter wildlife by snowmobiles in Yellowstone National Park, USA, for example, has created long-running controversies between the parks agency and conservation interests on the one hand, and snowmobile user groups and manufacturer associations on the other.

An equally or even more extreme example of wildlife disturbance through mechanised adventure activities is provided by the airboats in the Everglades and Great Cypress swamps in southeastern USA. These are large dinghies, which are driven by aircraft propellers powered by open-mounted engines. They travel fast and make an ear-shattering noise, forcing waterbirds to take flight in panic some distance ahead. Florida is also known for the high level of propeller damage inflicted on its manatee population by recreational boaters (Higham and Lusseau, 2004).

Inadvertent impacts of adventure tourism on wildlife

Many adventure tourism activities have no deliberate interactions with wildlife, and animals do not form part of their advertised attractions, but they may still cause impacts on the animals, whether they see them or not. Indeed, adventure tours which do not feature wildlife are perhaps more likely to cause such impacts than those which do, since the latter need to be aware of their effects if they are to approach the animals closely enough for a good view.

The impacts of various outdoor recreation activities on marine mammals, on birds, and on other wildlife, respectively, were reviewed by Higham and Lusseau (2004), Buckley (2004c), and Buckley (2004d). Impacts of particular adventure activities such as horse riding or off-road driving were reviewed by Newsome et al. (2004a) and Buckley (2004b). Information is also available on the impacts of adventure activities in particular ecosystems, notably the polar areas (Forbes et al., 2004; Snyder and Stonehouse, 2007). Some activities, certainly, can have severe population-scale impacts on particular animal species in a very short period. A single light-aircraft flight over a colony of white pelicans in Canada, for example, caused the immediate death of 88% of the eggs and chicks as the parent birds took flight in panic (Bunnell et al., 1981). The majority of impacts, however, are much more subtle and may occur cumulatively over a period of time. This applies, for example, to activities which disrupt the energetics of particular animal species, such as wildlife feeding for overwintering, or birds feeding for migration. Many impacts derive not directly from the adventure activity itself, but from its effect on interactions between different animals of the same or different species. For example, many kinds of quite minor disturbance can lead nesting birds of various species to leave their nests briefly, and even such brief absences may greatly increase the level of attack by predatory or scavenging birds.

Many of the impacts of adventure tourism on wildlife may not be visible to the tourists concerned. Driving on sandy beaches, for example, kills burrowing crabs, such as ghost crabs, by crushing them and their burrows; but since the crabs are camouflaged and are generally hidden under the sand during the day, drivers may never be aware of their presence. Noise from off-road vehicles can deafen lizards (Brattstrom and Bondello, 1983), but this would not necessarily be apparent even to an interested naturalist, let alone the vehicle drivers. Penguins approached by tourists may suffer significant stress, as shown by increased pulse rate and stress-hormone levels, but it takes specialist scientific equipment to detect these impacts. The same applies for the detection of increased heart rate in mountain sheep approached by hikers with or without dogs (MacArthur et al., 1982).

Conclusions

Animals do indeed have a role in adventure tourism; or more accurately, a number of different roles. There are tours where wildlife are the primary attraction, but where the process of watching them is itself adventurous. There are adventure tours through wildlife habitat, where animals form a significant subsidiary attraction. There are tours which use particular transport, access, or other technologies, normally associated with adventure activities, to watch wildlife. And finally, adventure tours may produce inadvertent and indeed invisible impacts on wildlife even though animals are not part of the product or attraction. Even though many adventure tourism products treat the natural environment principally as a giant adventure playground where the product relies only on the terrain rather than on the ecosystem, there are nonetheless many interactions between adventure activities and the natural environment, including its animal inhabitants.

Adventure activities can be a significant source of impacts on populations of particular animal species; and icon animal species can provide a major attraction for adventure tourism.

CASE STUDY 9.1: Sunchaser Eco-Tours, Khutzeymateen Grizzly Bears

Khutzeymateen Inlet, BC, Canada

Khutzeymateen is the northernmost national park on the west coast of British Columbia, Canada. It supports cool wet coniferous forest along the banks of a tidal marine inlet. Neighbouring inlets have largely been logged, and there was apparently a major conservation controversy over Khutzeymateen, which finally led to its declaration as a national park. The conservation advocacy was led by wildlife ecologists concerned for the grizzly bears, but they were assisted by two local charter boat operators who sponsored free trips for politicians to see the area for themselves.

When the park was indeed declared, these two operators, both small, were granted special concessions to take commercial tourists into the inner reaches of the inlet, where the bears feed on clams and tidal grasses. Both operators use sailing yachts which generate very little noise or wash even when travelling under auxiliary engine power. The tours are guided exclusively by the yacht owners, who are both very familiar with the area and know the individual bears. The yachts travel slowly and the tours take several days from the nearest port, with accommodation on board. There are also day tours which operate high-volume high-speed ferries from the same gateway port, but which are not permitted to enter the inner section of the inlet.

The yacht tours spend several days in the inner parts of the inlet, living on the yacht itself, with frequent excursions in a small inflatable dinghy to watch the bears from close range. At the head of the inlet there is a winding tidal river, and at high tide, the inflatable dinghy can navigate a considerable distance up this river. The riverbanks are shallow enough to see over at some points, but steep and higher at others. Bears can sometimes be seen in the distance, sometimes at very close range. At lower tide levels, the bears come down to tidal mudflats near the mouth of the river to dig for clams, which they do very successfully. Depending on the precise shape of the shoreline at that point and the temperament of the bear concerned, it is sometimes possible to drift very close. Different individual bears seem to occupy different areas along the shoreline, some at the head of the inlet and others further out towards the mouth. The latter are visible if they come out onto grassy areas along the shoreline, but not when they retreat into the forest. Males, females, and cubs of different ages can all be seen in different areas.

Continued

The principal purpose of this tour is to watch bears, so it would qualify both as wildlife tourism and nature tourism. It is educational, very low-impact, and has contributed significantly to conservation of the area and its wildlife, so it would qualify as ecotourism. It is in a remote area with access by float plane and yacht, and there is certainly an element of excitement and potential risk in watching grizzly bear only a few metres away, either from a small inflatable dinghy or on foot on the shore. It is the guides' skilled knowledge and experience which allows the safe management of such close encounters, which would be much more dangerous for an unaccompanied visitor who was not familiar with the behaviour of individual bears. For all these reasons, the tour therefore also qualifies as adventure tourism.

References
SunChaser Eco-Tours, 2009. <http://www.sunchasercharters.ca/>; (accessed 26.05.2009).

CASE STUDY 9.2: Natural Habitat Adventures, Madagascar

Giant chamaeleon, Madagascar

Madagascar is one of the world's most prized destinations for connoisseurs of bird and wildlife watching. It has a large number of endemic species, many of them regrettably endangered but still able to be found by suitably skilled local guides. It is particularly famous for its lemurs, birds, and chameleons. Natural Habitat Adventures (2009) is a large nature tourism operator based in Montana, USA and operating worldwide, principally though not exclusively for an American clientele. It offers tours to Madagascar, with experienced tour leaders and local on-site guides, to see a variety of both well- and lesser-known wildlife. The tour includes both the wetter north-eastern and drier south-western ecosystems, and visits both public national parks and smaller private and community reserves. It includes day hikes along forest trails, spotlighting at night, and boat rides to otherwise inaccessible areas. Wildlife species commonly seen include: rare lemurs such as the Greater Bamboo Lemur, the tiny Gray-brown Mouse Lemur, and Hubbert's Sportive Lemur; giant chameleons such as the green and brown Parsons Chameleon; rare frogs such as the bright vermilion tomato frog and the tiny *Mantidactylus*; endemic members of bird families such as couas, vangas, mesites, and ground rollers, and rare bird species such as Archbold's Newtonia, Benson's Rock Thrush, and Appert's Greenbul. Guests also see a wide range of vegetation types and plant species, including endemics such as the spiny octopus tree *Didiera*.

References
Natural Habitat Adventures, 2009. The nature people. <www.nathab.com/>; (accessed 25.02.2009).

CASE STUDY 9.3: Taj Safaris, India

Taj Safaris is a joint venture between the large Indian hotel corporation Taj Hotels and the South African-based wildlife tourism operator &Beyond (formerly Conservation Corporation Africa), which runs a series of private conservation reserves and up-market game-viewing lodges throughout eastern and southern Africa. Taj Safaris has constructed four new wildlife watching lodges on private landholdings adjacent to Bandhavgarh, Pench, Kanha, and Panna National Parks in central India. The key icon species and tourist drawcard is the Bengal tiger, which like all the world's tiger species is now endangered. Other icon species include gaur, one of the ancestral species of ox; nilgai, the Indian bluebuck; and a wide range of birds including wild peacock. The lodges are run in a style of rustic luxury, with traditional architecture and all the delicacies of local cuisine. Currently, unlike &Beyond's African operations, guests at Taj Safaris' lodges do not have exclusive access to private reserves. They do, however, have particularly skilled guides and drivers who are adept at giving their clients the best views of tigers and other wildlife.

CASE STUDY 9.4: Madikwe Game Reserve, South Africa

Madikwe Game Reserve is a consortium of adjacent private properties in the northwestern part of South Africa, adjacent to the border with Botswana. The properties run separate and competing tourist lodges but manage the land and wildlife cooperatively. This is modelled in many ways on the Sabi Sands reserve near Kruger National Park. Managing wildlife and habitat for tourism is a more difficult exercise for Madikwe than for Sabi Sands, however, because Madikwe is entirely self-contained, without the much larger adjacent public national park at Kruger which provides a buffer for animal populations. At Madikwe, therefore, predator–prey balances must be managed continuously through sales and purchase of particular wildlife species as required. Even with this intensive management, populations can fluctuate quite suddenly and substantially.

For a long time, for example, one of Madikwe's particular selling points was that it maintained a large and easily viewed population of the African wild dog or hunting dog, which is difficult to see in other reserves. The wild dog population expanded so successfully that it grew beyond the capacity of the Madikwe herbivore population to support it. For example, the reserve had been stocked with a number of the rare sable antelope as a particular tourist drawcard, but as a result of predation, the local sable population declined to a few individuals. The reserve managers addressed this issue by capturing and selling a significant proportion of the wild dogs. This was a well-justified and logical response. Unfortunately, however, shortly after these translocations, fighting broke out between different wild dog packs within the reserve, and in addition some animals escaped into surrounding cattle farming areas where they were presumably killed. As a result, the wild dog population in Madikwe fell rather drastically to quite a small number, so that it became much less likely that tourists would in fact see them.

Despite these difficulties, Madikwe does indeed contribute to the conservation of all the species which inhabit the reserve, endangered or otherwise. It does this by: contributing, albeit in a relatively small way, to the total extant populations of the species concerned; maintaining geographically and distinct sub-populations which are to some degree isolated from any potential disease outbreaks which might affect other populations; and providing an area of protected habitat in a region which is otherwise poorly protected. All of these represent clear contributions to conservation, funded by wildlife adventure tourism.

LOOKING BACK

1. What features of particular wildlife tours would also classify those products as adventure tourism?

2. What specific risks are associated with wildlife adventure tours, and what steps can tour operators, guides, and clients take to minimise those risks?

3. What impacts can adventure tourism create on wildlife, and by what mechanisms? How can these impacts be managed and minimised?

Whale Shark, Ningaloo, Australia

CHAPTER 10

Marine

KEY ISSUES

- types of marine adventure tourism
- diving tourism: reef, cold water, sharks, whales, deep ocean
- above-water adrenalin tourism: speedboats, jet boats, water ski, wakeboard, etc.
- above-water scenic tours: sailing, cruising, sea kayak, etc.
- above-water wildlife tours: coastal, expedition cruises

CONTENTS

CHAPTER SUMMARY

The marine adventure tourism sector is large and diverse. Broad divisions may be drawn. Some activities take place underwater, some on the surface. Some tours are motorised, others are not. Some offer adventurous travel to spectacular scenery, whereas others focus on skill-based activities. Many commercial tour products combine components from all these options.

There is a large global diving sector, much of it with a commercial component because of the need to use compressors. The largest component of the dive tourism industry relies on tropical and subtropical coral reef ecosystems, but there is a growing cool-water subsector and even polar ice-diving tours. There are growing specialist subsectors such as diving to watch sharks and large marine mammals. There are also commercial tours in submarines and deep ocean submersibles.

Above water, some marine adventure tour products focus on wildlife, such as whale watching tours. Some take clients to remote areas such as the Arctic and Antarctic for scenery and wildlife. Some involve active participation, such as sailing and sea kayaking. Some provide a short thrill ride, such as jet boats and paragliding. And some provide logistic support for skilled outdoor sports such as surfing.

RESEARCH REVIEW

There are four recent books of particular relevance to marine adventure tourism. The first, edited by Jennings (2007a) is on marine tourism and recreation generally, but many of the activities it examines may also be classified as adventure tourism. The second, a monograph by Cater and Cater (2007) is technically on marine ecotourism, but includes considerable information on marine tourism resources, activities, and management which is equally germane to the adventure sector. The third, edited by Higham and Lück (2008) focuses on tourism involving marine wildlife, but as noted in Table 10.1, much of this is marketed under an adventure label. The fourth is an encyclopaedia of marine tourism edited by Lück (2008), which includes several short entries relevant to marine adventure tourism. There is a brief entry on adventure tourism itself, and also one on marine ecotourism. Sailing, surfing, sea kayaking, stingrays, submersibles, and cruise ships and whale watching are also addressed. Sea kayaking tourism has also been described by Buckley (2006a) and Hudson and Beedie (2006). Dive tourism was also examined by Mograbi and Rogerson (2007), though principally as an example of pro-poor tourism.

The volume edited by Jennings (2007a) includes chapters on: sailing and cruising (Jennings, 2007b); single-day trips (Moscardo, 2007); tall-ship training tours (Easthope, 2007); motorboating (Jennings, 2007c); motorised water sports more generally (Richins, 2007); surfing and windsurfing (Ryan, 2007); diving and snorkelling (Dimmock, 2007); and sport fishing and game fishing (Killion, 2007). Commercial expedition yacht cruises have also been examined by Smith (2006).

The volume by Cater and Cater (2007) includes detailed descriptions of several marine adventure tours. These include shark watching and cage diving in South Africa (pp. 29, 69, 93); various types of tours in Australia's Great Barrier Reef (p. 52); cruise ships in the Antarctic (p. 66); snorkelling with whale sharks at Ningaloo in Australia (pp. 70–73); diving (pp. 81–85); whale watching (pp. 85–89); and sea kayaking (pp. 93–95); and both shallow water and deep ocean submarines (pp. 97–100). The controversies

Table 10.1   Marine Adventure Tours

Type of Tour	Example, Place	Principal Attraction	Depth and Air	Latitude	Access, Boat	Local Transport	Length Days	Operators Audited
Whale dive	Vava'u, Tonga	Wildlife	SCUBA	Tropical	Yacht	Tender	1–10	–
Whale shark	Ningaloo, Australia	Wildlife	Snorkel	Subtropical	Motor vessel	Motor vessel	One	King Dive, Ningaloo Blue
Dolphin swim	Akaroa, New Zealand	Wildlife	Swimming	Temperate	Motor vessel	Boat	One	–
Swim with seals	Galapagos, Ecuador	Wildlife	Swimming	Subtropical	Motor vessel	From land	Half	Betchart Expeditions
Shark dive	Port Lincoln, Australia	Adrenalin	SCUBA	Temperate	Motor vessel	Motor vessel	One	–
Manta dive	Maldives	Wildlife	SCUBA	Tropical	Dive boat	Dive boat	Half	Delphis Diving
Reef dives	Pan-tropical	Scenery	SCUBA	Tropical and subtropical	Dive boat	Dive boat	1–10	Taka Dive, Walindi
Kelp dives	Pan-temperate	Scenery	SCUBA	Temperate	Dive boat	Dive boat	1	–
Ice dives	Polar shelves	Scenery	SCUBA	Polar	Cruise boat	Tender	1 of 10	–
Glass-bottom	Cairns, Australia	Scenery	Surface	Tropical and subtropical	Boat or land	Glass boat	Half	Quicksilver Cruises
Submersibles	Various	Deep scenery	Surface pressure	Tropical to polar	Boat or land	Submarine	Half	–
Orca kayak	San Juan Is., USA	Wildlife	Surface	Temperate	Land	Sea kayak	5	Sea Quest

Continued

Table 10.1 Marine Adventure Tours—cont'd

Type of Tour	Example, Place	Principal Attraction	Depth and Air	Latitude	Access, Boat	Local Transport	Length Days	Operators Audited
Narwhal kayak	Baffin I., Canada	Wildlife	Surface	Polar	Speedboat	Sea kayak	10	Black Feather
Whale kayak	Alaska, USA	Wildlife	Surface	Polar	Boat or land	Sea kayak	10	Various
Whale cruise	South Shetland Is., UK	Wildlife	Surface	Polar	x cruise boat	Zodiacs	10	–
Seabird kayak	Svalbard, Norway	Wildlife	Surface	Polar	x cruise boat	Sea kayak	10	Aurora Expeditions
Arctic cruise	Svalbard, Norway	Scenery	Surface	Polar	x cruise boat	x cruise boat	10	Aurora Expeditions
Antarctic cruise	Antarctic Peninsula	Scenery	Surface	Polar	x cruise boat	x cruise boat	10	Explorer
Sailing charters	Various	Scenery, participation	Surface	All	Yacht	Yacht	1 to many	–
Tall-ship cruises	Various	Scenery or participation	Surface	All	Tall ship	Tall ship	1 to many	–
Coastal sea kayaks	Fiji, Turkey, etc.	Coastal scenery	Surface	All	Land	Sea kayak	1–10	Southern Sea Ventures
Surfing charters	Indonesia, Maldives, etc.	Skilled sport	Surface	Tropical	Charter boat	Charter boat	10–12	Mentawai Sanctuary
Surf resorts	Fiji, Maldives	Skilled sport	Surface	Tropical	Air or boat	Speedboat, dinghy	5–10	Dhonveli
Jet boat, speedboat	Coastal resorts	Thrill ride	Surface	All	Land	Jet boat, speedboat	1 h	–
Parasail	Dunk I., Australia	Thrill ride	Surface	Subtropical	Air, land	Speedboat	15 min	Dunk Island Resort

x cruise = expedition cruise.

surrounding feeding of and disturbance to marine wildlife are covered in particular detail. Also relevant is a table of commercial tourist submarines (p. 99) with information on the largest operator and the deepest dives. There is also a very extensive bibliography of marine tourism research publications.

BIG PICTURE

Introduction

A wide range of different types of marine tours is marketed as adventure. They range from short thrill-rides on high-powered jet boats or inflatables, to multi-week specialist dive or marine wildlife watching tours in remote ocean areas. They may be divided broadly into tours where the key activity or attraction is underwater, and those where it is entirely above water, though boat-based. Above-water tours may also usefully be divided according to the type of attraction involved. At one extreme are tours where the principal attraction is watching marine wildlife such as whales and dolphins, seals and sea lions, or a range of seabirds. In most of these tours, the clients take no part in operating the boat, acting only as passengers. Some tours, however, use sea kayaks to watch marine wildlife, and clients are attracted by both aspects of the experience.

Similarly, a wide variety of marine tours are on offer which involve ocean-going yachts of various types: either sail or motor yachts, ranging from fully crewed and catered to so-called bare-boat charters. For these tours, ocean scenery and the experience of being at sea are parts of the attraction, but the sailing activity itself may be equally important. There is then a suite of marine tours where the key attraction is an adrenalin-based activity. Some of these involve skilled and essentially sporting activities carried out by the commercial participants, with boat-based surfing tours in remote areas as a prime example. This example is considered further in the chapter on boardsports. In others, the commercial clients are principally passengers, with the skills provided by the tour operator. These include high-speed boat rides and activities such as paragliding.

Finally, there is an enormous range of commercial marine fishing tours. Some of these, such as deep sea big-game fishing, could be classified as a form of adventure tourism. From both a commercial market perspective and a government regulatory perspective, however, the recreational fishing industry is rather distinct from the rest of the marine tourism sector and is accordingly not considered here in any detail.

The main component of the below-water marine adventure tourism sector is the dive tourism industry, which has its own internationally recognised qualifications and certifications, and local legislation in most countries which prescribes licensing and safety procedures. For the vast majority of divers, the main attraction is the undersea environment, including marine plants and animals. Various motor-assisted options are available, including boat-towed manta-boarding, self-propelled underwater scooter devices of various kinds, and miniature submarines. None of these, however, are at all common; and arguably, even in these cases, the principal attraction is the undersea environment rather than the motorised activity.

Product types

A variety of different marine adventure tourism activities are listed in Table 10.1. Commercial tour products currently on offer range in duration from minutes to months, though the majority are either single-day or 1–2 weeks in length. They are available at all latitudes from polar to tropical; and though different activities are more commonplace at different latitudes, even this distinction is beginning to blur as new technologies make particular activities possible in more extreme environments and to a broader range of clients. Tropical and subtropical coral reefs, for example, are still the most popular sites for SCUBA diving tours, but cool water diving off temperate coastlines is growing rapidly in popularity, and there are now commercial tour operators offering trips to dive under the edges of the polar ice shelves.

Table 10.1 classifies the principal attractions of different marine adventure tours into four main categories. There are some where the key selling point, and the principal goal of the commercial clients, is to see a particular species of wildlife. Tours specifically to see whales or dolphins, sharks or stingrays, seals or seabirds provide examples. In the second category, the principal attraction can best be described as scenery, either above or below water, and including plants and animals as well as inanimate objects. Expedition cruises where the participants want to see icebergs or glaciers, or diving tours where the participants want to see the coral reefs, provide examples. In the third category, the key is active participation in an activity which involves skill and coordination, such as sailing or sea kayaking. Scenery and specific wildlife may also be part of the attraction, but it is because of the activity that the clients select this particular tour. Tours in the fourth category are also activity-based, but distinguished because the principal attraction is a short-term adrenalin boost. In some cases it is the clients themselves who carry out the activity; in others, they are simply passengers. Most of these activities involve skill, coordination, and a cool head, generally gained by extensive practice; but in many cases, the tour company provides a driver or operator who carries out the skilled component, with the clients simply experiencing the excitement. Distinctions between these categories are not clear-cut. For surfers, for example, each individual ride may be a short and adrenalin-intensive experience; but in a multi-day surfing tour, the emphasis is more on the skilled activity.

Some examples of particular activity subsectors are outlined in more detail in the following sections.

Diving

Diving is one of the most carefully controlled and most heavily studied types of marine adventure tourism (Buckley, 2006a, pp. 166–192; Cater and Cater, 2007; Dimmock, 2007). It is controlled largely through two major worldwide industry associations, the Professional Association of Diving Instructors (PADI, 2009) and the National Association of Underwater Instructors (NAUI, 2009). Nominally, NAUI is US-based whereas PADI is international, but in practice both operate worldwide. These two associations certify both divers and diving centres or diving tour operators. Except for introductory beginner dives or diver training courses, dive tour operators will only accept certified clients; and most diving tourists will only deal with certified dive centres and tour operators.

This system seems to work well, but diving accidents do occur none-theless, as reviewed in Chapter 4. Only a small proportion of such accidents, relative to diver hours, are in commercial dive tours, because most tours are very conservative in the depths and locations where they take clients to dive. Very few commercial dive tours, for example, are long and deep enough to require extended decompression stops on ascent, though all include a mandatory 3–5-minute halt at 5 m depth in all dives. Few dive in caves or in areas with strong currents. Multi-day liveaboard dive charters which take clients on, e.g. open-ocean night dives to submerged pinnacles, will generally only accept experienced clients and check their skills at a number of less risky dive sites first. Where they take clients on drift dives, using currents to carry divers past underwater scenery such as coral reef walls, they ensure that there is a boat on the surface to pick the divers up at the end, and the dive instructor will carry a brightly coloured inflatable marker buoy to ensure the group is visible when it ascends. Despite all these precautions, accidents do sometimes occur, but except in a few areas, the incidence of such events is generally lower than for some motorised terrestrial adventure activities.

Worldwide, the majority of certified divers live in temperate areas of Europe and North America; but the main geographic focus of the commercial dive tourism industry is in the colourful coral reef ecosystems in the warm and shallow seas of the tropical and subtropical. As wetsuit and drysuit technologies have improved in recent years, commercial dive tours in cold and even polar waters have also become more commonplace. Many experienced divers are also keen underwater photographers, and choose diving destinations in order to see and photograph particular marine organisms. Some focus on the rare and unusual, such as the pygmy seahorses of New Britain. Others prefer large and potentially dangerous marine wildlife. This is exemplified in particular by shark diving, as outlined in the following section.

Shark diving

For many divers, sharks have now become something to search for, rather than something to be scared of. Of course, the sharks have not stopped feeding merely because they have become objects for adventure tourism, so safety precautions are still paramount. Some sharks are much safer to swim with than others. Some can only be watched safely from inside a metal cage, which is lowered into the water from a crane on a shark diving boat.

The growth of shark watching as a form of adventure tourism is perhaps best shown by the existence of a *Shark Watchers' Handbook* (Carwardine and Watterson, 2002). This directory lists 24 different shark species which are routinely viewed by shark divers, and a global geographic directory of places where they can be seen (Table 10.2).

The actual experience of diving with sharks differs greatly depending on the species concerned. Divers off the deep ocean face of the ribbon reefs on the outer edge of Australia's Great Barrier Reef, for example, routinely see quite large sharks of various species, patrolling at depth. In shallower waters, blacktip and whitetip reef sharks are commonplace in many parts of the tropics. There are some areas where particular species of shark visit during their breeding season and can be observed at rest. One well-known example is provided by the endangered ragged-tooth shark, also known as sand tiger or gray nurse shark, which can be seen at Sodwana Bay in South Africa. There are some areas where schools or congregations of sharks are routinely seen, and many more where shark dive operators have encouraged such aggregations by routine chumming and feeding. In some of these cases, a dive guide will feed sharks underwater by hand whilst the dive clients watch. A chainmail gauntlet is an essential accessory. Finally, there are shark cage diving operations, where the tour operator deliberately attracts great white and other large and dangerous sharks to take food as close as possible to a suspended cage which protects the dive client. There

| Table 10.2 | Distribution of Shark Species Watched by Divers |

Shark Species	Europe and UK	America and Caribbean	Middle East and North Africa	East and South Africa	Australia or NZ	Asia and Pacific Islands
Ragged-tooth		*	*	*	*	*
Thresher			*			*
Basking	*					
Mako	*	*			*	
Great white		*		*	*	
Scalloped hammerhead		*	*	*		*
Great hammerhead		*		*	*	*
Caribbean reef		*				
Ocean whitetip		*	*		*	
Silky		*	*			
Dusky		*				
Galapagos		*			*	
Gray reef		*	*		*	*
Silvertip		*	*		*	*
Blacktip reef		*	*	*	*	*
Bull		*		*		*
Bronze whaler		*		*	*	*
Lemon		*				
Tiger		*		*	*	*
Whitetip reef		*	*		*	*
Blue	*	*			*	
Whale		*		*	*	*
Nurse		*				
Zebra/leopard				*	*	*
Horn		*				
Tawny		*				*

Data summarised from Carwardine and Watterson (2002), pp. 89–139.

* = present.

are well-known examples at Gansbaai in South Africa and at Port Lincoln in South Australia.

In addition to *The Shark Watchers' Handbook* mentioned above, there are published reports on a number of these shark diving operations. Both Cater and Cater (2007) and Higham and Lück (2008) mention cage dive tours. There is also an entry on shark dives in the *Encyclopaedia of Tourism and Recreation in Marine Environments* (Lück, 2008).

Information on shark diving sites, species, operators, and opportunities is provided in detail by Carwardine and Watterson (2002). Different sharks occur in different areas; but perhaps more importantly, different areas have been developed to a greater or lesser degree as diving destinations, and this influences how many good shark watching sites have been identified. Table 10.2, summarised from data presented by Carwardine and Watterson (2002), shows broadly which shark species can commonly be watched in which continents.

From an adventure tourism perspective, shark species may be considered in a number of different categories. There are species which are commonly seen in shallower waters, such as dives around coral reefs, throughout the tropics and subtropics. There are open ocean species which are more commonly encountered at offshore sites, either at submarine pinnacle dives, or from open-ocean boat dives using chumming as an attractant. Some of these occur principally in warmer waters, such as the hammerheads and shortfin mako, whereas others, such as the great white, are more common in colder waters. At many sites, particularly if chumming or feeding is used, these species can only safely be watched using shark cages. At other sites, however, dive tourism operators lead uncaged dives with the same species.

There are a number of shark species with more localised distributions, some of them still abundant but others are rare. According to Carwardine and Watterson (2002), for example, divers wishing to see sixgill sharks would have to go to Canada, whereas those keen to watch wobbegong or epaulette sharks would need to visit Australia. Ragged-tooth sharks and thresher sharks can be seen along the east coast of Africa, the Middle East, or some sites in Southeast Asia; lemon sharks principally in Central America and the Caribbean; and zebra or leopard sharks at Asia-Pacific sites.

Finally, there are two filter-feeding shark species which can be watched even by inexperienced divers or snorkellers in relative safety, namely, the whale and basking shark. Whale sharks have become an icon attraction in marine adventure tourism. They can be seen occasionally at a wide range of warm-water dive sites, but there are reliable aggregations at only a few sites, such as Donsol in the Philippines and Ningaloo in Western Australia. Basking sharks, in contrast, are commonly seen only in Europe, with dive sites in the UK and Portugal.

Whilst perhaps less common than diving with sharks, there are also various places in the world where snorkelling or diving with stingrays, eagle rays or manta rays provides an adventure tourism attraction. There is a dive site in the Maldives, for example, where divers can rest on a sandy bottom as manta rays swim just overhead. There is a site in Belize known as Stingray City (Shackley, 1998a) where the rays aggregate every day in order to be fed, and tourists can snorkel with them. There are similar sites in the Bahamas.

Whale shark watching

Whale sharks are the world's largest sharks, but they are filter feeders and generally inoffensive. It is therefore possible for tourists to swim or snorkel with them safely, as long as they stay far enough away to avoid an accidental blow from the very large and powerful tail. Whale sharks are also very beautiful animals, with a particular blue and white pattern on their skin which is reminiscent of sunlight filtering through shallow seawater. As a result, they are a very popular attraction for marine adventure tours.

There are several places around the world where whale sharks congregate at particular times of year in order to feed, and these are the sites where whale shark tourism ventures operate. The overall life history of whale sharks, however, is not fully studied or understood. This includes the factors which may threaten their populations, and the factors which may determine exactly when they arrive and leave at each of their shallow coastal feeding areas. Both these issues, needless to say, are critical for the whale shark tourism industry. The whale shark watching season is short, the boats are expensive to run and are used elsewhere during the rest of the year, and the tour operations incur a number of fixed expenses irrespective of income. As a result, they have to plan for a season when they think there will be a sufficient number of whale sharks to keep tourists satisfied. If the sharks do not show up when they are expected, this has significant economic consequences for the tourism enterprises.

Perhaps the best-known of the world's whale shark tourism destinations is Ningaloo reef off the coast of Western Australia. This industry has been described by Cater and Cater (2007), and its economics analysed by Davis et al. (1997). Two of the individual tour operators, Ningaloo Blue and King Dive, were described by Buckley (2006a). The Ningaloo reef is a World Heritage marine park, and whale shark tourism is regulated by the Western Australia Department of Conservation and Land Management. Operators must be licensed, and the number of operators is restricted. The management agency levies a fee on each tourist who takes a whale shark tour, and it is the tour operator's responsibility to collect the fees and return them monthly to the agency. Snorkelling is permitted but SCUBA diving equipment is not, supposedly to prevent tourists harassing whale sharks, but perhaps in reality to prevent tourists diving too deep in an excited attempt to follow the sharks, which can certainly dive far deeper and swim far faster than a human diver. SCUBA diving with whale sharks is permitted in other parts of the world.

The whale sharks do not surface and are not visible from a boat at any distance. In order to find them, the boat operators form syndicates who pay microlight spotter planes to search for the sharks, whilst the tour boats take their clients for a dive, swim, or snorkel on an area of coral reef en route to the usual whale shark viewing area. Once a whale shark is sighted, the boats converge on the area, unless several are sighted simultaneously. There is a protocol for boats to approach the whale sharks and for snorkellers once they are in the water, which is specified in marine park regulations. Under this protocol, each boat is allowed to remain close to a whale shark for up to 1 hour, before it must move away and give precedence to the next boat in line. In practice, however, the operators have an informal code under which each boat puts its snorkellers in the water for a mere 10 minutes in turn, but stands by for another turn if the whale shark remains in position. This is because all the operators have a second-trip-free guarantee if clients are not able to swim with the sharks. As a result, it is in all their interests to make sure that as many tourists as possible do get at least a brief swim with the whale sharks. Not all boat operators belong to the principal syndicate, so there is a certain degree of competition if only a few whale sharks are sighted on any given day.

Whale sharks are the icon which has catapulted Ningaloo and the entire surrounding Exmouth region from a small fishing village and associated military base, otherwise known only to a few surfers, to a major tourist destination in the central Western Australian coast. Even though the whale shark season itself is quite short, the area is available for dive tourism year-round.

Boat-based whale watching

Single-day boat tours to watch whales of various species are now available in many parts of the world. Many whale species are still endangered because of past (and current) whaling, and perhaps also because of underwater noise produced through submarine geophysical exploration and military exercises. From a whale watching perspective, the few countries that still permit and indeed encourage commercial or so-called scientific whaling, notably Norway and Japan, are the pariahs of the modern world. In 2007, an incident was widely reported in which a Japanese whaling vessel harpooned a Baird's Beaked Whale directly in front of a whale watching tourist boat (Japan Probe, 2007).

In North America, whale watching tours along the California and Oregon coastlines, as well as Mexico further south, rely principally on the gray whale migrations which move north along the coastline in March and back in December. In Australia, the principal species is the humpback whale. This species migrates north along both east and west coasts of Australia during June and July, and south again in September on the way to its summer feeding grounds in Antarctica. There is a significant tourism industry based on the whales' overwintering area in Hervey Bay in central southern Queensland, and another group of whale watching boats based in the Gold Coast area, a large coastal tourist town in far southeastern Queensland. Hervey Bay lies between the large sand mass of Fraser Island and the mainland coast. This site is within Queensland State coastal waters, and both commercial tour operators and private boats are subject to whale watching regulations, which prescribe approach distances, velocities, and times. Commercial tour operators are also required to report the approximate position of each whale sighting, using a system which divides the Bay area into large reference squares on a coarse grid. The whales at Hervey Bay are resting rather than migrating, and extended views are routinely possible. Under Queensland State law, the Gold Coast boats are not permitted to approach whales within Queensland State coastal waters, which extend about 5 km (3 nautical miles) offshore; but there is no legal barrier to whale watching in federal territorial waters further offshore, and this is in fact what these vessels do.

At Kaikoura in New Zealand, the principal attraction is the opportunity to watch sperm whales, which feed on squid at considerable depth and are only accessible to whale watching tourists at a very limited number of sites. Tourists can watch the whales either by boat or by helicopter. It seems likely that at least the helicopter-based tours may have a significant impact on the whale's behaviour. The whales have to remain on the surface long enough to replenish their oxygen supplies after extended deep dives in search of food, but when helicopters are present, they minimise their surface time and dive more steeply than otherwise. From the tour participants' perspective the advantages of the helicopter over a boat tour are that it can find and follow the sperm whales more easily, during the relatively short periods when they are on the surface; and that it provides a near-vertical view through the water surface so that the entire whale is visible, rather than a low-angle oblique view where much less of the animal can be seen.

In Glacier Bay, Alaska, humpback whales are routinely seen from single-day passenger cruise boats which travel up and down a long sound. Indeed, whales can even be seen from shore, from the national parks campground, on some occasions. A number of multi-day expedition cruises also provide opportunities to watch whales, including less commonly seen species, but the sightings are less reliable and whales are not the primary attraction for these cruises. A number of whale species, for example, may be seen in the Antarctic waters visited by expedition cruises such as those run by Explorer Shipping or Aurora Expeditions (Buckley, 2006a).

Whale watching by sea kayak

The coastal sounds around Vancouver Island and the San Juan Islands, near the Pacific Ocean border between Canada and the USA, are visited seasonally by particular pods of killer whales or orcas, which form the basis for a significant regional whale watching industry. There are particular places where orcas may regularly be seen from land, and there are a number of boat-based tours. There is also an area where motorised boats are prohibited in order to provide a resting place for the whales, but where paddle-powered sea kayaks are permitted. Several small companies operate multi-day sea kayak tours in this area, camping on various islands, which include good opportunities to watch orcas at very close range. Indeed, the orcas may even swim underneath the kayaks. Given that some of the whales are significantly larger than the kayaks, this can be quite an exciting experience. The structure and operations of one of these orca watching sea kayak tours are described by Buckley (2006a). Whales can also be seen from sea kayaks in many other parts of the world, but this seems to be the principal area where commercial trips are run specifically to watch killer whales.

One rather unusual adventure tour which provides opportunities to watch whales from sea kayaks is a multi-day tour using collapsible sea kayaks at the northern end of Baffin Island in the Canadian Arctic, which offers a good opportunity to see narwhal, the unicorn of the sea. One such tour is described by Buckley (2005b, 2006a). The Arctic Ocean scenery and the sea kayaking experience itself are also significant attractions for this tour, but narwhal are the main marketing icon and certainly contribute enormously to the overall participant experience. The narwhal are hunted by local Inuit using speedboats and high-powered rifles, and the narwhal tusks are apparently sold illegally to passengers on visiting cruise ships (Buckley, 2005b).

In other parts of the world, commercial sea kayaking tours may provide the opportunity to see other marine wildlife. Sea kayak adventure tours in Abel Tasman National Park at the northwest corner of New Zealand's South Island, for example, routinely encounter New Zealand fur seals, with good opportunities for close-range viewing. These tours have been described by Buckley (2006a) and by Cater and Cater (2007). Boat-supported sea kayak tours near Svalbard north of Norway provide opportunities to see large nesting colonies of seabirds and the possibility of encountering polar bears. One such tour offered by Aurora Expeditions and Southern Sea Ventures is described by Buckley (2006a).

Ocean coasts and islands by sea kayak

A number of adventure tourism operators worldwide offer commercial multi-day sea kayak trips where the key attraction is provided by the activity and the scenery rather than by any expectation of seeing unusual marine wildlife. Such tours are on offer, for example, in Australia, New Zealand, Fiji, Samoa, Turkey, the Kamchatka Peninsula in eastern Russia, Scotland, Alaska, Canada, and various parts of the USA. The operational structure of some of these sea kayaking tour products is described by Buckley (2006a). The sea kayaking sector is also analysed quite extensively by Cater and Cater (2007).

Some commercial sea kayaking operators offer only fully guided and catered tours in relatively remote locations. These are expensive because of the high client-to-guide ratio and the need either to bring in equipment by air for every trip, or to maintain an inventory of equipment which is only used seasonally. Other enterprises, in contrast, have an extended season or operate year-round, and also rent sea kayaks for unaccompanied trips, the sea kayak equivalent of the bare-boat charter. One such operator is Natural High Adventures in New Zealand (Buckley, 2006a; Cater and Cater, 2007). This company generates a high volume of sea kayaking business through various strategies, including: intensive local marketing in nearby Nelson, effectively an adventure gateway town; cross-marketing with its mountain-biking business; and selling short sea kayak tours to large international student groups visiting New Zealand from North America. The company offers sea kayak rentals, motorboat shuttles, guiding, catering, food delivery, accommodation bookings, camping equipment rentals, and bus shuttles as a suite of separately purchasable products, a strategy which seems to work well in a high-volume market.

Polar expedition cruises

The mainstream cruise industry (Dowling, 2006) is very much a social and relaxation market, though a few large cruise vessels do venture into Arctic and Antarctic waters. The expedition cruise market is a somewhat different subsector, aimed at providing an adventure experience, albeit one which is accessible to clients of all ages and fitness levels, and expect a high quality of service. Since only the hardiest and most experienced expeditioners can visit the polar oceans in a private yacht or sea kayak, travel on an expedition cruise vessel is effectively the only option for anyone else at all, no matter how fit they are.

The world's first expedition cruise vessel, originally named the Lindblad Explorer, came to the end of an eventful life when it sank in 2007 after colliding with an iceberg. It was owned and operated at the time by a company called Gap Adventures. Explorer Shipping, the company which had operated it for many years, had replaced the original vessel some years previously with the Explorer II, a slightly larger and more luxurious vessel. The Explorer was an ice-strengthened vessel, but not an icebreaker. Apart from the purpose-built Explorer II, most of the vessels used for polar expedition cruises are former Russian research ships, which became available for commercial tourism operations following the break-up of the former USSR. Some of these are fully equipped icebreakers, capable of cutting through the Arctic ice all the way to the North Pole. They are chartered by different adventure tourism operators at different times. One of these vessels, the Marina Svetaeva, was purchased for the 2008 season by the Australian-based company Aurora Expeditions, which had already been running Arctic and Antarctic expedition cruises for a number of years.

'Expedition cruise ship' is a label used in adventure tourism marketing rather than boat registries, but there are a number of characteristic features which do distinguish expedition cruises and vessels from their mainstream analogues. Expedition cruise ships are significantly smaller, typically carrying around 100 passengers rather than 1000 or more. They are designed for the severe weather and ocean seas commonplace at high latitudes. They carry a sufficient number of zodiacs or other outboard-powered inflatable rubber boats, with davits for rapid launching, so that they can quickly transport the entire complement of passengers to land and back to the expedition vessel, several times per day. This contrasts with the much larger mainstream cruise ships, which can only land their entire passenger complements at a dock or berth designed for that purpose, typically in an urban port.

Whilst mainstream cruise ships have an extensive social programme, and the facilities to support it, expedition cruise vessels commonly have a series of lectures by scientific experts who accompany the expedition specifically for that purpose. That is, they have an educational programme rather than a social programme. Mainstream cruise ships may indeed visit parts of Alaska, the Canadian Arctic, or the sub-Antarctic islands, but their principal itineraries focus on warmer waters and calmer climes. A large part of their programme consists of opportunities for the passengers to swarm ashore at coastal tourist towns, which could equally well have been reached by air and land. Expedition cruise ships, in contrast, typically travel to areas with no access other than by sea, and start their voyages from the closest available airport, such as Ushuaia at the southern tip of South America for voyages to the Antarctic peninsula, or Longyearbyen in Svalbard for trips into the European Arctic.

Except for the most upmarket of mainstream cruise ships (Dowling, 2006), a significant proportion of cruise ship passengers are relatively young and inexperienced travellers searching more for a social than an adventure experience. On expedition cruise vessels, in contrast, the majority of passengers are older, well-off and well-educated, and seeking a lifetime adventure experience, perhaps the culmination of many years of planning. They take a keen interest in the educational lecture programme, and they very quickly learn to identify different species of seabird or cetaceans. They have professional-standard binoculars and cameras, and when the captain announces a landing they are queuing up at the gangways, fully equipped, within seconds.

Surf charters

By far the majority of surfing is carried out as private land-based recreation, but there is a significant, growing and highly visible subsector which forms part of the commercial marine adventure tourism industry. The core of this subsector consists of multi-day liveaboard boat tours in tropical and subtropical seas, in areas where there is a long fetch of ocean to windward, and reefs or islands to convert ocean swells to rideable surf. Boat-based surf tours may also visit well-known breaks on larger islands or mainland coastlines, but only if they are relatively inaccessible by land, since one of the key selling points is the opportunity to surf high-quality but uncrowded waves (Buckley, 2002a, 2002b).

Where individual island surf breaks become popular as a result of boat-based tours, the tour operators may subsequently build island-based surf resorts as a more cost-effective way to capture the same sector of the surf tourism market. Some of these island surf resorts do also offer other tourist activities, but the main purpose of these is so that older, cash-rich time-poor surfers with family responsibilities will be able to bring their partners and children to the resorts. These activities also provide alternatives to keep the surfing clients happily occupied if there is no surf. Fishing and sit-on-top sea kayaks are the most common ancillary activities. A few island resorts also offer diving, but more commonly they would take advantage of nearby dive tourism operations, since diving is a much more heavily regulated activity than surfing, and requires much more expensive equipment and qualified instructors. Even with a full complement of such ancillary activities, the small island surf resorts are very different from large-scale luxury resorts in coastal tourist towns, where the emphasis is on relaxation and social activities.

Boat-based surf tours are currently available in areas such as the Maldives, Fiji, the Mentawai Islands in Indonesia, and the Montebello Islands off Western Australia. Most of these areas also have small and recently constructed surf resorts on the islands (Buckley, 2006a). Both the boat-based tours and the island resorts are relatively expensive; and most of them are marketed principally through a relatively small number, effectively an oligopoly, of specialist surf tourism retailers. Some of the resorts and boats have exclusive agreements with particular retailers, others not. The retail agencies advertise principally in specialist recreational surfing magazines, and on weather-forecast and surf-camera websites frequented by surfers (Buckley, 2002a, 2002b, 2003b, 2006a).

Over the past decade there have been some significant developments at the professional end of the surfing spectrum, and these may in due course become available as commercial surf tourism products. The main one is tow-in surfing, where experienced big-wave surfers, riding special tow-in boards with footstraps, use jet skis to tow them onto particularly large and powerful waves which they would be unable to paddle onto unaided. Once the surfer has caught the wave, the jet ski pulls away and the surfer continues the wave under gravity power alone. The footstraps are needed since on these very large waves, the board must travel at particularly high speed. The surfer uses the straps both to maintain the speed and to maintain control when travelling at high speed over a choppy water surface on the face of the wave. Tow-in surfing is now routine for big-wave surfers, professional surfers, and some surf competitions.

Even faster than tow-in surfboards, but currently restricted to a small number of skilled professional surfers, are hydrofoil surfboards where a tow-in board with footstraps is also equipped with a half-metre long fin which ends in a horizontal hydrofoil, an underwater wing. Once the board is moving fast enough, the entire board lifts out of the water, with only the hydrofoil and lower part of the fin remaining submerged. This allows for a very fast and smooth ride no matter how rough the water surface is. Using the hydrofoil boards, skilled surfers can ride large ocean swells well away from land, long before they break to form surf. The day may yet come when open-ocean hydrofoil surfing becomes a routine part of the panoply of commercial marine adventure tourism, but that day is still some way off.

If tow-in and hydrofoil surfing are thought of as power-assisted surfing, then sailboarding and kiteboarding may be thought of as wind-assisted surfing. Both are described more extensively in Chapter 11 on boardsports tourism. Neither sailboarding nor kiteboarding necessarily requires surf, and there are many exponents of each who restrict their recreation to lakes, bays, and sometimes rivers. Both sailboards and kiteboards, however, can be ridden in the surf or indeed in the open ocean, so those activities could be classified at least in part as marine adventure recreation; and to the extent that commercial tours may be available, as marine adventure tourism. In fact, however, as outlined in Chapter 11, there seem as yet to be relatively few commercial sailboarding or kiteboarding tours on offer.

Yachting and sailing

Ocean sailing must surely be one of the oldest subsectors of the marine adventure tourism industry. Individual travellers have paid for passage since the earliest days of ocean-going sailing craft, perhaps even since prehistoric times. The primary purpose of such voyages was commercial, but some of the passengers travelled for purely personal interests, and some left written accounts much more detailed than those in the ship logs (Newby, 1986). It is, of course, a far cry from the cramped quarters, uncertain navigation and hard tack of the early sailing ships, to modern fully crewed and catered luxury sailing charters with en-suite double cabins and skilled chefs. Only a small proportion of the commercial sailing tour industry, however, caters for the luxury end of the market. The majority relies on much more basic cruising yachts with old-style bunk berths, manually pumped marine toilets, saltwater ablutions, and fresh water only for drinking. A larger sector still, as measured by number of individual passengers, is the day-sailing market where yachts are built or modified to take the largest possible number of passengers for a short cruise of a few hours' duration, with no onboard accommodation except for a skeleton crew. There are also specialist subsectors, such as educational adventure tourism using tall ships, where most of the participants are of secondary school or university age and are taught to take part in sailing a traditional square-rigged sailing ship on a long-distance voyage, often with several changes of crew en route.

Whilst part of the market for sailing tours consists of experienced yachtsmen who have their own boats at home and simply want to sail in new waters, a significant proportion of clients consists of inexperienced sailors who either buy a day cruise on a fully crewed yacht, or join a friend who does have some sailing experience, for a bare-boat sailing holiday. Some examples of individual tourism products in each of these categories are summarised by Buckley (2006a) and Cater and Cater (2007). There are particular destination areas which have developed a large-scale and inter-nationally known bare-boat charter industry, such as the Greek islands, the Caribbean, Marlborough Sounds in New Zealand, and the Whitsunday Islands in Australia. Single-day cruises are also on offer at these destinations, to provide for tourists who want a sailing experience but do not have time, money, or expertise for a multi-day yacht charter. The majority of single-day sailing tours, however, are offered from marinas at mainstream coastal tourist towns and are marketed simply as a daytime activity for essentially urban tourists. That is, such tours would hardly qualify as adventurous to an experienced sailor, though they may still be perceived that way to the particular clients involved.

Coastal powerboat tours

A number of coastal tourist destinations worldwide offer short adrenalin-based rides in various high-speed powered watercrafts, including jet skis, jet boats, outboard-powered inflatables, and conventional speedboats powered either by outboard or inboard engines. Such tours appeal to essentially the same market sector as jet boat tours on rivers, such as the much-studied Shotover Jet operating from Queenstown in the South Island of New Zealand (Cloke and Perkins, 1998; Cater, 2006a). There is also a spectator tourist industry associated with professional offshore powerboat racing, but that is outside the scope of this volume.

Paragliding tours provide another type of short-duration commercial thrill ride available at a number of coastal island tourist resorts and tourist towns. In these tours, the client hangs in a harness below a small parachute which is towed behind a powerboat. The parachute is not independently steerable, and the client has no control over the activity. Some tours offer double as well as single harnesses. Typically the parachute and the client are lifted off directly from a beach and dropped back into shallow water after a 10–15-minute ride.

Game fishing

Small-scale fishing in near-shore marine waters is a major recreational activity in many countries, and this includes large numbers of low-volume, small-scale, single-day commercial fishing tours. These, however, would not generally be considered as part of the adventure tourism industry. In some areas, such as northern Australia and western Papua New Guinea, there are helicopter-access fishing tours which would qualify as adventure, but which are not marine. In tropical ocean waters worldwide, however, there is an upmarket sport-fishing sector known as game fishing or bill-fishing, with marlin and similar species as the principal targets (Killion, 2007). Much of this is carried out by wealthy private individuals using their own boats, but there is also a significant marine adventure tourism subsector based around this type of fishing. In market terms this is a specialised and largely self-contained subsector, which draws more on the recreational sport-fishing sector than on the commercial adventure tourism industry. To date, it has received relatively limited attention in the tourism research literature. Whilst some boats operate directly from ports or marinas, others operate in the open ocean, with one or more small high-speed catch boats operating from a single larger liveaboard mother boat where the clients live when not actually fishing. There are apparently also operations where the catch boats proceed to an offshore rendezvous point, for example, near an uninhabited offshore island, and the clients are brought in by helicopter or floatplane.

Submarines and submersibles

A number of commercial marine adventure tourism operators now offer trips in submarines or submersibles. Some of these descend to very considerable depths. According to Cater and Cater (2007) there are over 50 such operations worldwide. Most of these tourist submarines carry around 50 passengers and crew and stay in relatively shallow water, with maximum depth 100 m (Newbery, 1997). A few submersibles, however, can take one or two passengers to very great depths, e.g. to 1000 m or in one case potentially even to 6000 m (Laing and Crouch, 2008).

The largest submarine tour operator is Atlantis Adventures (2009), which currently has 11 sightseeing submarines in Hawaii, Guam, and the Caribbean, with over a million passengers per year. The principal deep ocean operator is Deep Ocean Expeditions (2009), which uses Russian MIR Class submersibles capable of successful descents to the deep ocean seabed. During 2009, this company offers dives to the seafloor under the North Pole, at a cost of just under US$100,000 per client.

Conclusions

The marine adventure tourism sector is large, diverse, and growing, in a similar manner to its terrestrial counterpart. Individual products range in price from tens of dollars to tens of thousands. New activities and improved equipment appear frequently, and more remote and previously inaccessible areas are being made available as part of commercial adventure tourism products. Many marine tours combine activities both above and below water, in latitudes from the equator to the poles. As in terrestrial ecosystems, there are conflicts between use of marine environments and wildlife for tourism, and use for primary production and other industries, notably the commercial fisheries and whaling industries, and effluents from land-based agriculture and manufacturing and urban waste treatment.

CASE STUDY 10.1: Sea Kayaking in the High Arctic

Polar expedition cruise operator Aurora Expeditions runs a joint venture with worldwide sea kayak tour operator Southern Sea Ventures to offer boat-supported sea kayak tours in the Norwegian High Arctic, around and north of Svalbard or Spitzbergen. Operational details of the tour are described by Buckley (2006a). Essentially, clients travel as part of Aurora Expeditions' Spitzbergen-circumnavigation cruise, but with the option to make local landings or sorties in sea kayaks rather than outboard-powered inflatables. They thus gain the experience of travelling silently amongst the Arctic ice at 82°N, under their own paddle power, but with the luxury of a warm and well-fed liveaboard expedition cruise ship as a base, instead of cold self-supported camping.

A self-supported sea kayak tour is offered by Black Feather Inc (2009) in the Canadian High Arctic, where polar bears are less of a threat than on Svalbard. The tour operates out of Pond Inlet on the northern tip of Baffin Island. It uses a speedboat to shuttle boats, guides, and clients to a particular bay, some days' paddling away, with a gentle gravel shore convenient for camping and assembling the collapsible Feathercraft® kayaks. The bay also offers unforgettable sighting of narwhal. Over the following few days the group paddles back to Pond Inlet, camping en route. Operational details are described by Buckley (2005b, 2006a).

LOOKING BACK

1. What similarities and differences are there between marine and terrestrial adventure tourisms from the perspective of a commercial tour operator?

2. What factors have led to the successful global spread of the two main diver certification programmes, run by PADI and NAUI, respectively? What differences are there between these programs? Are there other programs, and if so where do they operate? Have similar systems evolved for other types of adventure tourism and recreation? If so, which, and if not, why not, and would they be valuable?

3. How is marine adventure tourism regulated, in different regions and countries? Are such regulations successful in monitoring safety and minimising environmental impacts? How are they funded and enforced?

Mentawai Islands, Indonesia

CHAPTER 11

Boardsports

KEY ISSUES

- surf, snowboard, sailboard, kiteboard, wakeboard, skateboard, others
- social context, sector structure
- history, geography, economics
- products, prices, and volumes
- equipment
- safety
- marketing
- clothing

CONTENTS

CHAPTER SUMMARY

Boardsports include snowboarding, surfing, sailboarding, kiteboarding, skateboarding, and wakeboarding. Snowboarding is fully integrated into the commercial snow tourism industry and is now of comparable size to the skiing sector. Surfing includes not only a large individual outdoor recreation component but also a range of commercial tour products. There are as yet far fewer commercial tour products involving other boardsports.

Boardsports are heavily dependent on equipment, and advances in design and technology have opened up new activities and areas for inclusion in commercial tour products. Detachable fins on surfboards, and multi-piece masts on sailboards, for example, have made travel much easier.

Boardsports depend heavily on terrain and weather, so there is a very well-defined geography of boardsports tourism, with key icon areas for each activity. These areas are marketed heavily. There are also strong commercial cross-links with the fashion clothing industry and the entertainment sector.

There is an enormous range of prices for boardsports products, from short learner packages costing a few tens of dollars, to luxury all-inclusive expert packages costing tens of thousands. Safety, snow or wave quality, luxury, and exclusiveness are key factors.

RESEARCH REVIEW

There is remarkably little published research to date on boardsports tourism. This contrasts strongly with the ski industry, which has been studied extensively. There is a small literature comparing injury statistics in snowboarding and skiing (see Chapter 4). There is also a small literature on social and economic aspects of surfing, including surf tourism in some instances (Buckley, 2003b; Dolnicar and Fluker, 2003; Lazarow, 2007).

BIG PICTURE

Introduction

There is a particular skill to balancing on a moving board, adjusting speed and steering solely by shifting the weight on your feet. Surfboards, sailboards, kiteboards, snowboards, wakeboards, and skateboards are all different, but they are conveniently considered together under the general heading of boardsports. For boardsports which depend on natural terrain and weather, people routinely travel to particular geographic sites to take advantage of good conditions. Such travel now forms a significant component of the worldwide adventure tourism industry, and there are tour companies which specialise in packaging boardsports tours. Most of these involve only a single activity, but a few package multiple boardsports in a single trip. For indoor, street, urban, and flatwater boardsports there is less need to travel in search of suitable terrain. Tourism associated with these boardsports is therefore much smaller, connected principally to competitive events. The main focus here is therefore on the outdoor wind-, wave-, and snow-based boardsports and the associated commercial tourism subsectors.

The term boardsports is generally used to refer to sports which involve riding a single board, with the rider's feet placed across or diagonal rather than parallel to the board's centreline. That is, it includes snowboarding, surfing, windsurfing or sailboarding, kiteboarding, wakeboarding, skateboarding, and variants of these. It is distinguished from skiing, either on snow or water, where the skier generally has one ski for each foot, with the feet aligned parallel to the skis. Single-ski variants are also considered as skiing if the feet are parallel to the ski centreline. This includes waterskis where one foot is behind the other, and double-width snowskis with the bindings side-by-side but pointing forwards. Most skis require bindings, but barefoot waterskiing is still considered as skiing. Some boardsports use bindings, some do not, and some have options with or without bindings. Some boardsports rely purely on gravity, whereas others use sails, kites, or tow ropes to provide motive power.

Social context

The social context for boardsports differs between countries and has changed over time. In Australia, for example, a group of internationally competitive surfers known as the 'Bronzed Aussies' initially created a healthy and athletic image for surfers. This was followed by several decades where the stereotypical public perception of surfers in Australia was much more negative, e.g. as unemployed dropouts. Over the past two decades, however, the rapidly increasing popularity and prize money of professional competitive surfing, the dedication of a number of younger competitive surfers, and the continuing marketing campaigns by surf clothing manufacturers have recreated the image of surfers as athletes, and of professional surfing as a serious career option. In many developing nations throughout the Pacific region, surfing is perceived largely as a rich foreigners' sport, where tourists arrive on planes and chartered surf yachts, stay in surf lodges, and fly back to the city. For local youngsters living in villages near icon surfing sites, this is a lifestyle to be envied and emulated rather than despised, and to become a surfing guide is a common ambition.

Similar changes in the social context for snowboarding took place in Europe and North America over recent decades. Snowboarders were originally looked down upon both by skiers and by ski resort operators, who held a stereotypical view of snowboarders as young, rude, inexpert, and impoverished. As snowboarding grew in popularity with all age groups, however, and snowboarders showed off their skills on the slopes and halfpipes, ski resorts which had previously prided themselves on banning snowboarders were compelled by economic realities to change their policies. Indeed, snowboarding clients are now more numerous than skiers across the entire mountain resort industry. Snowboarding is now seen as entirely respectable rather than rebellious, particularly since the advent of so-called new-school skiing, where skiers now carry out manoeuvres previously practiced only by snowboarders. The final indicator of this changing social context is perhaps provided by the heliski industry, the most upmarket peak of the snow sports sector, which now caters equally to snowboarders and skiers.

Kiteboarding is a relatively new sport and the stereotypical image of kiteboarders is still that of delinquent adults, recklessly risking injury and family livelihoods through an extreme sport. The reality is rather different. The designs of kites and kite harnesses now incorporate a number of safety features; and since kiteboarding equipment is relatively expensive, the majority of kiteboarders are middle-aged and correspondingly cautious. Interestingly, when commercial sailboards first became available in the 1970s, sailboarders were looked down upon by yachtsmen and dinghy sailors. This perception has changed, firstly since sailboarding became an Olympic sport, and secondly since it became extremely popular throughout the lakes of many European nations.

Skateboards come in a wide variety of designs and sizes, but most of them require a very high degree of skill and balance to ride successfully. Skateboard competitions attract large audiences and are televised internationally. Historically, the stereotypical image of skateboarders was one of delinquent children and teenagers. In recent years, however, the wide availability of skateboard variants intended for family use, the production of motorised skateboards for city transport, and the construction of skate parks for urban recreation have given the sport a new aura of respectability.

In contrast to skateboarding and kiteboarding, wakeboarding is perceived simply as a close cousin to waterskiing, very much a mainstream sporting activity. One reason for this may be that ski boats, the vehicles to tow them, and the fuel to run them are expensive, so that waterskiing and wakeboarding are associated, in the public perception, with owning a boat and a four-wheel-drive vehicle.

Sector structure

The structure of the international boardsports tourism sector reflects these socio-economic and demographic differences, as well as the physical geography of terrain and weather conditions. As in many forms of tourism, there are both push and pull factors which may lead outdoor boardsports enthusiasts to travel in order to enjoy their particular adventure activity. In addition to differences in price and cost, the principal pull factors are related to surf, snow, water, and wind conditions. Expert snowboarders will pay to ride steep deep powder snow, especially if it has varied terrain features. Expert surfers will pay to surf long, clean, barrelling waves of a good size. Expert sailboarders and kiteboarders look for strong and consistent winds with either surf or flatwater depending on inclination. The principal push factor is commonly crowding. Even if snowboarders live next to snow-covered mountains, or surfers next to well-shaped waves, their enjoyment is lessened if their favourite sites or surf breaks are always heavily crowded, so they may travel simply to escape the crowds.

As with many forms of adventure tourism, the structure of the board-sports tourism sector may be thought of as a pyramid, with a large volume of relatively low-cost trips forming the base, and successively smaller volumes of higher-cost tours forming the apex. The lowest-cost but highest-volume types of trips involve self-drive domestic travel and camping or other budget accommodation. Surfers who go on extended surf safaris around the coast-lines of their own countries, for example, are still classified as part of the tourism sector. If they drive around the coastline of a neighbouring country, as many American and Europeans surfers do, they then become part of the international tourism industry. Sailboarders and kiteboarders may do the same. It is also possible for snowboarders to rely on snow tents for accommodation and snow shoes or split boards to climb to the top of rideable slopes. This, however, is relatively uncommon. Most snowboarders buy package tours to ski resorts in the same way as skiers; or if that is beyond their means, they take seasonal jobs at winter resorts where discounted lift tickets are part of the package.

Unlike snowboarding, where access to commercial lift infrastructure is essentially the entry level for the sport, there are rather few resorts built specifically for surfing, and these are relatively upmarket. Other than self-drive camping trips, the entry level for surf tourism is to travel to temperate or subtropical beach holiday destinations which also have good surf, and stay in any appropriate tourist accommodation from backpacker hostels to motels and hotels. For surfers without their own transport, there are also commercial surf safaris which take groups of surfers by bus from place to place, generally with fairly low-key accommodation. The nearest equivalent to this in the snowboarding sector would be the bus tours of so-called club fields in countries such as New Zealand. The club fields are small localised lift operations owned by local ski clubs, which generally do not include accommodation or any retail facilities. In fact, there are also a small number of tour operators who specialise in running backcountry snow camping trips for snowboarders, similar to those which they have historically offered for cross-country skiers. Typically these include avalanche safety training as an essential component. Tours such as these form only a miniscule proportion of the snowboarding sector as a whole.

As with most forms of adventure tourism, the leading edge of new product development is in the lower-volume, cash-rich, time-poor sector of the market, where relatively wealthy boardsports enthusiasts are prepared to pay significant sums for guided, fully catered luxury trips to international icon sites. For most snowboarders, the most desirable tour products are heliski packages based at purpose-built heliski lodges in mountain ranges which routinely experience an extended season of deep dry powder snow. For surfers, there are surf lodges with exclusive access to particular surf breaks in areas which routinely receive large long-fetch ocean swells; and there are luxury charter vessels which routinely run 10- to 12-day trips in the same regions, with greater flexibility to visit a wider range of surf breaks depending on conditions.

It is these fully packaged top-notch tours which dominate perceptions of the boardsports tourism industry in the eyes of government agencies, industry associations, and the public, probably because it is these types of tour which receive the greatest promotion and publicity. Such publicity includes feature articles and editorials in specialist sports and recreation magazines and in general travel magazines, and in both sports and travel newspaper features and television programmes. It also includes commercial promotions not only by the relevant tour operators themselves, but also by clothing and equipment manufacturers (Buckley, 2003b). The principal focus for the remainder of this chapter is hence on fully packaged and commercially promoted boardsports tour products. As noted earlier, however, these products form only the tip of the pyramid for the boardsports tourism sector as a whole. They rely on the much larger, lower-key and less visible independent boardsports travel and recreational sectors, which supply both the tour operator clientele, and the main markets for boardsports equipment and clothing manufacturers.

Geography

Like most types of adventure tourism, the boardsports tourism industry is greatly affected by geographic factors, both natural and human. The best surf, snow, wind, and water occur only at very specific sites, and commercial boardsports tour products are focussed on getting clients safely to and from those sites and keeping them comfortable whilst they are there. Especially at the upper end of the market, the overriding criterion in choosing a destination and tour is the quality of the surf or snow, wind or water at the destination, and the ability of the operators and guides to get their clients to the best local places and conditions at the best times of day. Safety and service quality are also significant considerations. These issues apply to the travel as well as the activity and accommodation components of the tour. Many boardsports, however, involve a significant element of risk, particularly at the expert level, and this may lead boardsports tourists to discount the potential risks involved in international travel, which they perceive as significantly lower. If every wave on a specific island reef break involves a very real risk of injury on the coral, or every snowboard run through untracked backcountry powder involves significant risk of triggering an avalanche or falling into a treewell, then the risks of aircraft hijacking or airport terrorist attacks may appear comparatively minor. Surf tourism to the Mentawai Islands off Western Sumatra in Indonesia, for example, was largely unaffected by bombings in Bali some years ago.

Precisely because outdoor boardsports can involve significant risk, however, safety during the activity itself is a key consideration for most boardsports tourists, especially those with family responsibilities. As in other outdoor sports and adventure tourism activities, most participants have a reasonable understanding of their relative capabilities and would not select a tour product or destination where they would put themselves or other participants at risk. Ageing surfers, for example, may well take a commercial tour to be able to surf good but uncrowded waves, but they also want waves that are well within their surfing ability so that they can gain maximum enjoyment from the lack of crowding. Similar considerations apply for backcountry or helicopter snowboarding: though most heliski companies advertise that any intermediate skier or boarder can successfully enjoy a helicopter package, they also go to some lengths to assess individual skill levels, and they restrict access to more difficult sites and slopes to experienced clients only. Even so, some clients overestimate their abilities, and tour operators maintain strategies to reassign them to different sites or take them to easier slopes or waves. This issue is also commonplace in other types of adventure tourism. Horse-riding tour operators, for example, report that their customers routinely overestimate their riding skills (Ollenburg, 2006).

Overall geographical patterns in boardsports tourism, as in other forms of adventure tourism (Chapter 2), are thus set by the interplay of natural and human geographic factors. Clients want the best conditions, and tour operators who can provide those conditions can command higher prices. Neither high costs nor high risks will put clients off completely, but either may serve as a deterrent. From the tour operator's perspective, therefore, destinations which are readily accessible for a majority of potential clients, and which have good infrastructure for rescue, emergency evacuation, and medical treatment if required, are broadly preferable. Sites which combine good conditions with good access, however, are likely to be crowded, unless the tour operator can gain exclusive rights over a particular site. This last option provides the rationale behind private resorts such as the Yellowstone Club, where ski slopes and lifts are available only to the Club's wealthy property owners. A similar though somewhat less expensive rationale applies to surf resorts with exclusive access to particular surf breaks, such as Tavarua in Fiji. More commonly, however, both boardsports clients and tourism enterprises must make trade-offs between the quality of conditions, the level of crowding, the degree of risk, and the cost of the experience. It is these factors, and their changing interactions, which determine the geography of the boardsports tourism sector at any one time. In addition, the way in which individual tourists and clients respond to these factors may also be mediated by marketing and fashion. Both destinations and tour operators wax and wane in popularity depending on how well they are known and how they are perceived.

Socio-economics

The economic scale of the boardsports industry depends strongly on precisely what components are included (see Chapter 1). The total annual turnover of the ski resort industry, of which over half is attributable to snowboarding, is measured in hundreds of billions of dollars. The total market capitalisation of surfwear manufacturing companies is measured in billions or tens of billions of dollars. The financial scale of specialist surf and snowboard tour operators, however, is far smaller, and for other boardsports the scale is smaller still. In the snowboard sector, the largest operators are heliski companies, which still cater principally for skiers but increasingly also for snowboarders. The annual turnover for these companies can be estimated quite accurately, at least for the industry leaders, because they are fully booked every season and their prices are posted on their websites and only rarely discounted. The largest heliski operator is Canadian Mountain Holidays (CMH), which operates 12 lodges over an 18-week season. Almost all the lodges have a capacity of 44 guests. Prices for a 1-week heliski package vary through the course of the season, but for most of the season are around Cdn$11,500 per person per week. These figures indicate a total annual turnover of around $100 million per annum. Most of the world's other heliski operators are significantly smaller than CMH, so the annual total turnover may be in the order of $200 million. Currently, the proportion of heliski clients riding snowboards is much smaller than at the ski resorts: perhaps 20% on average. This suggests that the heliboarding sector, as opposed to the heliski sector as a whole, may currently be worth around

$40 million per annum. The proportion of boarders, relative to skiers, is growing.

The surf tourism industry is somewhat more diffuse, and it is accordingly more difficult to estimate its annual turnover accurately. Very roughly, there are probably fewer than 50 full-time surf lodges worldwide and perhaps 100 full-time surf charter boats. Most of these are quite small and take groups of 10–12 clients on trips which last 10–12 days, with a couple of days' turn-around time at the end of each voyage. Prices for these trips are generally around US$3000, and the surfing season at different sites may range from a few months to year-round. These figures suggest that the annual turnover of the surf lodge and charter yacht industry might be around US$50 million per annum. There is also a significantly larger group of surfers who take local boats and stay in local accommodation near well-known surf breaks, but do not use purpose-built surf lodges and charter yachts. In addition to the costs of local lodges and yachts, nearly all these surfers also pay international airfares and gateway accommodation costs in order to take up their tour packages. In some cases, these international travel costs are as much or more than the cost of the local lodge or yacht, but in others they are much less.

Several recent attempts have been made to estimate the value placed upon local surf breaks and beaches by individual recreational surfers. This is a different economic approach, since it measures an estimated social welfare value, rather than hard cash passing hands in a commercial market. Estimates have been made for particular beaches in Australia (Lazarow, 2007) and France. Different beachgoers prefer different types of beach, so estimates such as these are fraught with methodological uncertainties unless surfers and surfing can be separated clearly from other beach uses and users. This can be achieved either by interviewing surfers specifically, or by studying sites which are used only for surfing. This approach has been used in Australia, for example, as one successful argument for the dedication of surfing reserves.

Just as boardsports tourism is heavily concentrated in particular geographic sites, associated economic activity is equally uneven. By far the majority of surfers, snowboarders, and other boardsports enthusiasts, particularly those who are wealthy enough to buy boardsports tours, live in the richer developed Western nations, or the newly industrialised nations such as Brazil. This, however, is changing rapidly, with both male and female surfers from countries such as Peru now found within the international professional rankings. The number of surfers and boarders in any particular country depends on factors such as: the size of the country, its cultural attitudes towards outdoor sports; the availability of suitable terrain and weather; and the history of the particular boardsports in the country concerned. Australia, for example, has a high proportion of surfers relative to its population because it has a warm climate, plenty of beaches, a largely coastal population, a strong enthusiasm for all kinds of sports, a culture which encourages beach recreation, and an extended history of surfing, which was introduced directly from Hawaii over half a century ago. Interestingly, despite having hardly any mountains and hardly any snow, Australia also has large numbers of snowboarders. Perhaps this indicates that cultural attitudes towards outdoor sports are more significant than local access to suitable terrain. But perhaps it may indicate merely that the Southern Alps in New Zealand are nearby and easy to get to.

Where there are good conditions for outdoor boardsports close by major population centres where those sports are popular, the emphasis is on individual recreation rather than on commercial tourism. Opportunities for tourism exist principally where people need to travel to get to the best conditions, whether domestically or internationally. Particular opportunities exist where there are barriers to easy individual access, e.g. because of transport, language, or ownership of the particular sites concerned. In most Pacific Islands, for example, rights of access to surf breaks are traditionally owned by local villagers who fish there; and physical access commonly requires a boat. Tour operators can provide both of these.

From an economic geography perspective, therefore, there are two main patterns in the boardsports tourism industry. There is a relatively large local circulation associated with domestic travel, and there are smaller flows associated with international travel to particular icon sites. As in most forms of international tourism, a large proportion of the total price paid stays in the country where the tourist originates, in the form of airfares, package prices, and agent commissions. Only those components which go to pay local suppliers in the destination country are actually transferred internationally, and even those components may then be transferred to a completely different country, depending on ownership structures for local suppliers. I have travelled with an Australian-owned company on an Arctic expedition cruise and sea kayak trip in Norwegian waters, for example, where the sea kayaks were owned by an Australian company, the expedition cruise vessel by a Russian, and bar bills were charged by a company in Cyprus. Similarly, the principal heliski/board operator in the Himalayas was established by an Australian and used Indian-owned helicopters with Swiss pilots and mechanics. Tracing the final distribution of financial flows associated with any particular holiday package purchase, in any form of tourism, is far from straightforward.

Retail prices paid for boardsports tours vary greatly, depending on the location, length, level of luxury, and type of transport. One-hour learn-to-surf packages sold to tourists in destinations such as Australia's Gold Coast, for example, typically cost around US$35 for 2–4 hours. Ten-day surf charters in

Indonesia's Mentawai Islands cost around US$300 per day, plus international airfares. Accommodation in surf lodges in Fiji, Samoa, or Tonga cost from one to several hundred US dollars per person per day. Helicopter snowboard packages in the Canadian Rockies cost well over US$1000 per person per day, plus airfares.

The range of variation in prices is matched by a corresponding range of variation in the means and interests of commercial boardsports tour clients. There are a few individuals who are wealthy enough to devote their entire lives to boardsports, but for most people there is a trade-off between money and time. In the boardsports tourism market, a distinction is commonly drawn between the so-called cash-rich, time-poor and time-rich, cash-poor segments. Not surprisingly, the latter segment, corresponding to the backpacker market in tourism more generally, can supply higher client volumes; whereas the former can support higher prices. In reality, however, many tourists do not fall clearly into one or other of these two segments. There are many surfers and snowboarders who are by no means wealthy and who rely on low-cost recreational opportunities for most of the time, but who will nonetheless save up for a surf yacht charter or a heliboard package once every 2 or 3 years.

Product structures

The structure of commercial tourism products shows considerable variation, with a range of different product types on offer for different activities and market subsectors. In the surf tourism industry, as outlined earlier, the lowest-priced products are 1-hour learn-to-surf lessons at major surfing destinations, using soft training boards supplied by the surf school. There are bus-based surf safaris along the coastlines of major surfing nations, generally with camping or low-key budget accommodation. There are international surf packages including airfares and local transport, accommodation, and surf guides. There are surf lodges at particular icon surf destinations, which cater solely or principally to surfers and their partners, and sometimes also offer a range of other ocean adventure activities such as sea kayaking and diving. And there are specialist surf yacht charters to less accessible surf breaks, with liveaboard accommodation and surfing skippers who know their areas well and can ensure that visiting surfers get the best waves available under the prevailing conditions, taking into account the surfers' expertise and interests.

In the snowboard tourism industry, there are basic resort and lift packages sold equally to skiers and snowboarders, with prices depending principally on the standard of accommodation. There are international packages which include airfares and transfers as well as the resort package. There are back-country tours and training clinics where skilled guides lead snowboarders cross-country to the slopes with the best snow, either on single-day excursions or on multi-day snow-camping or backcountry hut-based tours. There are snowcat and snowmobile-based tours where snowboarders are carried up fresh powder slopes by mechanised snow transport. And at the top of the market, there are helicopter tours ranging from a single shuttle to the top of a nearby mountain, to all-inclusive 1-week packages in purpose-built back-country heliski lodges. There are even heliski and heliboard tours which are based in luxury liveaboard cruise vessels equipped with their own helicopters. Details of product packaging in the heliski/board sector are examined further by Buckley (2006a, pp. 213–234).

For other boardsports activities, the commercial tourism sector is less well advanced. Other outdoor boardsports such as sailboarding and kite-boarding are more recent in origin, involve somewhat more expensive equipment, and make up smaller proportions of the boardsports tourism market as a whole. Some European nations, in particular, have large numbers of recreational sailboarders, and there are particular destinations which are well-known for their consistent wind and good conditions. The sailboarding tourism sector, however, still seems to be considerably smaller than either the surfing or snowboarding subsectors. Over the past decade, kiteboarding has replaced sailboarding to a large degree in many parts of the world, and kiteboards are much easier to transport than sailboards or even surfboards, but the market for kiteboarding tourism still appears to be quite small.

Sailboarders, kiteboarders, wakeboarders, and skateboarders do indeed travel with their boards, so all these activities are certainly included in the boardsports tourism sector. There are sporting associations for each of these activities, which run competitions at destinations around the world. There are large-scale non-competitive recreational events, similar to those described for other adventure activities by Buckley et al. (2006a). There are icon sites famous for particularly good conditions. For sailboarders, for example, there are sites known for flatwater speedsailing, sites known for high-wind freestyle riding, and sites known for ocean wavesailing. Since there is a high crossover between sailboarding and kiteboarding, many of these sites are also used by kiteboarders, and both sailboarders and kite-boarders travel specifically to ride at these sites. Indeed, these particular destinations are also magnets for amenity migration (Chapter 6). The population of Hood River, a small township on the Columbia Gorge in Oregon, USA, for example, includes a significant number of residents who moved there to sailboard and kiteboard in summer and snowboard in winter.

Relative to the snowboard and surfing sectors, however, there seem to be rather few tour operators offering commercial sailboard or kiteboard tours, and tour products advertised specifically to sailboarders and kiteboarders seem to be relatively unspecialised. The majority simply seem to offer travel and accommodation packages for well-known sailboarding and kiteboarding destinations, with no guides or equipment included. Clients are expected to bring their own gear and know how to use it. Sailboarding and kiteboarding lessons are indeed commercially available at well-known destinations, often in conjunction with retail equipment stores, but these seem neither to be sold as stand-alone tourism products in the same way as learn-to-surf lessons, nor included in integrated holiday packages in the same way as snowboard lessons.

Equipment

Boardsports tourism is heavily dependent upon equipment. There are differences between activities, between tour products, and between destinations as to whether clients are expected to bring all their own equipment, or whether rental equipment is available or included in a tour package. Resort-based snowboard packages, for example, may commonly include rental of snowboards, boots and bindings; and learn-to-surf lessons commonly include the loan of so-called softboards, which are large surfboards constructed out of the same soft foam as a bodyboard, less likely to injure either the participants or innocent bystanders. Surfboards are available for rent at a few well-known beach tourism destinations, but these rentals are aimed principally at beginners, and skilled surfers would nearly always bring their own boards. A few island surf lodges have surfboards available for loan or rent, usually with a substantial deposit in case of breakage, but once again most surfers would bring their own boards. Some heliski/heliboard operators now provide boards, but this is a relatively recent innovation, even though they have provided powder skis for a number of years. Travelling sailboarders and kiteboarders must generally bring their own equipment with them.

As with many types of outdoor sports and adventure activities, boards and associated equipment have experienced rapid technical evolution in recent years. Modern foam and fibreglass surfboards are barely half a century old, and during that time have undergone many changes in shape, size, fin layout, and attachment, and most recently materials. Both carbon fibre constructions and moulded plastic surfboards are now available, though individually shaped and glassed fibreglass boards are still by far the most frequent. Every part of a surfboard, and every different shape option for every part, has a specific name, and a good surfboard shaper can integrate all these different features to produce a board which will behave in a precisely predictable way when ridden by a particular surfer in given surf conditions. Professional surfers keep a selection of different boards, known as a quiver, to ride under different conditions; and many keen recreational surfers do the same. Depending on the skill and style of the surfer, there are also different designs with different names: thrusters, bonzers, single-fins, twinnies, fish, guns, rhino-chasers, mini-mals, longboards, and stand-up paddleboards. Whilst smaller surfboard shapers still shape each foam blank individually, larger manufacturers use machine shaping systems which cut each blank using a template, with a human shaper providing only the finishing touches. The fibreglass coating, however, is still applied by hand, including glassing on fins or, more commonly, glassing in fin boxes to take detachable fins.

The majority of sailboards, in contrast, are mass-produced one-design models manufactured using blow-moulded or rotation-moulded plastic. Part of the reason for this seems to be purely historical. The first commercial sailboards, the Windsurfer® brand, were made from moulded plastic, and this set a precedent. Later models by other manufacturers were also one-design productions. Even those manufactured using fibreglass were laid up into a hollow mould in the same way as a fibreglass yacht or kayak, rather than glassing the outside of a shaped foam core. Quite apart from precedent, there were reasons for this relating both to technical construction techniques and to the way in which the boards were used. From a technical perspective, the foam blanks used to shape surfboards were not thick enough for many of the sailboard designs, and there was not a sufficiently large market initially to induce the blank manufacturers to tool up for sailboard blanks. In addition, the blanks must be fitted with a central stringer, a thin slab of wood which runs from nose to tail throughout the entire depth of the board, and new and larger stringers would also have been required. The functional aspect was that the majority of sailboards are used for recreational sailing and racing in much the same way as small sailing dinghies. Dinghy sailors are used to one-design classes, and sailboards fitted into this scheme.

Almost as soon as the first Windsurfers® came on the market, however, people began modifying them to sail in high winds and to sail in the surf. These early boards had a single fin, and a central removable daggerboard which fitted through a slot in the hull. Larger fins and swept-back daggerboards were introduced for high-wind sailing, and other manufacturers introduced models where the daggerboard folded partly or completely into the hull. Common modifications for sailing in the surf included sawing the stern of the hull off to shorten the board, and bending up the nose to provide rocker.

These crude modifications soon lead to the production of new sailboard models designed specifically for the surf. Initially these were custom-built boards using similar glass-fibre or carbon-fibre construction to surfboards. This was possible because of innovations in sailboard technique, which allowed sailboarders to use much smaller boards, similar in dimensions to a waveski or longboard. Early designs were made with a thick, high-volume stern featuring a wide swallowtail shape and rounded rails. These, however, soon gave way to designs not dissimilar to a large surfboard, with sharp rails and multi-fin configurations. These boards were used for riding and jumping waves in high winds and were fitted with footstraps and fins, but no daggerboard. As sailboarders began to execute higher and more radical jumps, they found that fibreglass boards were unable to survive a heavy landing. More complex construction techniques were thus adopted, using kevlar and carbon fibre, a multi-layer core with various foams and honeycombs, vacuum bag compression during lay-up, and hot paint technologies as used for vehicles. Mast, boom, sail, and harness technologies improved at the same time, with the development of multi-piece carbon-fibre masts, adjustable-length, high-strength aluminium booms, fully battened Mylar® sails, and stronger and more flexible joints for attaching the sail rig to the board. Currently, as with surfboards, there are many different designs of sailboard and rig, intended for different conditions: raceboards, speedboards, waveboards, training boards, and so on.

Kiteboarding equipment has drawn on many different outdoor sports during the course of its evolution. There are two styles of board in common use. Twin-tip boards have evolved from wakeboards, and indeed some kiteboarders use wakeboard-style boot bindings. Most twin-tip kiteboards, however, have sailboard-style footstraps and are essentially rectangular in shape, with small wakeboard-style fins at each corner. Unidirectional boards, in contrast, resemble a small sailboard or a surfboard with footstraps and must be gybed rather than reversed when the kiteboarder changes direction. Kiteboard sails also fall into two major categories, with many refinements in each. Some kiteboarders favour a double-surface ram-air design similar to a paraglider sail or directional parachute. Much more common, however, are single-surface kites with a strong C-shaped curve, and an inflated leading edge and ribs, which act like battens. Different kites also have different line configurations, and harnesses have different attachments and safety release systems. All of these are still evolving quite rapidly at present.

There have also been bursts of evolution in the design of snowboards, bindings, and boots. One of the earliest snowboards, the Winterstick®, was a unidirectional board with a large shovel-shaped nose and a very deeply cut flaring swallowtail, with very soft bindings. These were soon replaced with bidirectional boards, symmetrical from end to end, with a multi-layer construction and considerable sidecut. A variety of bindings and boots are available, ranging from very rigid hard-shell boots for racing to much more flexible and softer boots for halfpipe and freestyle riding, and a range of intermediate designs for backcountry free-riding. Over the last few years, unidirectional boards have again appeared on the market, specialist designs intended for riding steep, deep powder-filled tree glades and similar terrain. Also available are split boards, which are snowboards divided longitudinally down the centre, with the two halves held in position by clamps which can be released to separate the halves. Binding attachments are set up so that the board can be ridden in conventional snowboard stance when the two halves are joined, or in skiing stance when they are separated, making it possible to hike uphill even through soft snow.

Unlike surfboards, sailboards, and kiteboards, it is very commonplace for tourists to rent snowboards rather than owning them. Indeed, even if they own their own board at home, they may still rent a board if they travel overseas. There seem to be three reasons for this. The first is simply that snowboards are a lot less breakable than surfboards. The second is that by far the majority of snowboarders ride in resorts where there is already an organised rental system for skis and skiing gear. And the third is that at most resorts, there is a sufficiently large volume of tourists every season to support a profitable snowboard rental business.

From a commercial tourism industry perspective, equipment may be important for either of two main reasons. The first is if it provides a barrier to boardsports tourism. Before multi-piece sailboard masts came on the market, for example, it was well-nigh impossible to travel with a sailboard; and even now, a sailboard and rig make a very bulky piece of baggage. When surfboard fins were glassed directly onto the board, there was always a high risk that they would be damaged or broken off completely during transit, and to minimise this risk, bulky protective packaging was needed. Once detachable fins became commonplace, it was far easier for surfers to travel with a single-padded board bag, known as a coffin, containing two or three surfboards and fin sets. Kiteboard and snowboard gear are quite manageable as baggage on international airlines, though it may prove bulky on a small shuttle plane.

The other way in which equipment is important for commercial tourism is if it provides commercial opportunities for sales or rentals. This applies not only to the boards themselves, but to the wide range of accessories and clothing which are needed for most boardsports, ranging from boardshorts to heliski suits. Indeed, the scale of the clothing industry associated with recreational surfing is considerably greater than the scale of commercial surf tourism (Buckley, 2003b). There is also a substantial snowboard clothing industry, though in relative terms this is not so significant, because of the financial scale of lift ticket and resort accommodation costs.

Marketing

The ways in which boardsports tourism are marketed broadly match the different constructions of tour products for different boardsports activities. For high-volume resort-based snowboard packages, the majority of marketing is through traditional travel distribution systems, with package holidays advertised in glossy colour brochures and sold principally through travel agents. It is also possible to buy both accommodation and lift tickets online. Data on the relative volumes of sales made either directly or through agents are proprietary, and do not seem to have been published in the tourism literature. Factors affecting the pricing of lift tickets, however, were analysed recently by Falk (2008). Resorts compete for recognition by hosting events and competitions in order to gain television and other media coverage.

Heliboarding operators, in contrast, rely much more heavily on marketing to an established customer base, adding to their clientele every year, but relying on a high level of repeat business. They advertise within ski and snowboard resorts, at gateway airports, and in specialist magazines. They send out lavishly illustrated electronic newsletters to existing customers. The largest operator, CMH, franchises out its marketing operations to individual agents in different countries, each with a fixed quota of places to sell. That is, if you live in Australia and you want to book with CMH, you can only do so through their Australian agent Travelplan®, even if you are a long-term repeat customer with direct individual connections at CMH. If the Australian quota has been sold, the only opportunity is for the Australian agent to trade quota informally with the agent from another country, such as Japan.

In contrast to snowboarding where the majority of tourism is tied to fixed-site resorts, most surfers make their travel arrangements independently and are not easily reached by mainstream tourism industry marketing. Pre-booked package surf tours, amenable to organised marketing, fall into four main categories: surf lodges, boat charters, bus safaris, and guided tours. The last of these, namely, package tours including airfare, accommodation, local transport, and a guide at a well-known destination, are relatively uncommon in the surfing sector. Bus safaris are aimed at more price-conscious surfers and are advertised largely through specialist surfing magazines.

For specialist and more upmarket surf lodges and boat charters, marketing generally follows a three-pronged approach: magazines, agents, and direct.

Worldwide, there are a small number of travel companies which specialise in surf travel and which act as agents for many of the lodges and boats. In some cases these are exclusive agencies, so that the lodge can only be booked through one particular travel company; but more commonly they are non-exclusive. Both the charter boats and surf lodges themselves, and the surf tour companies, advertise principally in specialist surf magazines. They also advertise on websites which are visited frequently by surfers, such as wave and beach webcams, weather and surf forecast sites, global surf directories, and surf competition sites. Often they may earn a weblink to their own site by providing sponsorship for a surfing event or a surf information site. In addition, they tweak their websites so as to boost their rankings in web searches for particular surf destinations. Some of these specialist surfing magazines have online editions which are pushed to large email lists, as well as printed magazine editions; and surf tour companies advertising in the printed editions can generally also obtain a listing and link in the online version, capitalising on the magazine's email list. For additional coverage, the tour companies may sponsor professional surfers and surf journalists to take their tours, so as to gain editorial coverage in surfing magazines, and acknowledgment in the credits of surfing movies, videos, and DVDs.

As with surfing and snowboarding, there are particular sites around the world which are renowned for consistently good kiteboarding or sailboarding conditions, and kiteboarders and sailboarders do indeed travel to visit those sites. For wavesailing, there is a degree of overlap with icon surfing sites: the island of Maui in Hawaii, for example, or Margaret River and Red Bluff in Western Australia. Columbia Gorge in Oregon, USA is known for high-wind freestyle sailboarding. Other well-known destinations include the Canary Islands and the Azores. There is a relatively small commercial tourism industry which specialises in bringing sailboarders and kiteboarders from around the world to these icon sites, and these companies advertise principally through specialised sailboard and kiteboard magazines, with links to their websites. As with other boardsports, there are strong marketing cross-links between tours, competitions and events, equipment manufacturers, and adventure entertainment such as movies and DVDs.

Cross-marketing of this type seems to be characteristic of the entire adventure tourism industry. In the case of boardsports it extends beyond the adventure sector itself. In North America and Europe, for example, snowboarding themes are used to advertise off-road vehicles and other consumer goods. In parts of the Australian coastline, surfboard themes are widespread in public signage, public park benches, and commercial amusement parks, in addition to surfboard and surf clothing shops. Surfing themes have even been used to advertise universities.

Clothing

One of the great commercial successes of the boardsports industry has been the spinoff of a large international clothing industry with boardsports themes. Best-known of these is the surfwear sector, headed by industry giants Billabong, Quicksilver, and RipCurl. Revenue from sales of surf-branded clothing to urban non-surfers far outstrips the financial scale of surf tourism or even surfboard manufacturing. There is also a sizeable clothing industry associated with snowboarding. These links were examined by Buckley (2003b), who argued that there is a strong fashion component to surf clothing, and a rather small number of surfwear manufacturers which dominate world markets for surf fashion, including urban streetwear as well as functional surfing gear. Each of the major surf clothing and equipment manufacturers sponsors surf competitions, teams of professional surfers, and surf trips to remote locations to produce magazine articles and surfing DVDs (Buckley, 2003b).

The principal market for branded surfwear and accessories is for non-surfers, and indeed, the big surfwear companies see themselves as being in the 'fashion apparel business' (Billabong, 2009). Selling surfwear to actual surfers also involves fashion, but functionality is a more basic requirement. For the urban streetwear market, clothing can be identical to no-name equivalents, and the brand name makes the mark-up. Surf fashion is not new – even by the 1960s, 'surf chic was a cultural phenomenon', according to the Quicksilver website. What is new in the 2000s is the growth in 'adventure' imagery – in lifestyles, clothing and accessories, and entertainment. Adventure is fashionable. Adventure tourism may have grown from outdoor recreation, but both have now become inseparable from the clothing, fashion, and entertainment sector. This is not immediately apparent to consumers and tourists; but a glance at corporate financial figures tells the story loud and clear.

Conclusions

Over the past two or three decades, boardsports have evolved rapidly from little-known low-key fringe recreational activities to multi-billion dollar business sectors with their own global competitions, specialist manufacturing and clothing sectors, multi-millionaire professional athletes, and large-scale international tourism industries. New boardsports have been added, and existing boardsports have developed new equipment designs and technologies. Boardsports pioneers have grown older, and aficionados of other adventure sports have taken up boardsports, generating a significant sector of older enthusiasts. As boardsports have overtaken other mainstream outdoor sports such as skiing, the cash-rich time-poor sector of boardsports tourism markets has grown to rival the time-rich cash-poor sector which gave these industries their start. It seems likely that these trends will continue, and we shall see further growth and further evolution of new boardsports over future years and decades.

CASE STUDY 11.1: Snowboarding at Niseko, Japan

Chairlifts at Niseko ski area, Japan, famous for its snow

Niseko is the largest ski and snowboard resort in Japan's northernmost main island of Hokkaido. It is renowned for heavy snowfall and is often put forward as a cheaper alternative to heliskiing in the Canadian Rockies. Niseko includes four separate ski and snowboard areas, linked by lifts, runs, and a road round the base of the mountain. Niseko is reached by a 3-hour road shuttle from the New Chitose airport, which for international visitors is reached via a domestic flight from Osaka or Tokyo Narita.

Niseko is a four-season tourism destination with a significant residential and investment property sector. Winter snow sports are the principal attraction, and indeed, 50% of the restaurants in the main ski village of Hirafu open only in winter. Marketing materials, however, including property and adventure magazines, also promote summer golfing and nature and cultural tourism experiences, and advertisements for property sales present summer as well as winter views. The small town of Kutchan is nearby, and many municipal and professional services, including medical facilities, are available only in Kutchan and not at Hirafu or elsewhere in the Niseko area. As in many North American and European ski resorts, it seems likely that Kutchan also acts as a dormitory town for service staff working in the Niseko ski villages themselves.

The Niseko resort areas all provide access to the mountain of Niseko Annupuri, 1308 m in elevation. There are over 20 individual lifts including 3 gondolas, and over 50 named individual runs. Two valleys are strictly off limits because of major cliffs, but other areas outside the controlled runs are opened sometimes, depending on conditions, and can be accessed through gates in the ski area boundaries. Some of these areas are used routinely as additional tree-skiing runs, whereas others are generally accessed only by groups with avalanche safety equipment and backcountry skills.

At a global scale, the ski and snowboard industry is heavily weighted in numerical terms towards Europe and North America. The resorts of Asia, Australasia, and the Andes are very much smaller. Japanese ski and snowboard resorts such as Niseko, however, form a significant and growing node of activity in the East. Because of their relatively high latitude, they may be somewhat more insulated against climate change than their Western counterparts – though since they are at low altitude and close to the ocean, patterns of climate change are likely to be complex.

LOOKING BACK

1. What individual sports can be included under the overall heading of boardsports, and how amenable is each to packaging as commercial adventure tourism products?

2. It has been argued that there are close financial links between boardsports, television, entertainment, and clothing fashion. Do you think this is correct and if so, what sort of links are they, and how could you test how strong they might be? Are there similar links for other types of adventure tourism, and if not, why should they have developed specifically for boardsports?

3. How would you estimate the economic scale of the boardsports adventure tourism sector specifically? In particular, what components would you include and why, and how would you distinguish tourism from individual recreation, for each of the individual boardsports you include?

Heliskiing in the Canadian Rockies

CHAPTER 12

Heliskiing

KEY ISSUES

- geography, climate, terrain

- principal product patterns

- daily, lodge and expedition models

- package components: vertical metres, equipment, guides, add-ons

- factors influencing client choice: snow quality, safety, service

- product differentiation between close competitors

CONTENTS

CHAPTER SUMMARY

Different heliski operators offer different tour products which reflect a small and identifiable set of successful strategies. The core of the market consists of high-volume, high-price, highly standardised 1-week all-inclusive lodge-based packages in the Canadian Rockies. These operators compete principally with each other, through subtle differences in the packages offered. Their model is also copied elsewhere. It relies heavily on advance bookings up to 2 years ahead. The second successful model strategy achieves high volume at a lower price with fewer fixed assets, by offering a flexible portfolio of single-day trips to less-experienced heliskiers drawn at short notice from nearby ski resorts. This model is common in New Zealand, but also copied elsewhere. The third strategy is to offer very high-priced, low-volume trips in areas with no fixed heliski infrastructure, aimed at highly experienced and particularly adventurous clients. These three models have evolved gradually, survived changes in the heliski industry, and are likely to be resilient to climate change.

BIG PICTURE

Introduction

Heliskiing is a specialist and relatively upmarket sector of the adventure tourism industry. Its specific constraints and relatively small size, essentially an oligopoly, provide a particular opportunity to analyse the strategies adopted by different operators and the factors which contribute to their success. This chapter examines: the precise product packaging strategies used by successful heliski tour operators; the product features which are key to those strategies; and whether product packages are largely identical across all operators, continuously variable across operators, or clumped into distinct and recognisable groups.

To carry out such a test requires data on: the operators, operating areas, tour products, product features, client characteristics, and client preferences. Some of this information is available from written sources, either printed or web-based; but most can only be obtained through direct observation of actual heliski tours and clients. A heliski tour, however, has no space for passive observers; everyone involved must be an active participant. This has the additional advantage that the observer is simply another client. The observations are unobtrusive, and unlikely to influence either operating practices or self-reported information from clients. Only the manager and senior staff, notably the lead heliski guide, will generally be aware of the research interests, since these interests are necessarily revealed in order to conduct detailed interviews.

Heliskiing is a high-priced and high-pressure adventure tourism activity with relatively little time for relaxation. Participant observation approaches are only possible for a researcher who can indeed participate fully. To be accepted by the clients and guides, the researcher must have sufficient skiing and/or snowboarding skills, and appropriate equipment, to keep up with their assigned helicopter group, or they will not be able to continue the tour. Most heliski operators assess their potential clients' expertise and experience before accepting a booking for a particular product, so as to ensure that their clients are capable and the heligroups are well matched (Buckley, 2006a). In addition, one of the implicit conditions of participant research is that the researcher should not do anything which would make any of the other clients uncomfortable; even including identifying oneself as a researcher.

Principal product patterns

A general description of the structure of the heliski industry, the basic operational aspects of heliskiing and heliboarding tour products, and structured field audits of a selection of such products were presented by Buckley (2006a). Key components are summarised in Tables 12.1 and 12.2. Broadly, there are two main types of product. In New Zealand the most common package is a single-day tour, generally without accommodation, specifying the number of runs rather than vertical elevation skied. In Canada and India, the most common product is a 1-week package, including luxury lodge accommodation, and specifying vertical elevation rather than number of runs. Further detail is provided below.

| Table 12.1 | Structure of Heliski Product Packages |

Operator, Package	Country, Area	Days, Metres*	Runs Per Day	Accom	Approx Full Capacity	Heli Group Size[†]	Guides Per Group
Mike Wiegele, deluxe	Canada, Rocky Mts	6.5, unlim	Unlim[§]	Indiv lodges	150	10	2
CMH, standard	Canada, Rocky Mts	6.5, 30,500	Unlim[§]	Group lodges	450	11	1
Himachal, standard	India, Himalayas	5, 30,500	Unlim[§]	Private hotel	30	5	1
Harris Mts, Odyssey	New Zealand	5, n/a[¶]	Varies[§]	Local hotel	Indef	4	1
Harris Mts, Max Vert	New Zealand	1, n/a[¶]	Indef[¶]	Various, in town	Indef	4	1
Harris Mts, basic	New Zealand	1, n/a[¶]	3	Various, in town	Indef	4	1
Methven, 1-day	New Zealand	1, n/a[¶]	5+	Local motels	Indef**	4	1

*Vertical metres included in package price: extra cost if exceeded.
[†]Number of clients per helicopter load, not including guide(s) or pilot.
[§]Not pre-determined, depends on guides, weather, and clients.
[¶]Structured and priced per run, not per vertical elevation skied.
**With more clients, they call in more guides and helicopters.
Data from Buckley (2006a).

Table 12.2	Key Features of Heliski Products and Marketing		
Operator, Country	**Marketing Channels**	**Avalanche Safety**	**Snow and Terrain**
Mike Wiegele, Canada	Email lists, competitions	Transceivers, two guides	Powder, tree and bowl
CMH, Canada	Exclusive country agents	Transceivers, guide, and tail-ender	Powder, tree and bowl
Himachal, India	Billboards in gateways	Transceivers, locator beacons, avalanche wings	Dry powder, up to 5000 m
Harris Mts, New Zealand	Via ski resorts	Transceivers	Variable, gully and spur
Methven, New Zealand	Via ski resorts	Transceivers	Variable, gully and spur

Data from Buckley (2006a).

Daily products

The daily products, exemplified by most of the New Zealand heliski operators, offer a portfolio of products on a day-by-day basis, with most clients booking at short notice. Individual clients even have the opportunity to switch from one product to another part way through the day concerned, since the principal difference between the products is the number of individual runs in the package. A key component of marketing strategies for these operators is to attract clients who are experienced skiers but inexperienced at heliskiing. The operators start by selling these clients the cheapest product in the portfolio, generally a three-run package; and then persuade them during the course of the day to upgrade to higher-priced products which include more runs, and to purchase additional days.

A number of identifiable factors are critical to the selection of this strategy. Some of these are geographical and others relate to target markets. Local geographical factors are as follows. The heliskiing terrain in New Zealand's South Island is close enough to gateway towns with tourist accommodation that there is no need to build specialist heliski lodges. Clients can ski in the resorts one day and on the heli slopes the next. This has the additional advantage that if heli operations are halted by strong winds, as typically happens several times a week, the day's flying is simply called off. Clients do something different for the day concerned, re-booking for a later date if their holiday schedule permits. Much of the terrain in the Southern Alps has no road access, and helicopters are in common use during summer. During winter, demand is much reduced, so helicopters are available to heliski operators on a day-by-day basis without incurring high costs for down days. The helicopters used are relatively small in capacity, so a commercially viable day's operation is feasible even with only a small number of clients. On days with a large number of bookings, e.g. because of pre-booked tour groups or because of a backlog from previous down days, the operators can use several helicopters simultaneously, and they maintain a stable of appropriately qualified heliski guides whom they can call upon at short notice.

The principal disadvantage of this model is that, in addition to uncertainty over the weather, heliski clients do not know in advance who they will be skiing with, how skilled their heli group will be, and how many runs it will do. This can be frustrating for skilled skiers and snowboarders used to the other product designs as outlined below, if they find themselves with an inexperienced group which rides slowly, requires gentle terrain, and makes only three runs. The operators do their best to avoid this situation, but often there may be no alternative. There is generally a midday lunch stop which allows some restructuring of the heligroups, but even this does not always provide opportunity for more skilled clients to move into more skilled groups and make more runs. If a group of adequately fit and wealthy clients books jointly, they may have the option to charter their own guide and helicopter for the entire day. This costs considerably more but allows the group to make as many runs as they are able, sometimes up to three times the maximum and seven times the minimum number of runs in the routine retail packages.

One feature of the market which was important for the New Zealand operators in the 1990s and early 2000s was a supply of relatively wealthy Japanese clients who were already skilled at skiing in powder snow at Japanese resorts, and who routinely included a few days heliskiing in a New Zealand ski holiday. During 2007, however, changing economic conditions in Japan apparently caused a significant drop in the number of Japanese clients for New Zealand heliskiing operations, with significant economic impacts. The global economic downturn in 2008–2009 has also had negative effects.

Lodge model

The lodge model is best known from the Canadian Rockies, where the world's two largest heliski operators both offer week-by-week packages which include accommodation and meals in special-purpose heliski lodges, as well as an adequate, though not indefinite quota of heliski runs. Largest of all, as measured by client capacity, is Canadian Mountain Holidays (CMH), which operates over a dozen independent lodges, most of them designed for 44 clients, across a number of different ski terrain concession areas. The largest single operation is that run by Mike Wiegele Helicopter Skiing (MWHS). Similar week-long packages have been offered for a number of years in the Indian Himalayas, but based in a hotel in a mountain summer resort town, rather than a purpose-built lodge. One of the two principal Alaskan heliski operators, Chugach Heliski, has also adopted the lodge model recently, with part of its operations based in a backcountry lodge, as well as those based in city hotels. General descriptions of CMH, MWHS, and Himachal Helicopter Skiing (HHS) are available in Buckley (2006a). Because the CMH and MWHS products are very similar, they compete on fine details of service and safety, as outlined later in this chapter.

There seem to be two key factors underpinning the lodge model. Most important is that the heliski terrain is a considerable distance from the nearest ski resort, so that it is uneconomical and impractical to ferry clients backwards and forwards from resort accommodation. The second is that clients who are paying high prices for heliskiing also expect a high standard of accommodation and catering, and purpose-built lodges make it possible for heliski operators to provide these. In addition, since there is no one at the lodges except heliski staff and clients, the company can schedule the lodge's entire operations around the needs and desires of its skiers and snowboarders. For example, this may include early morning stretching sessions, video playback of the day's runs in the bar every evening, and so on. The third factor is somewhat more subtle but equally critical. The cost of maintaining exclusive access to the heliski terrain, generally through lease concession arrangements with public land management agencies, is not insignificant. In addition, the helicopters are stationed full-time at the heliski areas during the winter season, with associated costs. Lodge staff and guides must also be hired well in advance for the heliski season, so there is a high fixed salary cost. This cost structure is very different from the day-by-day model in New Zealand. The major operators in the Canadian Rockies, Alaska, and the Himalayas, therefore, need to book their entire year's programme up as fully as possible, far in advance – typically a year or more. The week-by-week inclusive product package helps to achieve this, as clients must make a significant deposit in order to secure a place and are then unlikely to cancel.

The significance of these factors can be tested by examining heliski operations where not all of them apply simultaneously. The large New Zealand operator Harris Mountains Heliski, for example, taken over some years ago by The Helicopter Line (THL), used to offer a 1-week inclusive package under the name of 'Odyssey', specifically to appeal to clients who were used to the North American lodge model. Accommodation was provided in a hotel between two of the major ski resorts, and the package included days heliskiing and days' resort skiing, to take account of likely down days through strong winds. Since the Odyssey clients made up only a small proportion of the total, however, there was no guarantee how many individual runs they would get each day, so the package components and price were continually readjusted during the week. Not surprisingly, this approach did not prove popular either with clients or with the office staff doing the accounting. The physical environmental conditions were not conducive to the all-week inclusive package arrangements; the local infrastructure made it unnecessary; and the interaction with daily clients made it unwieldy.

In the Himalayas, HHS uses an existing hotel rather than a purpose-built lodge, but there is no ski resort nearby and the heliski clients come solely for that purpose. In addition, the hotel has few other clients during winter, and a number of ground-floor rooms are modified into a heliski operations area, with two helipads immediately adjacent. A ski resort has in fact recently been proposed at Manali, the base for the HHS operations. If this goes ahead it would change both the operations and market dynamics of the heliski operations. It appears, however, that there is considerable local opposition to the proposal and significant doubt as to whether it will proceed (Singh, 2008). In Alaska, heliski operations have historically run from hotels in Anchorage. One of the operators now offers a lodge-based product, but it appears that the lodge was originally built for salmon fishing, and the lodge-based heliski product has evolved from a previous combination product which included fishing for king salmon, and skiing on the granular spring snow known as corn snow.

Expedition model

There is good skiable snow in many parts of the world which are not currently accessible through any kind of organised ski infrastructure. A number of companies specialise in taking heliskiers and boarders to these more remote areas, using a variety of logistic arrangements. At the upper end of the market are heliski tours based on luxury motor yachts such as the Absinthe (2009), which operates in the Coast Ranges of British Columbia, Canada from a helipad on the yacht. Similar arrangements have been used for some years to support the production of extreme skiing movies, but it is only recently that they have been offered to commercial clients. For sufficiently wealthy clients, this approach could also be used in areas such as Greenland, Svalbard, and Patagonia.

In areas remote from the coast, and hence generally blessed with drier powder snow, various tour companies charter helicopters to take one or two groups of clients per season into remote and otherwise unskied areas. There are several such operations in the Himalayas and various mountain ranges in Russia, for example. Finally, there are one or two specialist tour operators who offer unusual, low-volume heliski products rather different from the high-volume daily and lodge models described above. One example is provided by Tatchu Surf Adventures (2009) based on Vancouver Island in British Columbia, Canada, which offers a combination of surf and snowboard holiday using charter helicopter access.

From a product packaging perspective, the distinguishing feature for all of these is that they provide exclusive opportunities available only to a few. There are some skiers and snowboarders who want 'more of the same' and routinely purchase many consecutive weeks at CMH or MWHS every year. There are others who prefer greater variety, even at greater risk of poor conditions, and it is these who provide the clientele for the boat-based, expedition-style and other unusual heliski tour products.

Client preferences

What heliskiers and heliboarders want can be summed up in three words: snow, safety, service. The relative priorities ascribed to each of these, however, differ between individual clients. More precisely, each individual client has different preference functions for each of these key components of the product. For most clients, these preference functions include an inflection point or threshold. The marginal increase in client satisfaction for a unit improvement in the product parameter concerned is higher below this level, and lower above it. In simple terms, each client expects a certain minimum standard of snow quality, safety, and service in order to be satisfied with the heliskiing holiday experience they have purchased. Above these thresholds, they will still be glad of continuing improvement, but the effect is less.

These thresholds differ between individual clients because of factors such as capability, prior experience, and risk aversion. For first-time or relatively inexperienced heliskiers and boarders, the opportunity to make first tracks on powder snow, irrespective of the quality of the powder, is a sufficient inducement to leave the packed snow of the ski resorts. For most clients, the possibility of superb conditions is balanced against the probability of reliably good conditions. A destination with a possibility of superb conditions but a significant risk of poor snow or weather will rank lower than a destination where snow quality is consistently and reliably high, even if never quite so perfect as the less reliable site. For the most fanatic powder skiers and snowboarders, snow quality overrides all other considerations and there is no upper threshold. They will travel anywhere in search of the most perfect powder snow, lighter and deeper than any they have experienced previously, restricted only by their available funds.

For those skiers and snowboarders who have been caught in an avalanche, barely escaped being caught, or even witnessed one at close range, considerations of safety may well be paramount. The same applies for those who have been trapped in a tree well or helped to rescue someone from such a trap; those who have suffered an injury on a remote snow slope and needed assistance; or those who are skiing for the first time in more difficult terrain than usual, e.g. steep tree-covered slopes with cliffs, or slopes steep enough to cause continual sloughing of surface snow, as in some of the Alaskan heliski areas. The components of safety programmes in commercial heliskiing and boarding operations have been described by Buckley (2006a) and need not be reiterated here. It does appear that amongst experienced heliski clients, some operators are perceived as providing the highest level of safety which can reasonably be expected in a potentially risky activity, whereas other operators are perceived as so-called cowboys for whom safety is a more secondary consideration.

The level of safety which a heliski operator can provide is strongly dependent on the area in which it operates, since this influences terrain, snow patterns, avalanche characteristics, weather patterns, types of helicopter available, helicopter maintenance, helicopter landing techniques, communications, emergency backup options, general infrastructure, health and medical infrastructure, and so on. Clients balance these considerations, insofar as they are aware of them, against considerations of snow quality. Even in a single geographic area, however, competing heliski tour operators may take different approaches to safety, as demonstrated by the comparison between CMH and MWHS. In that particular case, the key difference is the additional margin of safety provided by a second trained guide at the rear of the group, relative to a nominated client carrying a second safety pack and acting as a guide substitute. Adding the second guide reduces the number of clients in the helicopter by 10%, with a consequent effect on price. This is not the only difference which affects prices: the distinction between a package which includes unlimited vertical elevation skied and one with additional charges above a predefined maximum quota is also significant, but smaller.

For clients who are accustomed to travelling in five-star luxury, the quality of accommodation may be a significant consideration. Certainly, as CMH has redeveloped its various lodges over the years, it has routinely transformed them from relatively rustic backcountry lodges to much more luxurious establishments, similar to upmarket boutique hotels. The individual residences at the MWHS Blue River Village are even more spacious and would put many luxury serviced apartments to shame. The Holiday Inn in Manali, base for the Himachal Helicopter Skiing operations, is also well set up, with the additional bonus of an astonishing Himalayan panorama direct from the breakfast table. Meals provided in the CMH, MWHS, and HHS packages are at a very high standard of table d'hôte dining.

Product differentiation under close competition

CMH and MWHS offer very similar products in the same market segment and are hence in direct competition. They have fine-tuned their product packages to provide some differentiation. The characteristics of their principal or standard products were compared in Table 12.1. Both also offer more expensive and exclusive products, but those contribute only a small proportion of their customers.

The most significant differences are that the MWHS package includes unlimited vertical elevation skied, and two guides per heligroup, but costs correspondingly more. Other than snow quality, it is these three factors – safety, price, and vertical – which are key to purchasing decisions for most heliski clients. Essentially, MWHS provides a product which includes slightly more and also costs slightly more, so that value for money seems similar.

Both operators offer a 6.5-day package including luxury lodge accommodation and meals. Both provide powder skis and avalanche transceivers, with training in search techniques. Both offer morning stretch classes and carry water and electrolytes on the helicopters. Both sell Avalung® breathing apparatus and a range of heliski clothing. Both have customer loyalty programmes with a free helisuit after one million vertical feet, which corresponds to about seven 1-week packages.

There are differences in lodge design, availability of snowboards, communications facilities, charges for guest laundry and for tuning, and waxing skis and boards.

Conclusions

Heliskiing is one of the more expensive subsectors of the adventure tourism industry. Unlike many other subsectors, there are two very different but equally successful product designs. In the Rockies and Himalayas the standard is a 1-week all inclusive package, typically booked a year or more in advance. In New Zealand the standard is a single-day tour booked on arrival. In the Canadian Rockies, the two main operators offer very similar products, and fine-tune components of their packages so as to differentiate them.

LOOKING BACK

1. What kinds of adventure tourism activities make use of helicopters, and how? Are they more common in particular countries, and if so, why?

2. What kind of clientele do heliskiing operations attract, and how do the operators reach their clients and maintain repeat business? What other avenues can you suggest?

3. What components make up the marketable features of a retail heliski/board product? How do different operators package these components to create a range of competitive products?

PART 4

Conclusions

CHAPTER 13

Adventure Tourism Trends

Kiteboarding, newly popular
boardsport

KEY ISSUES

- historical evolution

- differences between regions and activity subsectors

- adventure destinations and events

- product portfolios and combination packages

- ever-increasing luxury

- exploratories and expeditions

- climate change, reduced security, and global financial change

CONTENTS

CHAPTER SUMMARY

Trends in the adventure tourism sector may usefully be considered in three major categories. There are new adventure activities which become possible with the development of new or improved equipment. There are external global trends such as climate change and economic disruption which influence the adventure tourism sector. And there are essentially social trends which seem to have arisen within the industry itself.

During the first decade of the current millennium, the main internal trends in adventure tourism have been: growth in adventure destinations and adventure events; development of larger and more complex multi-activity product portfolios and combo product packages; a trend to more and more upmarket luxury products; and a growing number of tours marketed as expeditions or exploratories.

These trends may in themselves reflect the particular socio-economic and political circumstances of recent decades, in particular the increased holiday time available to relatively well-off baby boomers who want interesting new experiences but in comfort and safety. In view of the global economic contraction in 2008–2009, we may anticipate a significant slow-down or reversal in at least some of these trends.

RESEARCH REVIEW

Tourism products change over time. Different generations, as well as different ethnic and socio-economic groups, take different types of holidays. Some changes are driven by tourism opportunities available, some by demands and fashions (Buckley, 1996). Product development has been described in a wide variety of tourism subsectors, including farm (Che et al., 2005; Ollenburg, 2007), film (Carl et al., 2007), food (Hashimoto and Telfer, 2006), wine (Getz and Brown, 2006), heritage (Ho and McKercher, 2004), hot springs (Lee and King, 2006), sports (Higham, 2005), cultural (McIntosh, 2004; Notzke, 2004), and urban tourism (Rogerson, 2006). The development of tourism destinations has also received attention (Butler, 2006; Chaisawat, 2006; Formica and Uysal, 2006; Hernández and León, 2007), along with branding and marketing (Henderson, 2007) and competitiveness (Lee and King, 2006). The actual process of product development was considered by Pechlaner et al. (2006), but was not mentioned, for example, in the list of tourism knowledge research propositions put forward by Xiao and Smith (2007).

Product development in the adventure tourism sector, however, does not seem to have been examined previously, though Page et al. (2006) did describe how adventure tourism is marketed in Scotland. Indeed, even the structure and characteristics of adventure tourism products have largely been ignored until recently (Buckley, 2006a, 2007a), let alone the processes by which those products are developed. As with other subsectors, there has been more attention to the development of adventure destinations (Cater, 2006a) than to the development of retail products. There is also some reference to the development of products in the outdoor recreation literature (Fennell, 2002), but the focus of that literature is on private individual recreation and on non-profit entities such as schools, rather than on commercial tourism.

BIG PICTURE

History

Throughout the history of the civilised world, there have been adventurous travellers who visited far-flung parts of the globe and needed transport, accommodation, food, and guides along the way. Some of these were driven by religious, military, or commercial reasons, but others were simply curious about art and architecture, nature and culture in other countries and continents. Some of these travellers were adventurous in any sense of the word, and their journals have become classics of travel writing. The majority of modern commercial adventure tourism pales into insignificance in comparison with the exploits of explorers and adventurers such as Ibn Battuta or Wilfred Thesiger (Newby, 1986).

There was also an era of expeditionary travel driven principally by geographic and political aims, as the nations of Europe competed to investigate and annex new areas of territory in the rest of the world. This was followed by an era when national teams competed to lay claim to adventurous firsts, such as reaching the North and South Poles, climbing Mt Everest, or rafting the length of the Yangtze River in China. Indeed, this pursuit of expeditionary firsts still continues, though there is now less focus on competition between countries, and more on competition between commercial sponsors and their teams.

The commercial adventure tourism industry seems to have had multiple beginnings, as the equipment, opportunities, and demand for different types of adventure activity arose at different times and in different places. Places for tourists on Arctic voyages, for example, have apparently been available commercially since 1871 (Marsh, 2000). The whitewater rafting industry apparently developed after the Second World War, using army-surplus pontoons to make rafts. Commercial outfitters who provided pack and riding horses, equipment, and guides have operated in the USA since the days of the Wild West. The commercial canoe tour industry in Canada presumably evolved from the days of early exploration by the so-called Voyageurs. Indeed, the Canadian canoe tour company Blackfeather takes its name from the Voyageurs' insignia. In east and southern Africa, and perhaps also in India, the modern-day game lodges and safaris can trace their ancestry directly to the days of colonial big-game hunting, where wealthy Europeans and later Americans would pay local safari operators to provide in-country logistics, and famous hunters to act as guides. Because of these different histories, as well as different geographies, the adventure tourism industry has developed somewhat different regional signatures in different continents and subcontinents, in much the same way as the ecotourism sector (Buckley, 2003a, 2009a); though the signature seems to be reflected more in the portfolio of products on offer, than the way products are structured within any one activity (Buckley, 2006a).

The modern era of commercial adventure tourism can perhaps be dated to the 1970s, when companies offering one type of guided adventure tour began to realise that there were parallel markets for other types of adventure activity in the same region, and hence began to diversify their product ranges. One well-known example is provided by World Expeditions (formerly Australian Himalayan Expeditions), operating in Nepal. Initially, the company focused on guided mountain treks in the Himalayas, but as whitewater rafting gained popularity (Knowles and Allardice, 1992), the company diversified into new activities and new countries. Other tour operators followed similar strategies, and this led in due course to the multi-country, multi-activity operation which has become one of the principal business models for the modern-day adventure tourism industry.

Over the past two or three decades, as adventure tourism has grown to become a significant component of the mainstream tourism sector, it has also developed more structure, as business and marketing models have been adapted to logistic constraints and client demands. There are relatively unspecialised high-volume low-skill adventure products which are sold through mainstream travel agents. There are some companies which rely on location, with both ground and sales operations in recognised adventure capitals or adventure gateways, where tourists buy a holiday to the gateway and then purchase individual adventure tours once they arrive. There are global outdoor travel and tourism packagers and retailers, who offer an extensive and commonly worldwide portfolio of nature, culture, and adventure-based products which they market directly to retail consumers. Some of these tours may be run using their own equipment and staff, but the majority are run by local on-the-ground or on-the-water operators who own and maintain the equipment and provide the skilled guides. These local operators may market their products exclusively through a single retail packager or through a number of such companies; and they may or may not also carry out their own direct marketing under their own name. Similarly, individual guides may work exclusively for a particular local operator, or they may work for a number of different operators at the same destination, depending on each day's demands. Operations where supply is limited by external constraints and demand exceeds supply, can generally rely solely on direct marketing to an established clientele, with some selling out the season's entire places a year or more ahead. And a very few are in such demand that they have allocated quotas to different countries of origin, with exclusive agents in each of these countries appointed to sell that specific quota. An example is provided by Canadian Mountain Holidays (2009).

Industry-scale trends

The development of new products in any particular sector of the tourism industry may be considered at four main scales: product, company, destination, sector. Individual tourism enterprises continually revise both their individual products and their overall product portfolios. Destinations attempt to market themselves through the combined strengths of local tourism operators. And at regional and global scale, the types of product offered in an entire tourism subsector change over time, as noted at the outset. Some of the product developments in the global adventure tourism industry are related principally to the development of new equipment: either entirely new, as in the case of snowboards and later kiteboards; or improved, as in the case of diving and kayaking gear (Buckley, 2006a). Other product developments, however, are related to social rather than technological change.

Over the past two decades, in particular, a number of trends have become identifiable within the adventure tourism sector (Buckley, 2005c, 2006a). These are explored in more detail later, but in summary they are: adventure destinations and events; multi-activity portfolios and combo products; increasing luxury; and exploratory and expedition-style products. There are also global-scale trends external to, but strongly affecting the adventure tourism industry: notably climate change, global redistribution of wealth, and increasing security risks in international travel.

External trends affecting adventure tourism

Superimposed on internal tourism trends within the adventure tourism industry itself, there are larger-scale changes in the physical environment and global social structures, which are beginning to affect the adventure tourism sector. On the physical side, the principal current concern is global climate change. On the socio-economic side, the key concern is change in the relative wealth of different social groups in different countries, and the consequences for travel patterns and preferences. The links between adventure tourism and climate change can be categorised in a number of different ways, as outlined in Chapter 8. At the broadest scale there are perhaps three major issues, though these are not entirely disjunct. The first is long-haul travel to adventure areas, and associated costs and offset measures. The second is changes to natural resources at adventure destinations, either directly or indirectly through social mechanisms. The third is changes in the behaviour of individual tourists because of the social aspects of climate change.

Currently, large-scale changes in the distribution of wealth are occurring through three major mechanisms. The first is the enormous economic growth in countries such as India and China. National per capita GNP is still relatively low in these nations, but because of income inequities and large populations overall, they now have a very substantial cohort of very wealthy individuals, and moderately wealthy middle classes which are enormous in scale. There is a growing interest in adventure tourism in both these countries, and we can anticipate that they will soon contribute a significant proportion of the global adventure tourism clientele, both domestically and internationally. The second group of newly wealthy tourists derives from Russia and surrounding nations. It appears that many of the assets of the former USSR are now in private hands, and this has produced a class of very wealthy individuals who are investing heavily in international real estate and also travelling extensively and expensively.

The third major economic change, during 2008, has been the problems experienced by the global finance sector. These have greatly diminished the value of discretionary savings held by many of the baby-boomer generation in North America and Europe, which supplied a large proportion of the mid to upper end of the nature and adventure tourism markets. This loss in perceived individual financial security seems to have affected travel patterns and plans much more than changes in fuel prices and long-haul travel costs.

A significant proportion of the global adventure tourism industry involves international travel, and this is heavily dependent on currency exchange rates. These fluctuate in ways which do not seem to be predictable, even to professional forex traders. These fluctuations are now so substantial that it has become a significant consideration, in purchasing any form of overseas holiday, whether to pay for it well in advance or at the last possible moment. Many of the smaller tour operators now include a clause in their purchase contracts under which they are entitled to add a last-minute surcharge if exchange rates change unfavourably by too large a margin.

Last but by no means least, international adventure travel is affected severely by war, terrorism, and political instabilities. There are some adventure activities, such as big-wave surfing on coral reef breaks, where the activity itself carries a significant element of physical risk, and in consequence, commercial tour clients may pay relatively less attention to risks such as aircraft hijackings and airport bombings. For most tourists, however, including commercial adventure tourists, security is a prime consideration in choosing any holiday destination. A very small number of travellers may actively seek out dangerous, corrupt, or politically unstable destinations, but by far the majority avoid them.

It is not only that physical risk increases in such circumstances. In addition, if the foreign affairs portfolios in the governments of tourists' countries of origin issue warnings or advisories about particular destination countries, then this commonly invalidates travel insurance for those areas. Thus an increased risk of injury, loss, or inconvenience is coupled with a reduced opportunity for medical treatment or evacuation, or compensation for losses. Where such advisories provide grounds to invoke the cancellation clauses of a travel insurance policy, therefore, this may well prove a preferable course of action. In the longer term, when a regime dangerous to tourists is maintained for many years, as in the case of Uganda under Idi Amin, tourists simply stop visiting and it takes a long time for infrastructure and confidence to be rebuilt subsequently.

Adventure destinations and events

A growing number of tourism destinations, at various scales, have begun to market themselves as adventure capitals, offering a range of different commercial adventure tourism products at the same destination. Coupled with this is an increasing number of adventure events, not necessarily competitive, which aim to attract large numbers of adherents to utilise mainstream facilities at the destinations concerned. For the mainstream accommodation and hospitality sector, adventure events fulfil much the same function as non-adventure events, such as conferences and conventions, spectator sporting events, and so on.

Associated with such events are multi-sport adventure races, which combine several aspects of the commercial tourism and recreation sectors. Most of these events include out-of-town as well as local competitors, and the former need transport and accommodation in the same way as any other tourist. Most of the adventure activities concerned require specialised equipment, and adventure races are commonly sponsored by outdoor equipment retailers or manufacturers, for whom they simply represent a sales technique. Competitions also provide a mechanism for persuading customers to upgrade from entry-level to top-end adventure products, with the latter being considerably more expensive. In addition, if the companies sponsoring the races are either structured as franchises or form syndicates so as to run a series of races at different geographic locations, then each race provides a pool of tourists who will then travel to the other race destinations.

Both destinations and events may be marketed by regional or local tourism promotion agencies or associations, public or private, but they depend on private commercial operators to provide the retail products at the destination, and generally also to run adventure events. At the same time, the companies offering these products commonly advertise their location at the destination concerned, and/or association with the adventure event; contribute funding to joint promotions; and co-brand their own marketing materials. Adventure events and destinations are thus part of the development of retail adventure tourism products and vice versa.

A number of tourist destinations worldwide are now known specifically for their adventure opportunities. Queenstown, New Zealand seems to have been one of the earliest to structure its marketing campaigns around an adventure theme, and for some years it has claimed to be the adventure capital of the world (Cater, 2006a). There are numerous other destinations, however, which also offer a portfolio of adventure activities and market themselves as adventure capitals of particular geographic areas (Buckley et al., 2006a). These include Cairns in Australia, Voss in Norway, Chamonix in France, Bozeman and Moab in the USA, and Pacific Harbour in Fiji. Some of these have added an adventure theme to existing attractions; some have repositioned themselves as adventure destinations; and some have sought to market themselves as adventure destinations from the outset.

There are also areas, such as the coastline near Geraldton in Western Australia, which at one time used an adventure theme in their marketing, but have now abandoned it. It would be interesting to know why. Victoria Falls in Zimbabwe, in contrast, is still marketed and indeed known for its adventure opportunities as well as sightseeing; but it has lost popularity for political and security reasons, and is now facing strong competition from Livingstone in Zambia on the other side of the river, which markets itself as the new adventure capital of Africa (Buckley et al., 2006a).

Whilst adventure branding does seem to have been a successful marketing tool for those destinations which have adopted it to date, the label is now being claimed by an increasing number of destinations with rather little justification, either because they are small and have only local markets, or because adventure is only a minor component of their tourism portfolio. The Coral Coast of Fiji and the Gold Coast of Australia, for example, rely principally on beach resorts, but are still seeking to use an adventure label in their marketing mix. It seems possible, therefore, that the impact of terms such as 'adventure capital' could be eroded to the point where they no longer have significant meaning or marketing value.

Meanwhile, however, the staging of adventure events is still in a strong growth phase. Exponents of a particular adventure activity assemble at a single destination, which is usually but not necessarily perceived as an adventure destination more generally, in order to take part in a specific event. Such events may be competitive, but not necessarily so. Essentially, they represent an extension of outdoor sporting events to encompass recreational adventure activities, such as off-road driving, mountain biking, parachuting, and kayaking. Examples at Moab, USA include the 24 Hours of Moab mountain bike race, the Moab Boogie skydiving festival, and the Easter Jeep Safari 4WD trail rally.

There are also an increasing number of so-called adventure races, multi-sport competitive events inspired by long-running televised competitions such as the Raids Gauloises, the Eco-challenges, and the Speights Coast-to-Coast in New Zealand. In Australia at least, these events are organised and promoted by outdoor sports equipment retailers, such as the recently established Anaconda retail chain, presumably as a way to increase both their customer base and the number and price of items bought by individual customers.

Adventure events seem to fulfil several roles simultaneously. They help to provide custom for tourist accommodation and services over the event itself. They help to market the destination more generally, beyond the immediate period of the event. And commonly, they are used as opportunities to sell and promote outdoor recreational equipment. These links provide one of the most intriguing opportunities to examine the way in which private individual outdoor recreation links the commercial adventure tourism sector with the equipment-manufacturing sector.

Portfolios and combo packages

A significant trend at a number of adventure destinations is for a single major adventure tourism operator to take over retail marketing of a range of different adventure activities, offering them either as a portfolio or as combination products. In the single-destination portfolio approach, clients select from a range of activities and products offered by a single retailer.

In the combination approach, clients can buy a single product package which includes several different activity components. This approach seems to be particularly common at heavily visited adventure destinations or adventure capitals, as a key strategy for competition between different adventure tourism operators. There seem to be three main subsidiary mechanisms for this approach. A company which already offers one activity can simply start to offer new activities from scratch, by buying new equipment, applying for any new operating permits required, and hiring new guides if needed. The second approach is for one company to buy up or take over other operators in their entirety, including the products they offer. The third is for a group of operators at the same destination to form a marketing syndicate, packaging together individual products offered by each so as to form a combined product offered by them all. The best-known example of this approach is the so-called Awesome Foursome in Queenstown, New Zealand, which includes bungy jumping, jet-boating, whitewater rafting, and a helicopter flight.

A number of larger-scale adventure tourism operators have extended the portfolio approach from a single destination to a wide portfolio of products in different countries. Ideally, their aim is to establish a regular clientele of tourists who will take many individual trips with the same company. To encourage this, these companies typically also offer discounts for repeat trips and incentives for bringing new clients. One feature of establishing a faithful long-term clientele is that the individual clients get older each year and start to demand greater levels of luxury. Indeed, there seems to be a general trend for the more successful nature and adventure tour operators to move continually upmarket. Whether they do this to keep the same clients, or whether they do it to attract new and more wealthy clients once they have established a reputation for quality, does not seem to have been investigated. Relatively few tour operators, however, attempt to offer both upmarket and down-market products at the same time; and those which do, generally do so under different names, so as not to damage or dilute the brand image associated with the upmarket products. Companies which offer both consumptive and non-consumptive adventure tourism products, such as hunting safaris and photographic safaris, use a similar approach. Typically, however, as one company moves upmarket in its offerings, others move in to pick up the more down-market niches.

Moving upmarket, increasing luxury

As the adventure tourism industry has continued to grow, it has also gone increasingly upmarket. This applies both for the sector as a whole and at the scale of individual companies. At the sector-wide scale, more and more expensive and luxurious options are being offered in more and more remote places. Some of these have been well publicised generally, such as space and sub-space tourism, and guided climbs of Mount Everest and the Seven Summits (Hales, 2006). Others are currently promoted only to aficionados, such as heliskiing in remote areas of west-coast Canada and Alaska, accessed from a luxury motor vessel (Absinthe, 2009).

The trend to increasing luxury is discernible at all levels in the adventure tourism sector. Game and wildlife-watching lodges, once relatively rustic affairs, now feature aromatherapy spas and five-star dining in addition to the wildlife-viewing opportunities. The surfing sector, once perceived as the province of the time-rich but cash-poor, has grown to include luxury island lodges and boat charters in remote areas, marketed very much to the cash-rich, time-poor. At the upper end of the commercial surf tourism market, luxury support vessels and jetskis for tow-in surfing in remote ocean surf breaks are already available for professional surfers, and no doubt will soon become part of the commercial tourism sector (Chapter 11). Most recently, helicopter surfing has been attempted, though as yet not very successfully.

At the scale of individual tour companies and products, it has become commonplace that whenever a lodge or vessel is refurbished, the level of luxury is increased, often significantly (Buckley, 2006a, p. 156). Companies which once offered bare-bones guiding now offer fully catered tours with support crews. Even backpacking has moved from a dollar-a-day survival-scratching independent activity to a large international industry courted assiduously by national tourism promotion agencies, with global marketing systems, organised coach itineraries, service and quality standards for accommodation, and a wide range of add-on activities. The same applies for closely associated products, whether guidebooks such as the *Lonely Planet*® series (Buckley, 2008a), or so-called overlander bus and truck tours through Africa and Asia (Buckley, 2006a, pp. 399–401).

As these companies continue to move upmarket, new operators move in beneath them to offer the more basic low-cost products to new generations of cash-poor clients. In addition, many adventure tour operators now offer very short and hence relatively inexpensive adventure tour products. Examples include: a 2-hour raft trip as well as a full-day experience; a half-day, three-run heliskiing option as well as a week-long package; a 1-hour surfing or kiteboarding lesson as well as multi-day courses; or a brief resort dive experience as well as week-long specialist dive charters.

For the adventure tourism sector as a whole, therefore, the financial structure can still be perceived as a triangle or pyramid, with low-skill, low-price, short-duration, high-volume trips close to major tourist gateways representing the base, and high-skill, high-price, low-volume products in remote areas representing the apex (Figure 13.1). Under this conceptual model, the trends outlined above would be represented as follows: firstly, continuing upward growth of the apex as more and more expensive products are added to the overall market mix; secondly, gradual progression by individual tour operators from the base towards the apex; and thirdly, continuing entry of new participants, at all levels but particularly near the base, providing growth in the overall size and volume of the pyramid.

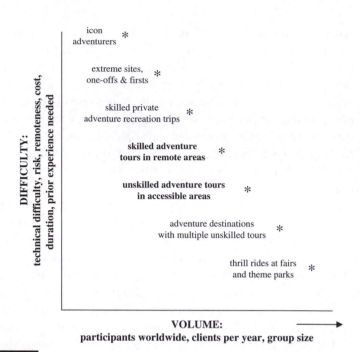

FIGURE 13.1   *The adventure tourism product pyramid.*
From Buckley (2007a)

As a general trend, therefore, it seems that increasingly expensive adventure tourism products have been offered over recent years, and that this increase will continue. In addition, in any particular adventure tourism activity subsector, financially successful operators offer successively more luxurious products. We can also anticipate that in future, such companies will offer increasingly higher proportions of their overall product portfolios near the top end of the price range in that subsector.

There are likely to be two critical complexities: geographic and generational. There are likely to be different patterns and trends for different adventure activities and combinations in different geographic regions; and it is also likely that the particular financial position and aspirations of the baby-boomer generation have influenced the growth of luxury adventure products, and that this trend may thus be reversed once that generation ceases to travel, or if their investments shrink in value owing to the current global economic downturn.

Exploratories and expeditions

Many adventure tourism companies make continuing efforts to emphasise an adventurous component in their products, in the shape of flexibility and uncertainty. In one sense, this is making a virtue of necessity. Expedition cruises to Arctic or Antarctic regions, for example, do indeed need to adapt their daily itinerary to local conditions (Buckley, 2003a, pp. 186–193, 2006a, pp. 153–165). Wildlife watching tours, whether by sea kayak or off-road safari, cannot actually guarantee that clients will see any particular animal species, so they advertise the possibility, or the search (Buckley, 2005b). Some operators have taken this one step further, deliberately making the search into a challenge for the clients, as in the 'star bird' lists provided by Taj Safaris (2009). Similar approaches have been advocated, or adopted, for some national parks.

In addition, as tour operators try out new products, they may offer trial runs as exploratories. Where a new retail tour product offered by a particular operator simply involves assembling a new combination of local accommodation, transport, and activity providers, the retail packager will generally send one of their guides or other staff to test it in advance, before taking paying clients. Where a new retail offering involves setting up completely new on-ground logistics, or chartering group transport, or any other component which is too expensive to test out in advance, then the retail tour operator may offer it as an exploratory tour. Essentially, this represents a disclaimer, telling clients that the company cannot necessarily guarantee either the promised attractions or a smooth itinerary. Sometimes, exploratories are offered at a discounted price to take account of these uncertainties, but not always. Since the term exploratory has gained a certain cachet, with its connotations of adventure and uniqueness, tour companies may even be able to sell such trips at a price premium, especially if major retail competitors do not yet offer comparable packages. Some examples include: Coastal Adventures (2009), Ibex Expeditions (2009), Sicklebill Safaris (2009), and Wilderness Travel (2009).

Some commercial outdoor tour operators take this concept one step further by offering a variety of firsts: first ascents of mountaineering routes; first descents of rivers, gorges, or mountain snow slopes; or first traverses of hiking, cross-country skiing, or sea-kayaking routes, as commercial tourism products. The critical distinction is that for these trips, there are no on-ground providers and no previous trips even by private expeditions or recreational groups. The commercial trip thus qualifies as an expeditionary first, which gives the paying clients something over and above a regularly repeated tour (Buckley, 2006a, p. 34). Given the high cost of mounting adventure expeditions in the more remote parts of the world, selling commercial places now provides a realistic alternative or addition to corporate sponsorship.

One example is provided by a group of cross-linked companies which specialise in offering commercial first descents of rivers in western China and Tibet. Trading variously as Earth Science Expeditions, Shangri-La River Expeditions, or Last Descents (2009), the individuals concerned have explored a number of relatively inaccessible river gorges in the eastern Himalayas over the past 15 years (Buckley, 2006a, pp. 35–49; Bowerman, 2008). Other operators in the same activity sector and indeed the same region do also run first descents, though not as a primary business. Well-established adventure tour operators in a variety of activity sectors also advertise new opportunities, such as diving under polar ice, crossing Greenland on skis, heliskiing new runs or terrain, surfing new breaks, and so on.

It seems, therefore, that there is a trend for adventure tourism advertising materials to feature more and more firsts, uncertainties, exploration, and expeditions. It also appears that more and more first ascents, descents, traverses, etc., are now financed at least partly through selling commercial tour places. As a result, the number of opportunities for commercial tour clients, either unskilled or suitably skilled depending on the activity concerned, to take part in expeditionary firsts has increased over recent years, and this seems to be continuing.

Conclusions

Adventure tourism now forms about a fifth of the tourism industry, which in aggregate makes up about a tenth of global GNP (Buckley, 2006a). It has also gained a well-recognised place in the social structures of modern societies (Swarbrooke et al., 2003; Cater, 2006a). Trends in such an industry are hence worthy of research from a wide variety of academic disciplines, including economic, demographic, and psychological perspectives as well as product and business development and marketing. The trends identified above reflect some of the more immediate research issues related to the commercial structure of the adventure tourism sector, an aspect which appears to have been largely neglected in tourism research to date. Conceptually, some of them will be relatively straightforward to test, others more difficult. In practice, nearly all of them will involve difficult and extensive data collection exercises which may well be beyond the reach of any individual researcher, except perhaps for localised subsets of the sector. Accordingly, this concluding chapter is intended not only as an analysis of trends; but also as an invitation for tourism researchers to turn their attentions to the adventure subsector and consider how these trends might be tested.

CASE STUDY 13.1: Combo Products: Awesome Foursome, Shearwater Adventures

The world's best-known combination product is in Queenstown, New Zealand, where a number of operators combine to offer the so-called Awesome Foursome: helicopter, bungy-jump, jet-boat ride and whitewater rafting (Cater, 2006a). In that case, the individual experiences are owned and operated by different enterprises, but each of them, and many travel agents, markets the package as a whole. Another example is provided by Shearwater Adventures in Victoria Falls, Zimbabwe, which offers a portfolio of adventure activities packaged in a variety of different combinations (Buckley, 2006a, pp. 90–93). Shearwater Adventures started solely as a local rafting and canoeing company, but now claims to be Africa's largest adventure tourism operator. At an even broader level, there is a continuing trend to cross-marketing not only between different adventure tourism products, but also between tourism, fashion, clothing, and entertainment (Buckley, 2003b); and between day-time adventure tours and night-time entertainment venues in the same destination (Cater, 2006a).

CASE STUDY 13.2: Increasing Luxury: Game-Watching Lodges

Reception area, Wilderness Safaris North Island, Seychelles

The trend to ever-increasing luxury in adventure tourism products is well exemplified by the African safari industry. Historically, private game lodges deliberately cultivated the ambience of a colonial-era hunting safari, with style, comfort, and service but not the modern trappings of urban or resort luxury. Examples include: Selati Lodge in the Sabi Sabi private reserve near South Africa's Kruger National Park; the Desert Rhino Tented Camp operated by Wilderness Safaris in Namibia; and Klein's Camp operated by &Beyond (formerly Conservation Corporation Africa) near Serengeti National Park in northern Tanzania. The recently refurbished Kirkmans Kamp, run by &Beyond in the Sabi Sands area, has deliberately adopted the same motif. Tiger-watching lodges built by Taj Safaris at Pench and Bhagvan National Parks in India, designed in conjunction with &Beyond, have also followed colonial-era Indian architectural styles. In a number of other recently constructed lodges, however, a very different style has been adopted, with plunge pools, aromatherapy spas, and massage facilities as standard. Examples include: Earth Lodge at Sabi Sabi, or the Al Maha Lodge in the Dubai Desert Conservation Reserve.

One particularly good example of this trend to luxury is Wilderness Safaris' North Island Lodge in the Seychelles. Though offering a different experience from the company's game-viewing lodges in Botswana and Namibia, stays at North Island are sold through the same marketing system

Continued

and at least partly to the same clientele. North Island is a privately owned island which Wilderness Safaris, with four other investors, is rehabilitating from an abandoned coconut plantation to a conservation reserve. Feral animals have been removed; removal of weeds and restoration of native vegetation has commenced; and three endangered wildlife species have successfully been reintroduced. These land management measures are funded by a top-end tourist lodge, with 11 extremely spacious and well-equipped private oceanfront villas, each with their own butler, plus a large central restaurant where menus are only 'suggestions' and you can, in theory, order anything you like. All this comes at a price, currently around US$5000 per day.

References

North Island, 2009. <www.north-island.com/>; (accessed 25.02.2009).

LOOKING BACK

1. What major trends are identifiable within the adventure tourism sector? Are these different from trends in the tourism industry more broadly, and if so how?

2. One of the identified trends suggested in this volume is that tour clients expect more and more luxury. Why might this be the case?

3. Chapter 23 in Buckley (2006a) *Adventure Tourism*, identified 17 tourism destinations marketing themselves as 'adventure capitals'. How many of these places still make that claim? How many others have also made similar claims more recently? What justification do they provide? What activities do they offer?

References

Absinthe, 2009. <http://www.eaheliskiing.com/heli-skiing/heli-skiing-absinthe-yacht> (accessed 05.06.09).

Adventure Collection, 2009. <http://www.adventurecollection.com/home> (accessed 05.06.09).

Aitkens, M., 1990. Have snowboard will soar. The Physician and Sports Medicine 18, 114–120.

Allison, W.R., 1996. Snorkeler damage to reef corals in the Maldive Island. Coral Reefs 15, 215–218.

Alpizar, F., 2006. The pricing of protected areas in nature-based tourism: a local perspective. Ecological Economics 56, 294–307.

Amo, L., Lopez, P., Martin, J., 2006. Nature-based tourism as a form of predation risk affects body condition and health state of Podarcis muralis lizards. Biological Conservation 131, 402–409.

Anderson, G.R.V., Forbes, M.A., Pirzl, R.M., 1996. A national overview of the development of whale watching in Australia. In: Encounters with Whales 1995 Proceedings. Australian Nature Conservation Agency, Canberra.

Anderson, S., 2000. Expedition health and safety: a risk assessment. Journal of the Royal Society of Medicine 93, 557–562.

Archabald, K., Naughton-Treves, L., 2001. Tourism revenue sharing around national parks in Western Uganda: early efforts to identify and reward local communities. Environmental Conservation 28, 135–149.

Arnould, E., Price, I., 1993. River magic: extraordinary experience and the extended service encounter. Journal of Consumer Research 20, 24–45.

Asoh, K., Yoshikawa, T., Kosaki, R., Marschall, E.A., 2004. Damage to cauliflower coral by monofilament fishing lines in Hawaii. Conservation Biology 18 (6), 1645–1650.

Atlantis Adventures (2009). Experienced by over 12 million passengers. <http://www.atlantisadventures.com> (accessed 06.04.09).

Azqueta, D., Sotelsek, D., 2007. Valuing nature: from environmental impacts to natural capital. Ecological Economics 63, 22–30.

Baldacchino, G. (Ed.), 2006. Extreme Tourism: Lessons from the World's Cold Water Islands. Elsevier, Oxford, p. 292.

Barnes, J., Burgess, J., Pearce, D., 1992. Wildlife tourism. In: Swanson, T.M., Barbier, E.B. (Eds.), Economics for the Wilds: Wildlife, Wildlands, Diversity and Development. Earthscan, London, pp. 136–151.

Barnes, J.I., Jager, J.L.V., 1996. Economic and financial incentives for wildlife use on private land in Namibia and the implications for policy. South African Journal of Wildlife Research 26, 37–46.

Barnes, J.I., Schier, C., Van Rooy, G., 1999. Tourists' willingness to pay for wildlife viewing and wildlife conservation in Namibia. South African Journal of Wildlife Research 29, 101–111.

Beach, D.W., Weinrich, M.T., 1989. Watching the whales. Oceanus 32, 84–88.

Beale, C.M., Monaghan, P., 2004. Human disturbance: people as predation-free predators? Journal of Applied Ecology 41, 335–343.

Bebbington, J., Brown, J., Frame, B., 2007. Accounting technologies and sustainability assessment models. Ecological Economics 61, 224–236.

Becken, S., 2008. Climate change – beyond the hype. Tourism Recreation Research 33, 351–353.

Becken, S., Hay, J., 2007. Tourism and Climate Change. Channel View, Clevedon.

Becken, S., Simmons, D.G., 2002. Understanding energy consumption patterns of tourism attractions and activities in New Zealand. Tourism Management 23, 343–354.

Beedie, P., 2003. Mountain guiding and adventure tourism: reflections on the choreography of the experience. Leisure Sciences 22, 147–167.

Beedie, P., Hudson, S., 2003. Emergence of mountain-based adventure tourism. Annals of Tourism Research 30, 625–643.

Beeton, S., Benfield, R., 2002. Demand control: the case for demarketing as a visitor and environmental management tool. Journal of Sustainable Tourism 10, 497–513.

Bejder, L., Samuels, A., 2003. Evaluating impacts of nature-based tourism on cetaceans. In: Gales, N., Hindell, M., Kirkwood, R. (Eds.), Marine Mammals: Fisheries, Tourism and Management Issues. CSIRO Publishing, Collingwood, pp. 229–256.

Bejder, L., Dawson, S.M., Harraway, J.A., 1999. Responses by Hector's dolphins to boats and swimmers in Porpoise Bay, New Zealand. Marine Mammal Science 15, 738–750.

Bell, M., 2001. Understanding circulation in Australia. Journal of Population Research 18, 1–18.

Bennett, J., Harley, D., Worley, M., Donaldson, B., Andrew, D., Geering, D., Povey, A., Cohen, M., 2000. Watching Wildlife in Australia. Lonely Planet, Melbourne.

Bennett, M.A., Kriwoken, L.K., Fallon, L.D., 2003. Managing bushwalker impacts in the Tasmanian wilderness World Heritage Areas, Australia. International Journal of Wilderness 9, 14–27.

Bentley, T., Page, S.J., 2001. Scoping the extent of adventure tourism accidents. Annals of Tourism Research 28, 705–726.

Bentley, T., Page, S.J., 2008. A decade of injury monitoring in the New Zealand adventure tourism sector: a summary risk analysis. Tourism Management 29 (5), 857–869.

Bentley, T., Macky, K., Edwards, J., 2006. Injuries to New Zealanders participating in adventure tourism and adventure sports: an analysis of Accident Compensation Corporation (ACC) claims. The New Zealand Medical Journal 119 (1247), 1–9.

Bentley, T., Meyer, D., Page, S.J., Chalmers, D., 2001b. Recreational tourism injuries among visitors to New Zealand: an exploratory analysis using hospital discharge data. Tourism Management 22, 373–381.

Bentley, T., Page, S.J., Edwards, J., 2008. Monitoring injury in the New Zealand adventure tourism sector: an operator survey. Journal of Travel Medicine 15, 395–403.

Bentley, T., Page, S.J., Laird, I.S., 2000. Safety in New Zealand's adventure tourism industry: the client accident experience of adventure tourism operators. Journal of Travel Medicine 7, 239–245.

Bentley, T., Page, S.J., Laird, I.S., 2001a. Accidents in the New Zealand adventure tourism industry. Safety Science 38, 31–48.

Bentley, T., Page, S.J., Laird, I., 2003. Managing tourist safety: the experience of the adventure tourism industry. In: Wilks, J., Page, S.J. (Eds.), Managing Tourist Health and Safety in the New Millennium. Pergamon. Elsevier Science, Oxford, pp. 85–100.

Bentley, T., Page, S.J., Meyer, D., Chalmers, D., Laird, I., 2001c. How safe is adventure tourism in New Zealand: an exploratory analysis. Applied Ergonomics 32, 327–338.

Berger, I.E., Greenspan, I., 2008. High (on) technology: producing tourist identities through technologized adventure. Journal of Sport and Tourism 13, 89–114.

Berrow, S.D., 2003. Developing sustainable whalewatching in the Shannon Estuary. In: Garrod, B., Wilson, C. (Eds.), Marine Ecotourism: Issues and Experiences. Channel View, Clevedon, pp. 198–203.

Berrow, S.D., Holmes, B., Kiely, O.R., 1996. Distribution and abundance of bottle-nosed dolphins Tursiops truncatus (Montagu) in the Shannon Estuary. Biological Environments 96B, 1–10.

Bertram, E., Muir, S., Stonehouse, B., 2007. Gateway ports in the development of Antarctic tourism. In: Snyder, J., Stonehouse, B. (Eds.), Prospects for Polar Tourism. CAB International, Wallingford, pp. 123–146.

Billabong, 2009. Billabong. <http://www.billabong.com.au> (accessed 06.04.09).

Birtles, R.A., Arnold, P.W., Dunstan, A., 2002. Commercial swim programs with dwarf minke whales on the northern Great Barrier Reef, Australia: some characteristics of the encounters with management implications. Australian Mammalogy 24, 23–38.

Bisht, H., 1994. Tourism in Garhwal Himalaya: with Special Reference to Mountaineering and Trekking in Uttarkashi and Chamoli Districts. Indus Publishing Company, New Delhi.

Black Feather, (2009). The Wilderness Adventure Company. <http://www.blackfeather.com> (accessed 25.02.2009).

Blane, J.M., Jaakson, R., 1994. The impact of ecotourism boats on the St Lawrence beluga whales. Environmental Conservation 21, 267–269.

Blom, A., 2000. The monetary impact of tourism on protected area management and the local economy in Dzanga-Sangha (Central African Republic). Journal of Sustainable Tourism 8, 175–189.

Blumberg, K., 2008. Internationalisation in adventure tourism: the mobility of people, products and innovations. In: Coles, T., Hall, C.M. (Eds.), International Business and Tourism. Routledge, Oxon, pp. 181–194.

Boggild, A.K., Costiniuk, C., Kain, K.C., Pandey, P., 2007. Environmental hazards in Nepal: altitude illness, environmental exposures, injuries, and bites in travelers and expatriates. Journal of Travel Medicine 14, 361–368.

Booth, K.L., Cullen, R., 2001. Managing recreation and tourism in New Zealand mountains. Mountain Research and Development 21, 331–334.

Borge, L., Nelson, W.C., Leitch, J.A., Leistritz, F.L., 1991. Economic impact of wildlife-based tourism in Northern Botswana. North Dakota State University, Agricultural Experiment Station, p. 88.

Borrie, W., Roggenbuck, J., 2001. The dynamic, emergent, and multi-phasic nature of onsite wilderness experiences. Journal of Leisure Research 33, 202–228.

Bourdeau, P., Corneloup, J., Mao, P., 2002. Adventure sports and tourism in the French mountains: dynamics of change and challenges for sustainable development. Current Issues in Tourism 5, 22–32.

Bowerman, K., 2008. Part 2. In: Pellegrini, T. (Ed.), Fast Track, Week 44. BBC News, London.

Bowker, J.M., 2001. Outdoor Recreation by Alaskans: Projections for 2000 Through 2020. USDA Forest Service, Pacific Northwest Research Station, Portland, USA.

Bowker, J.M., English, D.B.K., Donovan, J.A., 1996. Toward a value for guided rafting on southern rivers. Journal of Agricultural and Applied Economics 28, 423–432.

Boyd, S.W., Butler, R.W., 1999. Definitely not monkeys or parrots, probably deer and possibly moose: opportunities and realities of ecotourism in Northern Ontario. Current Issues in Tourism 2, 123–137.

Boyle, P., Halfacree, K. (Eds.), 1998. Migration into Rural Areas: Theories and Issues. John Wiley & Sons, Chichester.

Bratton, R., Kinnear, G., Korolux, G., 1979. Why people climb mountains. International Review of Sport Sociology 4, 23–36.

Brattstrom, B.H., Bondello, M.C., 1983. Effects of off-road vehicle noise on desert vertebrates. In: Webb, R.H., Wilshire, H.G. (Eds.), Environmental Effects of Off-Road Vehicles: Impact and Management in Arid Regions. Springer Verlag, New York, pp. 167–206.

Breivik, G., 1996. Personality, sensation seeking and risk taking among Everest climbers. International Journal of Sport Psychology 27, 308–320.

Broderick, J., 2009. Voluntary carbon offsets: a contribution to sustainable tourism? In: Gössling, S., Hall, C., Weaver, D. (Eds.), Sustainable Tourism Futures. Routledge, New York, pp. 169–199.

Brookes, A., 2001. Doing the Franklin: wilderness tourism and the construction of nature. Tourism Recreation Research 26, 11–18.

Broome, L.S., 2001. Density, home range, seasonal movements and habitat use of the mountain pygmy-possum Burramys parvus (Marsupialia: Burramyidae) at Mount Blue Cow, Kosciuszko National Park. Austral Ecology 26, 275–292.

Brown, I., 1989. Managing for adventure recreations. Australian Parks and Recreation 25, 37–40.

Buckley, R.C., 1993. International trade, investment and environment: an environmental management perspective. Journal of World Trade 27, 102–148.

Buckley, R.C., 1996. Investing in the Future: Practical Tourism Research Solutions. Tourism and Technology. QIDC, Singapore.

Buckley, R.C., 1998a. Ecotourism megatrends. Australian International Business Review 1998, 52–54.

Buckley, R.C., 1998b. Tools and indicators for managing tourism in parks. Annals of Tourism Research 26, 207–210.

Buckley, R.C., 1999a. The law in green conflicts. Environmental and Planning Law Journal 16, 100–101.

Buckley, R.C., 1999b. Green Guide to White Water. CRC Tourism and Griffith University, Gold Coast.

Buckley, R.C., 2000. Green Guide for 4WD Tours: Best-Practice Environmental Management for 4WD and Off-Road Tours. CRC Tourism. Griffith University, Gold Coast.

Buckley, R.C. (2002a). Surf tourism and sustainable development in Indo-Pacific Islands. I. The industry and the islands. Journal of Sustainable Tourism 10, 405–424.

Buckley R.C. (2002b). Surf tourism and sustainable development in Indo-Pacific Islands. II. Recreational capacity management and case study. Journal of Sustainable Tourism 10, 425–442.

Buckley, R.C., 2003a. Case Studies in Ecotourism. CAB International, Wallingford, p. 264.

Buckley, R.C., 2003b. Adventure tourism and the clothing, fashion and entertainment industries. Journal of Ecotourism 2, 126–134.

Buckley, R.C., 2003c. Environmental inputs and outputs in ecotourism: geotourism with a positive triple bottom line? Journal of Ecotourism 2, 76–82.

Buckley, R.C., 2004a. Skilled commercial adventure: the edge of tourism. In: Singh, Tej V. (Ed.), New Horizons in Tourism. CAB International, Wallingford, pp. 37–48.

Buckley, R.C., 2004b. Environmental impacts of motorized off-highway vehicles. In: Buckley, R.C. (Ed.), Environmental Impacts of Ecotourism. CAB International, Wallingford, pp. 83–98.

Buckley, R.C., 2004c. Impacts of ecotourism on birds. In: Buckley, R.C. (Ed.), Environmental Impacts of Ecotourism. CAB International, Wallingford, pp. 187–209.

Buckley, R.C., 2004d. Impacts of ecotourism on terrestrial wildlife. In: Buckley, R.C. (Ed.), Environmental Impacts of Ecotourism. CAB International, Wallingford, pp. 211–228.

Buckley, R.C. (Ed.), 2004e. Environmental Impacts of Ecotourism. CAB International, Wallingford, p. 389.

Buckley, R.C., 2005a. Recreation ecology research effort: an international comparison. Tourism Recreation Research 30, 99–101.

Buckley, R.C., 2005b. In search of the narwhal: ethical dilemmas in ecotourism. Journal of Ecotourism 4, 129–134.

Buckley, R.C., 2005c. Social trends and ecotourism. Journal of Ecotourism 4, 56–61.

Buckley, R.C., 2006a. Adventure Tourism. CAB International, Wallingford, p. 528.

Buckley, R.C., 2006b. Adventure tourism research: a guide to the literature. Tourism Recreation Research 31, 75–83.

Buckley, R.C., 2007a. Adventure tourism products: price, duration, size, skill, remoteness. Tourism Management 28, 1428–1433.

Buckley, R.C. (Ed.), 2007b. Climate Response. Griffith University, Gold Coast and Brisbane. ISBN 978-1-921291-11-1.

Buckley, R.C., 2008a. Testing take-up of academic concepts in an influential commercial tourism publication. Tourism Management 29 (4), 721–729.

Buckley, R.C., 2008b. Climate change: tourism destination dynamics. Tourism Recreation Research 33, 354–355.

Buckley, R.C., 2008c. Misperceptions of climate change damage coastal tourism: case study of Byron Bay, Australia. Tourism Review International 12, 71–88.

Buckley, R.C., 2009a. Ecotourism: Principles and Practices. CAB International, Wallingford, p. 368.

Buckley, R.C., 2009b. Whitewater tourism. In: Prideaux, B., Cooper, M. River Tourism. CAB International, Wallingford, pp. 181–196.

Buckley, R.C., 2009c. Environmental management. In: Buckley, R.C. (Ed.), Ecotourism: Principles and Practices. CAB International, Wallingford, pp. 117–174.

Buckley, R.C., 2009c. Evaluating the net effects of ecotourism on the environment: a framework, first assessment and future research. Journal of Sustainable Tourism. doi 10.1080/09669580902999188.

Buckley, R.C., Araujo, G., 1997. Green advertising by tourism operators on Australia's Gold Coast. Ambio 26, 190–191.

Buckley, R.C., King, H.J., 2003. Visitor-impact data in a land-management context. In: Buckley, R.C., Pickering, C.M., Weaver, D. (Eds.), Nature-Based Tourism, Environment and Land Management. CAB International, Wallingford, pp. 89–99.

Buckley, R.C., Littlefair, C., 2007. Minimal-impact education can reduce actual impacts of park visitors. Journal of Sustainable Tourism 15, 324–325.

Buckley, R.C., King, N., Zubrinich, T., 2004. The role of tourism in spreading dieback disease in Australian vegetation. In: Buckley, R.C. (Ed.), Environmental Impacts of Ecotourism. CAB International, Wallingford, pp. 317–324.

Buckley, R.C., Ollenburg, C., Johnson, J., 2006a. Adventure destinations. In: Buckley, R. (Ed.), Adventure Tourism. CAB International, Wallingford, pp. 412–428.

Buckley, R.C., Pickering, C., Warnken, J., 2000. Environmental management for alpine tourism and resorts in Australia. In: Godde, P.M., Price, M.F., Zimmerman, F.M. (Eds.), Tourism and Development in Mountain Regions. CAB International, Wallingford, pp. 27–45.

Buckley, R.C., Pickering, C.M., Weaver, D. (Eds.), 2003. Nature-Based Tourism, Environment and Land Management. CAB International, Wallingford, p. 213.

Buckley, R.C., Robinson, J., Carmody, J., King, N., 2008b. Monitoring for management of conservation and recreation in Australian protected areas. Biodiversity and Conservation 17, 3589–3606.

Buckley, R.C., Sander, N., Ollenburg, C., Warnken, J., 2006b. Green change inland amenity migration in Australia. In: Moss, L. (Ed.), The Amenity Migrants. CAB International, Wallingford, pp. 278–294.

Buckley, R.C., Zhong, L-S., Cater, C., Chen, T., 2008a. Shengtai luyou: cross-cultural comparison in ecotourism. Annals of Tourism Research 35, 945–968.

Bunnell, E.I., Dunbar, D., Koza, L., Ryder, G., 1981. Effects of disturbance on the productivity and numbers of white pelicans in British Columbia – observations and models. Colonial Waterbirds 4, 2–11.

Burfeind, D.D., Stunz, G.W., 2006. The effects of boat propeller scarring intensity on nekton abundance in subtropical seagrass meadows. Marine Biology 148, 953–962.

Burger, J., Gochfeld, M., Niles, L.J., 1995. Ecotourism and birds in coastal New Jersey: contrasting responses of birds, tourists and managers. Environmental Conservation 22, 56–65.

Burnley, I., Murphy, P., 2004. Sea Change: Movement from Metropolitan to Arcadian Australia. UNSW Press, Sydney.

Butler, R. (Ed.), 2006. The Tourism Area Life Cycle: Applications and Modifications, Volume 1. The Tourism Area Life Cycle: Conceptual and Theoretical Issues, Volume 2. Cromwell Press, Great Britain.

Butler, R.W., 2004. Geographical research on tourism, recreation and leisure: origins, eras and directions. Tourism Geographies 6, 143–162.

Butler, R.W., Boyd, S.W. (Eds.), 2000. Tourism and National Parks: Issues and Implications. John Wiley & Sons, Chichester.

Buultjens, J., Davis, D., 2001. Managing for sustainable commercial whitewater rafting in Northern New South Wales, Australia. Journal of Tourism Studies 12, 40–50.

Byrnes, T.A., Warnken, J., 2006. Greenhouse gas emissions from marine tours: a case study of Australian tour boat operators. Journal of Sustainable Tourism 14, 255–270.

Byrnes, T.A., Buckley, R., Arthur, M., submitted for publication. Environmental management for fishing, sailing and diving tours. Ambio.

Camp, R.J., Knight, R.I., 1998. Rock climbing and cliff bird communities at Joshua Tree National Park, California. Wildlife Society Bulletin 26, 892–898.

Canadian Mountain Holidays, 2009. <http://www.canadianmountainholidays.com/> (accessed 14.1.09).

Carl, D., Kindon, S., Smith, K., 2007. Tourists' experiences of film locations: New Zealand as 'Middle-Earth'. Tourism Geographies 9, 49–63.

Carlson, C., 2001. A Review of WhaleWatching Guidelines and Regulations Around the World. International Fund for Animal Welfare, Yarmouth Port, USA.

Carlson, L.H., Godfrey, P.J., 1989. Human impact management in a coastal recreation and natural area. Biological Conservation 49, 141–156.

Carwardine, M., Watterson, K., 2002. The Shark Watchers Handbook. Princeton University Press, Princeton NG, p. 287.

Cater, C., 2006a. World adventure capital. In: Buckley, R. (Ed.), Adventure Tourism. CAB International, Wallingford, pp. 429–442.

Cater, C.I., 2006b. Playing with risk? Participant perceptions of risk and management complications in adventure tourism. Tourism Management 27, 317–325.

Cater, C., Cater, E., 2007. Marine Ecotourism: Between the Devil and the Deep Blue Sea. CAB International, Oxford, P. 307.

Cater, C., Cloke, P., 2007. Bodies in action: the performativity of adventure tourism. Anthropology Today 23, 13–16.

Ceron, J., Dubois, G., 2009. Tourism and climate change mitigation: which data is needed for what use? In: Gössling, S., Hall, C., Weaver, D. (Eds.), Sustainable Tourism Futures. Routledge, New York, pp. 84–101.

Cessford, G.R., 2002. Perception and reality of conflict: walkers and mountain bikes on the Queen Charlotte Track in New Zealand. In: Arnberger, A., Brandenburg, C., Muhur, A. (Eds.), Monitoring and Management of Visitor Flows in Recreational and Protected Areas. Proceedings of the Conference held at Bodenkultur University Vienna, Austria. Institute for Landscape Architecture and Landscape Management, Bodenkultur University, Vienna, pp. 102–108.

Chaisawat, M., 2006. Policy and planning of tourism product development in Thailand: a proposed model. Asia Pacific Journal of Tourism Research 11, 1–16.

Chavez, D.J., 1996a. Mountain biking: direct, indirect, and bridge building management. Journal of Park and Recreation Administration 14, 21–35.

Chavez, D.J., 1996b. Mountain Biking: Issues and Actions for USDA Forest Service Managers. United States Department of Agriculture, Forest Service, California.

Che, D., Veeck, A., Veeck, G., 2005. Sustaining production and strengthening the agritourism product: linkages among Michigan agritourism. Agriculture and Human Values 22, 225–234.

Chen, H., Hwang, S.N., Lee, C., 2006. Visitors' characteristics of guided interpretation tours. Journal of Business Research 59, 1167–1181.

Cheron, E., Ritchie, B., 1982. Leisure activities and perceived risk. Journal of Leisure Research 14, 139–154.

Chhetri, P., Arrowsmith, C., Jackson, M., 2004. Determining hiking experiences in nature-based tourist destinations. Tourism Management 25, 31–43.

Cigna, A.A., 1993. Environmental management of tourist caves. Environmental Geology 21, 173–180.

Cioccio, L., Michael, E.J., 2007. Hazard or disaster: tourism management for the inevitable in northeast Victoria. Tourism Management 28, 1–11.

Clayton, C., Mendelsohn, R., 1993. The value of watchable wildlife: a case study of McNeil River. Journal of Environmental Management 39, 101–106.

Cloke, P., Perkins, H.C., 1998. Cracking the canyon with the awesome foursome: representations of adventure tourism in New Zealand. Environment and Planning D: Society and Space 16, 185–218.

Coastal Adventures, 2009. Sea kayaking tours. <http://www.coastaladventures.com/tours.html> (accessed 02.03.09).

Cole, D., 1981. Managing ecological impacts at wilderness campsites. An evaluation of techniques. Journal of Forestry 79, 86–89.

Cole, D.N., 2004. Impacts of hiking and camping on soils and vegetation: a review. In: Buckley, R.C. (Ed.), Environmental Impacts of Ecotourism. CAB International, Wallingford, pp. 41–60.

Cole, D.N., Hendee, J.C., 1990. Ecological impacts of wilderness recreation and their management. Wilderness Management (1990), 425–466.

Constantine, R., 1999. Effects of Tourism on Marine Mammals in New Zealand. Science for Conservation: 106. Department of Conservation, Wellington, New Zealand.

Constantine, R., 2000. Increased avoidance of swimmers by wild bottlenose dolphins (Tursiop truncatus) due to long-term exposure to swim-with-dolphin tourism. Marine Mammal Science 17, 689–702.

Cooper, C., Fletcher, J., Wanhill, S., Gilbert, D., 2008. Tourism: Principles and Practice. Pearson, London, p. 704.

Cope, R., 2003. The international diving market. Travel and Tourism Analyst 6, 1–39.

Corkeron, P.J., 1995. Humpback whales (Megaptera novaeangliae) in Hervey Bay, Queensland: behavior and responses to whale-watching vessels. Canadian Journal of Zoology 73, 1290–1299.

Corne, N.P., 2009. The implications of coastal protection and development on surfing. Journal of Coastal Research 25, 527–434.

Costa, C.A., Chalip, L., 2007. Adventure sport tourism in rural revitalisation: an ethnographic evaluation. In: Weed, M. (Ed.), Sport and Tourism: A Reader. Routledge, New York, pp. 133–151.

Cox, T.M., Ragen, T.J., Vos, E., Baird, R.W., Balcomb, K., Barlow, J., Cranford, T., et al., 2006. Understanding the impacts of anthropogenic sound on beaked whales. Journal of Cetacean Research and Management 7, 177–187.

Coxon, C., 2006. Safety in the dive tourism industry of Australia. In: Wilks, J., Pendergast, D., Leggat, P.A. (Eds.), Tourism in Turbulent Times: Towards Safe Experiences for Visitors. Elsevier, pp. 199–216.

Crawford, D.W., Jackson, E.L., Godbey, G., 1991. Leisure activities and perceived risk. Journal of Leisure Research 14, 139–154.

Croft, D.B., 2000. Sustainable use of wildlife in Western New South Wales: possibilities and problems. Rangeland Journal 22, 88–104.

Curtin, S., 2003. Whale-watching in Kaikoura: sustainable destination development? Journal of Ecotourism 2, 173–195.

Danielsen, F., Burgess, N.D., Balmford, A., 2005a. Monitoring matters: examining the potential of locally-based approaches. Biodiversity and Conservation 14, 2507–2582.

Danielsen, F., Jensen, A.E., Alviola, P.A., Balete, D.S., Mendoza, M., Tagtag, A., Custodio, C., Enghoff, M., 2005b. Does monitoring matter? A qualitative assessment of management decisions from locally-based monitoring of protected areas. Biodiversity and Conservation 14, 2633–2652.

Davidson, L., 2002. The 'spirit of the hills': mountaineering in northwest Otago, New Zealand, 1882–1940. Tourism Geographies 4, 44–61.

Davis, D.C., Tisdell, C.A., 1995. Recreational scuba diving and carrying capacity in marine protected areas. Ocean and Coastal Management 26, 19–40.

Davis, D.C., Tisdell, C.A., 1996. Economic management of recreational scuba diving and the environment. Journal of Environmental Management 48, 229–248.

Davis, D.C., Tisdell, C.A., 1998. Tourist levies and willingness to pay for a whale shark experience. Tourism Economics 5, 161–174.

Davis, D.C., Banks, S., Birtles, A., Valentine, P., Cuthill, M., 1997. Whale sharks in Ningaloo Marine Park: managing tourism in an Australian marine protected area. Tourism Management 18, 259–271.

Deep Ocean Expeditions, (2009). Innovators in submersible expeditions and adventure. <http://www.deepoceanexpeditions.com> (accessed 06.04.09).

De Walt, K.M., de Walt, B.R., 2002. Participant Observation: A Guide for Fieldworkers. Rowman Altamira, Lanham, p. 285.

Deibert, M., Aronsson, D., Johnson, R.J., Ettlinger, C., Shealy, J., 1998. Skiing injuries in children, adolescents and adults. Journal of Bone and Joint Surgery [American Volume] 80, 25–32.

Delle Fave, A., Bassi, M., Massimini, F., 2003. Quality of experience and risk perception in high-altitude rock climbing. Journal of Applied Sport Psychology 15, 82–98.

Dewhurst, H., Thomas, R., 2003. Encouraging sustainable business practices in a non-regulatory environment: a case study of small tourism firms in a UK national park. Journal of Sustainable Tourism 11, 383–403.

Dijst, M., Elbersen, B., Willis, K., 2005. The challenge of multifunctional land use in rural areas. Journal of Environmental Planning Management 48, 3–6.

Dimmock, K., 2007. Scuba diving, snorkeling, and free diving. In: Jennings, G. (Ed.), Water-based Tourism, Sport, Leisure, and Recreation Experiences. Elsevier, Oxford, pp. 128–147.

Dixon, J.A., Scura, L.F., Van't Hof, T., 1993. Meeting ecological and economic goals: marine parks in the Caribbean. Ambio 22, 117–125.

Dolnicar, S., Fluker, M., 2003. Behavioural market segments among surf tourists: investigating past destination choice. Journal of Sport and Tourism 8, 186–196.

Domagalski, T.A., Steelman, L.A., 2007. The impact of gender and organizational status on workplace anger expression. Management Communication Quarterly 20, 297–315.

Dowling, R.K., 2006. Cruise Ship Tourism. CAB International, Wallingford, p. 441.

Dowling, R.K., Sharp, J., 1997. Conservation–tourism partnerships in Western Australia. Tourism Recreation Research 22, 55–60.

Duane, T.P., 1999. Shaping the Sierra: Nature, Culture and Conflict in the Changing West. University of California Press, Berkeley.

Duane, T.P., 2004. Success and challenges: managing growth in the Sierra Nevada. In: Taylor, L., Ryall, A. (Eds.), Sustainable Mountain Communities. The Banff Centre, pp. 11–18.

Duffus, D., 1996. The recreational use of grey whales in southern Clayoquot Sound, Canada. Applied Geography 16, 179–190.

Duffus, D.A., Dearden, P., 1993. Recreational use, valuation, and management of killer whales (Orcinus orca) on Canada's Pacific Coast. Environmental Conservation 20, 149–156.

Eagles, P.F.J., McCool, S.F., 2002. Tourism in National Parks and Protected Areas: Planning and Management. CAB International, Oxford.

Easthope, G., 2007. Sail training adventures. In: Jennings, G. (Ed.), Water-based Tourism, Sport, Leisure, and Recreation Experiences. Elsevier, Oxford, pp. 207–220.

English, D.B.K., Bowker, J.M., 1996a. Economic impacts of guided whitewater rafting: a study of five rivers. Water Sources Bulletin 32, 1319–1328.

English, D.B.K., Bowker, J.M., 1996b. Sensitivity of whitewater rafting consumers surplus to pecuniary travel cost specifications. Journal of Environmental Management 47, 79–91.

Ewert, A.W., 1985. Why people climb: the relationship of participant motives and experience level to mountaineering. Journal of Leisure Research 17, 241–250.

Ewert, A.W., 1989. Outdoor Adventure Pursuits: Foundations, Models and Theories. Publishing Horizons, Scottsdale, AZ.

Ewert, A.W., 1994. Playing the edge: motivation and risk taking in a high-altitude wildernesslike environment. Environment and Behaviour 26, 3–24.

Ewert, A.W., Hollenhorst, S., 1989. Testing the adventure model: empirical support for a model of risk recreation participation. Journal of Leisure Research 21, 124–139.

Ewert, A.W., Hollenhorst, S.J., 1997. Adventure recreation and its implications for wilderness. International Journal of Wilderness 3, 21–26.

Ewert, A.W., Jamieson, L., 2003. Current status and future directions in the adventure tourism industry. In: Wilks, J., Page, S.J. (Eds.), Managing Tourist Health and Safety in the New Millennium. Pergamon, Oxford, pp. 67–83.

Ezzedine, K., Heenen, M., Malvy, D., 2007. Imported cutaneous melioidosis in traveler, Belgium (letter to the editor) (clinical report). Emerging Infectious Diseases 13 (6), 946–948.

Fahey, B., Wardle, K., Weir, P., 1999. Environmental effects associated with snow grooming and skiing at Treble Cone Ski Field. Science for Conservation 120, 49–62.

Falk, M., 2008. A hedonic price model for ski lift tickets. Tourism Management 29 (6), 1172–1184.

Farmer, R.J., 1992. Surfing: motivations, values and culture. Journal of Sport Behavior 15, 241–257.

Farris, M.A., 1998. The effects of rock climbing on the vegetation of three Minnesota cliff systems. Canadian Journal of Botany 76, 1–10.

Federiuk, C.S., Schlueter, J.L., Adams, A.L., 2002. Skiing, snowboarding, and sledding injuries in a northwestern state. Wilderness and Environmental Medicine 13, 245–249.

Feher, P., Meyers, M.C., Skelly, W.A., 1998. Psychological profile of rock climbers: state and trait attributes. Journal of Sport Behavior 21, 167–180.

Fennell, D., 2002. Ecotourism Programme Planning. CAB International, Wallingford.

Fennell, D., Dowling, R., 2003. Ecotourism Policy and Planning. CAB International, Oxford.

Findlay, K.P., 1997. Attitudes and expenditures of whale watchers in Hermanus, South Africa. South African Journal of Wildlife Research 27, 57–62.

Finlay, L., 2002a. "Outing" the researcher: the provenance, process and practice of reflexivity. Qualitative Health Research 12, 531–545.

Finlay, L., 2002b. Negotiating the swamp: the opportunity and challenge of reflexivity in research practice. Qualitative Research 2, 209–230

Fix, P., Loomis, J.B., 1997. The economic benefits of mountain biking at one of its Meccas: an application of the travel cost method to mountain biking in Moab, Utah. Journal of Leisure Research 39, 342–352.

Fluker, M.R., Turner, L.W., 2000. Needs, motivations, and expectations of a commercial whitewater rafting experience. Journal of Travel Research 38, 380–389.

Folke, J., Hammer Ostrup, J., Gössling, S., 2006. Ecotourist choices of transport modes. In: Gössling, S., Hultman, J. (Eds.), Ecotourism in Scandinavia: Lessons in Theory and Practice. CAB International, Wallingford, pp. 154–165.

Forbes, B., Monz, C., Tolvanen, A., 2004. Ecological impacts of tourism in terrestrial polar ecosystems. In: Buckley, R.C. (Ed.), Environmental Impacts of Ecotourism. CAB International, Wallingford, pp. 155–170.

Formica, S., Uysal, M., 2006. Destination attractiveness based on supply and demand evaluations: an analytical framework. Journal of Travel Research 44, 418–430.

Franklin, A., Crang, M., 2001. The trouble with tourism and travel theory? Tourist Studies 1, 5–22.

Frechtling, D.C., 2006. An assessment of visitor expenditure methods and models. Journal of Travel Research 45, 26–36.

Fredman, P., Herberlein, T.A., 2003. Changes in skiing and snowmobiling in Swedish Mountains. Annals of Tourism Research 30, 485–488.

Freeman, A.N.D., 2004. Constraints to community groups monitoring plants and animals in rainforest revegetation sites on the Atherton Tablelands of far north Queensland. Ecological Management and Restoration 5, 199–204.

Frohoff, T.G., 2005. Stress in dolphins. In: Bekoff, M. (Ed.), Encyclopedia of Animal Behavior. Greenwood Publishing Group, New York, pp. 1158–1164.

Fyall, A., Garrod, B., 2005. Tourism Marketing: a Collaborative Approach. Channel View, Clevedon, p. 383.

Garrick, J.G., Kurland, L.T., 1971. The epidemiological significance of unreported ski injuries. Journal of Safety Research 3, 182–187.

Garrod, B., Fennell, D.A., 2004. An analysis of whalewatching codes of conduct. Annals of Tourism Research 31, 334–352.

Getz, D., Brown, G., 2006. Benchmarking wine tourism development. International Journal of Wine Marketing 18, 78–97.

Giard, D., 1997. The situation regarding nature sport tourism in mountain areas. Cahiers Espaces (1997): 48–57.

Gibson, C., 2008. Locating geographies of tourism. Progress in Human Geography 32 (3), 407–423.

Giese, M., 1996. Effects of human activity on Adelie penguins, Pygoscelis adeliae, breeding success. Biological Conservation 75, 157–164.

Giese, M., 1998. Guidelines for people approaching breeding groups of Adelie penguins. Polar Record 34, 287–292.

Giese, M., Riddle, M., 1999. Disturbance of emperor penguin Aptenodytes forsteri chicks by helicopters. Polar Biology 22, 366–371.

Giese, M., Handsworth, R., Stephenson, R., 1999. Measuring resting heart rates in penguins using an artificial egg. Journal of Field Ornithology 70, 59–53.

Gilbert, D., Hudson, S., 2000. Tourism demand constraints: a skiing participation. Annals of Tourism Research 27, 906–925.

Gjerdalen, G., Williams, P., 2000. An evaluation of the utility of a whale watching code of conduct. Tourism Recreation Research 25, 27–37.

Glorioso, R.S., 1999. Amenity migration in the Sumava Bioregion, Czech Republic: implications for ecological integrity. In: Godde, P.M., Price, M.F., Zimmerman, F.M. (Eds.), Tourism and Development in Mountain Regions. CAB International, Wallingford, pp. 275–296.

Godde, P.M., Price, M.F., Zimmerman, F.M. (Eds.), 2000. Tourism and Development in Mountain Regions. CAB International, Wallingford.

Goeft, U., Alder, J., 2000. Mountain bike rider preferences and perceptions in the south-west of Western Australia. CALM Science 3, 261–275.

Goeldner, C.R., Brent Ritchie, J.R., 2005. Tourism: Principles, Practice, Philosophies. Wiley, New York, p. 590.

Gordijn, H., De Vries, A., 2004. Tweede woningen in het buitenland (Second homes abroad). Ruimte in Debat 1, 16–17 (in Dutch), cited in Djist et al., 2005.

Gordon, J., Leaper, R., Hartley, F.G., Chappell, O., 1992. Effects of Whale Watching Vessels on the Surface and Underwater Acoustic Behavior of Sperm Whales off Kaikoura, New Zealand. Department of Conservation, Wellington, New Zealand.

Gössling, S., Hall, C., Weaver, D. (Eds.), 2009. Sustainable Tourism Futures. Routledge, New York.

Goulet, C., Regnier, G., Grimard, G., Valois, P., Villeneueve, P., 1999. Risk factors associated with alpine skiing injuries in children: a case–control study. American Journal of Sports Medicine 27, 644–650.

Gray, M., Kalpers, J., 2005. Ranger based monitoring in the Virunga-Bwindi Region of East-Central Africa: a simple data collection tool for park management. Biodiversity and Conservation 14, 2723–2741.

Green, E., Donnelly, R., 2003. Recreational scuba diving in Caribbean marine protected areas: do the users pay? Ambio 32, 140–144.

Grijalva, T.C., Berrens, R.P., Bohara, A.K., Jakus, P.M., Shaw, W.D., 2002. Valuing the loss of rock climbing access in wilderness areas: a national-level, random-utility model. Land Economics 78, 103–120.

Gyimothy, S., Mykletun, R.J., 2004. Play in adventure tourism: the case of Arctic trekking. Annals of Tourism Research 51, 855–878.

Hadley, G.L., Wilson, K.R., 2004. Patterns of small mammal density and survival following ski-run development. Journal of Mammalogy 85, 97–104.

Hadwen, W.L., Hill, W., Pickering, C.M., 2007. Icons under threat: why monitoring visitors and their ecological impacts in protected areas matters. Ecological Management and Restoration 8, 177–181.

Hadwen, W.L., Hill, W., Pickering, C.M., 2008. Linking visitor impact research to visitor impact monitoring in protected areas. Journal of Ecotourism 7, 87–93.

Hagel, B.E., Goulet, C., Platt, R.W., Pless, B., 2004. Injuries among skiers and snowboarders in Quebec. Epidemiology 15, 279–286.

Hales, R., 2006. Mountaineering. In: Buckley, R.C. (Ed.), Adventure Tourism. CAB International, Wallingford, pp. 260–285.

Hall, C., 2008. Tourism and climate change: knowledge gaps and issues. Tourism Recreation Research 33, 339–350.

Hall, C., Higham, J., 2005. Tourism, Recreation and Climate Change. Channel View, Clevedon.

Hall, C.M., McArthur, S., 1991. Commercial whitewater rafting in Australia: motivations and expectations of the participants and the relevance of group size for the rafting experience. Australian Journal of Leisure and Recreation 1, 25–31.

Hall, C.M., Page, S.J., 2006. The Geography of Tourism and Recreation: Environment, Place and Space. Routledge, London.

Hall, M., Wouters, M., 1994. Managing nature tourism in the Sub-Antarctic. Annals of Tourism Research 21, 355–374.

Hammit, W.E., Cole, D.N., 1997. Wildland Recreation: Ecology and Management. Wiley, New York.

Hanley, N., 2002. Rationing an open-access resource: mountaineering in Scotland. Land Use Policy 19, 167–176.

Hanley, N., Koop, G., Alvarez-Farizo, B., Wright, R.E., Nevin, C., 2001. Go climb a mountain: an application of recreation demand modelling to rock climbing in Scotland. Journal of Agricultural Economics 51, 36–52.

Hanley, N., Shaw, W.S., Wright, R.E., 2003. The New Economics of Outdoor Recreation. Edward Elgar, Cheltenham.

Harriott, V.J., Davis, D., Banks, S.A., 1997. Recreational diving and its impact in marine protected areas in eastern Australia. Ambio 26, 173–179.

Hashimoto, A., Telfer, D.J., 2006. Selling Canadian culinary tourism: branding the global and the regional product. Tourism Geographies 8, 31–55.

Hawkins, J.P., Roberts, C.M., 1992. Effects of recreational scuba diving on fore-reef slope communities of coral reefs. Biological Conservation 62, 171–178.

Hawkins, J.P., Roberts, C.M., 1993. Effects of recreational scuba diving on coral reefs: trampling on reef flat communities. Journal of Applied Ecology 30, 25–30.

Hawkins, J.P., Roberts, C.M., 1994. The growth of coastal tourism in the Red Sea: present and future effects on coral reefs. Ambio 23, 503–507.

Hawkins, J.P., Roberts, C.M., 1997. Estimating the carrying capacity of coral reefs for recreational scuba diving. In: Lessios, H.A., Macintyre, I.G. (Eds.) Proceedings of the Eighth Coral Reef Symposium, Vol. 2, 1923–1926. Smithsonian Tropical Research Institute, Panama.

Hawkins, J.P., Roberts, C.M., Van't Hof, T., De Meyer, K., Tratalos, J., Aldam, C., 1999. Effects of recreational scuba diving on Caribbean coral and fish communities. Conservation Biology 13, 888–897.

Heberlein, T.A., Breymeyer, A., Noble, R., 1996. Recreation and tourism management in protected areas. In: Breymeyer, A., Noble, R., Dee, S. (Eds.), Biodiversity Conservation in Transboundary Protected Areas: Proceedings of an International Workshop, Bieszczady and Tatra National Parks, Poland, May 15–25, 1994, pp. 203–209. National Academics Press, Washington.

Heino, R., 2000. What is so punk about snowboarding? Journal of Sport and Social Issues 24, 176–191.

Hendee, J.C., Dawson, C.P., 2002. Wilderness Management, third ed. Fulcrum, Golden, Colorado.

Henderson, J.C., 2007. Uniquely Singapore? A case study in destination branding. Journal of Vacation Marketing 13, 261–274.

Hernández, J.M., León, C.J., 2007. The interactions between natural and physical capitals in the tourist lifecycle model. Ecological Economics 62, 184–193.

Hertz, R., 1996. Introduction: ethics, reflexivity and voice. Qualitative Sociology 19, 1–3.

Hertz, R. (Ed.), 1997. Reflexivity and Voice. Sage, Thousand Oaks.

Higginbottom, K., 2004. Wildlife Tourism: Impacts, Management and Planning. Common Ground Publishing, Altona.

Higgins, B.R., 1996. The global structure of the nature tourism industry: ecotourists, tour operators, and local businesses. Journal of Travel Research 35, 11–19.

Higham, J. (Ed.), 2005. Sport Tourism Destinations: Issues, Opportunities and Analysis. Elsevier, Oxford.

Higham, J., Lusseau, D., 2004. Ecological impacts and management of tourist engagements with cetaceans. In: Buckley, R. (Ed.), Environmental Impacts of Ecotourism. CAB International, Wallingford, pp. 171–186.

Higham, J.E.S., Lück, M., 2008. Marine Wildlife and Tourism Management. CAB International, Wallingford.

Higham, J.E.S., Lusseau, D., 2007. Urgent need for empirical research into whaling and whale watching. Conservation Biology 21, 554–558.

Ho, P.S.Y., McKercher, B., 2004. Managing heritage resources as tourism products. Asia Pacific Journal of Tourism Research 9, 255–266.

Hoegh-Guldberg, O., Mumby, P.J., Hooten, A.J., Steneck, R.S., Greenfield, P., Gomez, E., Harvell, C.D., Sale, P.F., Edwards, A.J., Caldeira, K., Knowlton, N., Eakin, C.M., Iglesias-Prieto, R., Muthiga, N., Bradbury, R.H., Dubi, A., Hatziolos, M.E., 2007. Coral reefs under rapid climate change and ocean acidification. Science 318 (5857), 1737.

Hollenhorst, S., Schuett, M.A., Olson, D., Chavez, D.J., 1995. An examination of the characteristics, preferences, and attitudes of mountain bike users of the national forests. Journal of Park and Recreation Administration 13, 41–51.

Holloway, J.C., 2004. Marketing for Tourism. Prentice-Hall, London, p. 510.

Holmes, N., Giese, M., Kriwoken, L.K., 2005. Testing the minimum approach distance guidelines for incubating Royal penguins Eudyptes schlegeli. Biological Conservation 126 (3), 339–350.

Holt, M.M., Noren, D.P., Veirs, V., Emmons, C.K., Veirs, S., 2009. Speaking up: killer whales increase their call amplitude in response to vessel noise. The Journal of the Acoustical Society of America 125 (1), EL27–EL32.

Holyfield, L., 1999. Manufacturing adventure: the buying and selling of emotions. Journal of Contemporary Ethnography 28, 3–32.

Howard, J., 1999. How do SCUBA diving operators in Vanuatu attempt to minimize their impact on the environment. Pacific Tourism Review 3, 61–69.

Hoyer, K., 2000. Sustainable tourism or sustainable mobility? The Norwegian case. Journal of Sustainable Tourism 8, 147–160.

Hoyt, E., 2000. Whale-Watching 2000: Worldwide Tourism Numbers, Expenditures, and Expanding Socioeconomic Benefits. International Fund for Animal Welfare, Crowborough.

Hudson, S., 2002. Sport and Adventure Tourism. Haworth Hospitality Press, New York.

Hudson, S., Beedie, P., 2006. From Inuits in skin boats to Bobos on the high seas: the commodification of sea kayaking through tourism. Tourism in Marine Environments 2, 65–77.

Hughes, R., 2001. Animals, values and tourism – structural shifts in United Kingdom dolphin tourism provision. Tourism Management 22, 321–330.

Hunter, L.M., Boardman, J.D., Saint Onge, J., 2004. The Association Between Natural Amenities, Rural Population Growth and Long-term Residents' Economic Well-Being. University of Colorado at Boulder, Institute of Behavioural Sciences, Research Program on Environment & Behaviour, Working Paper EB2004-0005. University of Colorado, Boulder, CO, p. 38.

Ibex Expeditions, 2009. Expeditions and exploratories. <http://www.ibexexpeditions.com/expeditions-exploratories.html> (accessed 03.02.09).

Illich, I.P., Haslett, J.R., 1994. Responses of assemblages of Orthoptera to management and use of ski slopes on upper subalpine meadows in the Austrian Alps. Oceologia 97, 470–474.

Jaakson, R., 1988. River recreation boating impacts. Journal of Waterway, Port. Coastal and Ocean Engineering 114, 363–367.

Jack, S.J., Ronan, K.R., 1998. Sensation seeking among high and low risk sports participants. Personality and Individual Differences 25, 1063–1083.

Jakus, P., Shaw, W.D., 1996. An empirical analysis of rock climber's response to hazard warnings. Risk Analysis 16, 581–585.

Jameson, S.C., Ammar, M.S.A., Saadalla, E., Mostafa, H.M., Riegl, B., 1999. A coral damage index and its application to diving sites in the Egyptian Red Sea. Coral Reefs 18, 333–339.

Janik, V.M., Thompson, P.M., 1996. Changes in surfacing patterns of bottlenose dolphins in response to boat traffic. Marine Mammal Science 12, 597–602.

Japan Probe, 2007. Whale-watching tourists watch in horror as whaling ship harpoons and kills whale. <www.japanprobe.com/?p=2601>; (accessed 11.06.09).

Jenkins, O.H., 2003. Photography and travel brochures: the circle of representation Tourism Geographies 5, 305–328.

Jennings, G., 2003. Marine tourism. In: Hudson, S. (Ed.), Sport and Adventure Tourism. Haworth Hospitality Press, Binghamton, pp. 125–164.

Jennings, G., 2007a. Water-based Tourism, Sport, Leisure, and Recreation Experiences. Elsevier, Oxford, p. 260.

Jennings, G., 2007b. Sailing/cruising. In: Jennings, G. (Ed.), Water-Based Tourism, Sport, Leisure, and Recreation Experiences. Elsevier, Oxford, pp. 23–45.

Jennings, G., 2007c. Motorboating. In: Jennings, G. (Ed.), Water-Based Tourism, Sport, Leisure, and Recreation Experiences. Elsevier, Oxford, pp. 46–63.

Jim, C.Y., 1989. Visitor management in recreation areas. Environmental Conservation 16, 19–32.

Johnson, B., Edwards, T., 1994. The commodification on mountaineering. Annals of Tourism Research 21, 459–478.

Johnson, J., 2004. Impacts of tourism-related in-migration: the Greater Yellowstone region. In: Buckley, R. (Ed.), Environmental Impacts of Ecotourism. CAB International, Wallingford, pp. 171–186.

Johnson, J., Godwin, I., 2006. Ice climbing. In: Buckley, R.C. (Ed.), Adventure Tourism. CAB International, Wallingford, pp. 245–259.

Johnson, J., Rasker, R., 1995. The role of economic and quality of life values in rural business location. Journal of Rural Studies 11, 405–416.

Johnson, J., Maxwell, B., Aspinall, R., 2003. Moving nearer to heaven: growth and change in the Greater Yellowstone region, USA. In: Buckley, R.C., Pickering, C., Weaver, D.B. (Eds.), Nature-Based Tourism, Environment and Land Management. CAB International, Oxford, pp. 77–88.

Johnson, R.J., Ettlinger, C.F., Shealy, J.F., Meader, C., 1997. Impact of super sidecut skis on the epidemiology study of skiing injuries. Sportverletz Sportschaden 11, 150–152.

Kane, M.J., Zink, R., 2007. Package adventure tours: markets in serious leisure careers. In: Weed, M. (Ed.), Sport and Tourism: A Reader. Routledge, New York, pp. 207–223.

Karxzmarski, L., Cockcroft, V.G., McLachlan, A., Winter, P.E.D., 1998. Recommendations for the conservation and management of humpback dolphins, *Sousa chinensis* in the Algoa Bay Region, South Africa. Koedoe 41, 121–130.

Kastenholz, E., 2004. 'Management of demand' as a tool in sustainable tourist destination development. Journal of Sustainable Tourism 12, 388–408.

Kayastha, S.L., 1997. Tourism and environment in the Himalayan region. In: Nag, P., Kumra, V.K., Singh, J. (Eds.), Geography and Environment: Volume Two. Regional Issues. Concept Publishing Company, India.

Kerkvliet, J., Nowell, C., 2000. Tools for recreation management in parks: the case of the Greater Yellowstone's blue-ribbon fishery. Ecological Economics 34, 89–100.

Killion, L., 2007. Sport fishing and big game fishing. In: Jennings, G. (Ed.), Water-based Tourism, Sport, Leisure, and Recreation Experiences. Elsevier, Oxford, pp. 112–127.

King, R., Beeton, S., 2006. Influence of mass media's coverage of adventure tourism on youth perceptions of risk. Tourism Culture and Communication 6, 161–169.

Knopf, R.C., Peterson, G.L., Leatherberry, E.C., 1983. Motives for recreational river floating: relative consistency across settings. Leisure Research 5, 6–17.

Knowles, P., Allardice, D., 1992. White Water Nepal. Menasha Ridge, Birmingham. Alabama and Rivers Publishing, Surrey.

Kovacs, K.M., Innes, S., 1990. The impact of tourism on harp seals (Phoca groenlandica) in the Gulf of St. Lawrence, Canada. Applied Animal Behaviour Science 26, 15–26.

Laden, G.D.M., Purdy, G., O'Rielly, G., 2007. Cold injury to a diver's hand after a 90-min dive in 6°C water. Aviation. Space and Environmental Medicine 78, 523–525.

Laing, J., Crouch, G., 2008. Submersible. In: Lück, M. (Ed.), The Encyclopaedia of Tourism and Recreation in Marine Environments. CAB International, Wallingford, pp. 457–458.

Lamers, M., Stel, J., Amelung, B., 2007. Antarctic adventure tourism and private expeditions. In: Snyder, J., Stonehouse, B. (Eds.), Prospects for Polar Tourism. CAB International, Wallingford, pp. 170–187.

Lamprey, R.H., Reid, R.S., 2004. Expansion of human settlement in Kenya's Maasai Mara: what future for pastoralism and wildlife? Journal of Biogeography 21, 997–1032.

Landau, D., Splettstoesser, J., 2007. Antarctic tourism: what are the limits? In: Snyder, J., Stonehouse, B. (Eds.), Prospects for Polar Tourism. CAB International, Wallingford, pp. 197–209.

Last Descents, 2009. Rafting in China. Your adventure of a lifetime may save a river. <http://www.lastdescents.com/> (accessed 05.06.09).

Laws, E., Semone, P., 2009. The Mekong: developing new tourism region. In: Prideaux, B., Cooper, M. (Eds.), River Tourism. CAB International, Wallingford, pp. 55–73.

Lazarow, N., 2007. The value of coastal recreational resources: a case study approach to examine the value of recreational surfing to specific locales. Journal of Coastal Research 50, 12–20.

Lazarow, N., Miller, M.L., Blackwell, B., 2008. The value of recreational surfing to society. Tourism in Marine Environments 5, 145–158.

Lee, C.F., King, B., 2006. Assessing destination competitiveness: an application to the hot springs tourism sector. Tourism and Hospitality: Planning and Development 3, 179–197.

Lemelin, R.H., Smale, B., 2006. Effect of environmental context on the experience of polar bear viewers in Churchill, Manitoba. Journal of Ecotourism 5, 176–191.

Leung, Y., Marion, J., 1999a. Spatial strategies for managing visitor impact in national parks. Journal of Park and Recreation Administration 17, 2–38.

Leung, Y.F., Marion, J.L., 1999b. Characterizing backcountry impacts in Great Smoky Mountains National Park, USA. Journal of Environmental Management 57, 193–203.

Leung, Y.F., Marion, J.L., 1999c. Assessing trail conditions in protected areas: application of a problem-assessment method in Great Smoky National Park, USA. Environmental Conservation 26, 270–279.

Leung, Y.F., Marion, J.L., 1999d. The influence of sampling interval on the accuracy of trail impact assessment. Landscape and Urban Planning 43, 167–179.

Leung, Y.F., Marion, J.L., 2004. Managing impacts of camping. In: Buckley, R.C. (Ed.), Environmental Impacts of Ecotourism. CAB International, Wallingford, pp. 245–258.

Levy, A.S., Hawkes, A.P., Hemminger, L.M., Knights, S., 2002. An analysis of head injuries among skiers and snowboarders. Journal of Trauma 53, 695–704.

Lew, A.A., Hall, C.M., 1998. The Asia-Pacific ecotourism industry: putting sustainable tourism into practice. In: Hall, C.M., Lew, A. (Eds.), Sustainable Tourism: A Geographical Perspective. Addison Wesley Longman Ltd, Harlow.

Lewis, A., Newsome, D., 2003. Planning for stingray tourism at Hamelin Bay, Western Australia: the importance of stakeholder perspectives. International Journal of Tourism Research 5, 331–346.

Li, W., 2004. Environmental management indicators for ecotourism in China's nature reserves: a case study in Tianmushan Nature Reserve. Tourism Management 25, 559–564.

Liddle, M.J., 1997. Recreation Ecology: The Ecological Impact of Outdoor Recreation. Kluwer Academic Publishers, Dordrecht.

Lindberg, K., McCool, S., Stankey, G., 1997. Rethinking carrying capacity. Annals of Tourism Research 24, 461–465.

Lipscombe, N., 1999. The relevance of the peak experience to continued skydiving participation: a qualitative approach to assessing motivations. Leisure Studies 18, 267–288.

Littlefair, C.J., 2004. Reducing impacts through interpretation, Lamington National Park. In: Buckley, R.C. (Ed.), Environmental Impacts of Ecotourism. CAB International, Wallingford, pp. 297–307.

Livet, R., 1997. From sports diving to underwater tourism. Cahiers Espaces 1997, 62–68.

Lockwood, M., Worboys, G., Kothari, A., 2006. Managing Protected Areas: A Global Guide. Earthscan, London.

Loeffler, T.A., 2004. A photo elicitation study of the meanings of outdoor adventure experiences. Journal of Leisure Research 36, 536–556.

Loomis, J., 2006. A comparison of the effect of multiple destination trips on recreation benefits as estimated by travel cost and contingent valuation methods. Journal of Leisure Research 38, 46–51.

Lück, M. (Ed.), 2008. The Encyclopedia of Tourism and Recreation in Marine Environments. CAB International, Wallingford, p. 587.

Lusseau, D., Higham, J., 2004. Managing the impacts of dolphin-based tourism through the definition of critical habitats: the case of bottlenose dolphins (Tursiops spp) in Doubtful Sound, New Zealand. Tourism Management 25, 657–667.

Luzar, E.J., Diagne, A., Gan, C., Henning, B.R., 1995. Evaluating nature-based tourism using the new environmental paradigm. Journal of Agricultural and Applied Economics 27, 544–555.

Luzar, E.J., Diagne, A., Gan, C.E.C., Henning, B.R., 1998. Profiling the nature-based tourist: a multinomial logit approach. Journal of Travel Research 37, 48–55.

Lynch, P., Jonson, P., Dibben, M., 2007. Exploring relationships of trust in 'adventure' recreation. Leisure Studies 26, 47–64.

MacArthur, R.A., Giest, V., Johnston, R.H., 1982. Cardiac and behavioural responses of mountain sheep to human disturbance. Journal of Wildlife Management 46, 351–358.

McCann, R.M., Giles, H., 2007. Age-differentiated communication in organizations: perspectives from Thailand and the United States. Communication Research Reports 24, 1–12.

McCool, S.F., Lime, D.W., 2001. Tourism carrying capacity: tempting fantasy or useful reality. Journal of Sustainable Tourism 9, 372–388.

McCool, S.F., Moisey, R.N. (Eds.), 2001. Tourism, Recreation and Sustainability. CAB International, Oxford.

McCool, S.F., Stankey, G.H., 2001. Managing access to wildlands for recreation in the USA: background and issues relevant to sustaining tourism. Journal of Sustainable Tourism 9, 389–399.

McIntosh, A.J., 2004. Tourists' appreciation of Maori culture in New Zealand. Tourism Management 25, 1–15.

McIntyre, N., 1992. Involvement in risk recreation: a comparison of objective and subjective measures of engagement. Journal of Leisure Research 24, 64–71.

McIntyre, N., Roggenbuck, J.W., 1998. Nature/person transactions during an outdoor adventure experience: a multi-phasic analysis. Journal of Leisure Research 30, 401–422.

McIntyre, N., Jenkins, J., Booth, K., 2001. Global influences on access: the changing face of access to public conservation lands in New Zealand. Journal of Sustainable Tourism 9, 434–450.

MacLellan, L.R., 1999. An examination of wildlife tourism as a sustainable form of tourism development in North West Scotland. International Journal of Tourism Research 1, 375–387.

McNamee, M.J., 2007. Philosophy, Risk and Adventure Sports. Routledge, Oxon, p. 202.

Machold, W., Kwasny, O., Gabler, P., 2000. Risk of injury through snowboarding. Journal of Trauma 48, 1109–1114.

Machold, W., Kwansy, O., Eisenhardt, P., Kolonja, A., Bauer, E., Lehr, S., Mayr, W., Fuchs, M., 2002. Reduction of severe wrist injuries in snowboarding by an optimized wrist protection device: a prospective randomized trial. Journal of Trauma 52, 517–520.

Macnab, A.J., Smith, T., Gagnon, F.A., Macnab, M., 2002. Effect of helmet wear on the incidence of head/face and cervical spine injuries in young skiers and snowboarders. Injury Prevention 8, 324–327.

Malcolm, M., 2001. Mountaineering fatalities in Mt Cook National Park. New Zealand Journal of Medicine 114, 78–80.

Mallett, J., 1998. Plenary Address. Seventh World Congress of Adventure Travel and Ecotourism. Ecuador, Quito.

Mallick, S.A., Driessen, M.M., 2003. Feeding of wildlife: how effective are the 'keep wildlife wild' signs in Tasmania's national parks? Ecological Management and Restoration 4, 199–237.

Mangun, J.C., Mangun, W.C., 2002. Wildlife watchers in the western United States: a structural approach for understanding policy change. Human Dimensions of Wildlife 7, 123–137.

Manning, R., 1999. Studies in Outdoor Recreation, second ed. Oregon UP, Corvallis.

Manning, R.E., 2004. Managing impacts of ecotourism through use rationing and allocation. In: Buckley, R. (Ed.), Environmental Impacts of Ecotourism. CAB International, Wallingford, pp. 273–286.

Manning, R.E., Ballinger, N.L., Marion, J., Roggenbuck, J., 1996. Recreation management in natural areas: problems and practices, status and trends. Natural Areas Journal 16, 142–146.

Mansergh, I.M., Scotts, D.J., 1989. Habitat continuity and social organization of the mountain pygmy-possum restored by tunnel. Journal of Wildlife Management 53, 701–707.

Marion, J.L., Rogers, C.G., 1994. The applicability of terrestrial visitor impact management strategies to the protection of coral reefs. Ocean and Coastal Management 22, 153–163.

Marsh, J., 2000. Tourism and national parks in polar regions. In: Butler, R.W., Boyd, S.W. (Eds.), Tourism and National Parks: Issues and Implications. John Wiley & Sons, Chichester, pp. 125–136.

Marshall, A.J., Nardiyono, Engstrom, L.M., Pamungkas, B., Palapa, J., Meijaard, E., Stanley, S.A., 2006. The blowgun is mightier than the chainsaw in determining population density of Bornean orangutans (*Pongo pygmaeus morio*) in the forests of East Kalimantan. Biological Conservation 129, 566–578.

Martin, P., Priest, S., 1986. Understanding the adventure experience. Journal of Adventure Education 3, 18–21.

Mason, P., 2007. 'No better than a band-aid for a bullet wound!': the effectiveness of tourism codes of conduct. In: Black, R., Crabtree, A. (Eds.), Quality Assurance and Certification in Ecotourism. CAB International, Wallingford, pp. 46–64.

Massyn, P.J., 2008. Citizen participation in the lodge sector of the Okavango Delta. In: Spenceley, A. (Ed.), Responsible Tourism: Critical Issues for Conservation and Development. Earthscan, London, pp. 225–237.

Matsumoto, K., Miyamoto, K., Sumi, H., Sumi, Y., Shimizu, K., 2002. Upper extremity injuries in snowboarding and skiing: a comparative study. Clinical Journal of Sport Medicine 12, 354–359.

Mbaiwa, J.E., 2008. The realities of ecotourism development in Botswana. In: Spenceley, A. (Ed.), Responsible Tourism: Critical Issues for Conservation and Development. Earthscan, London, pp. 205–223.

Medio, D., Ormond, R.F.G., Pearson, M., 1997. Effect of briefings on rates of damage to corals by scuba divers. Biological Conservation 79, 91–94.

Mehmetoglu, M., 2007. Typologising nature-based tourists by activity – theoretical and practical implications. Tourism Management 28 (3), 651–660.

Meyer, E., 1993. The impact of summer and winter tourism on the fauna of alpine soils in western Austria. Revue Suisse de Zoologie 100, 519–527.

Mike Wiegele Helicopter Skiing, 2009. Wiegele world is powder. <http://www.wiegele.com> (accessed 04.02.09).

Milazzo, M., Badalamenti, F., Fernandez, T.V., Chemello, R., 2005. Effects of fish feeding by snorkellers on the density and size distribution of fishes in a Mediterranean marine protected area. Marine Biology 146 (6), 1213–1222.

Miller, K., 2007. Compassionate communication in the workplace: exploring processes of noticing, connecting, and responding. Journal of Applied Communication Research 35, 223–245.

Miller, P.J.O., Biasson, N., Samuels, A., Tyack, P.L., 2000. Whale songs lengthen in response to sonar. Nature 405, 903.

Mmopelwa, G., Kgathi, D.L., Molefhe, L., 2007. Tourists' perceptions and their willingness to pay for park fees: a case study of self-drive tourists and clients for mobile tour operators in Moremi Game Reserve, Botswana. Tourism Management 28, 1044–1056.

Mograbi, J., Rogerson, C.M., 2007. Maximising the local pro-poor impacts of dive tourism: Sodwana Bay, South Africa. Urban Forum 18, 85–104.

Moore, S.A., Smith, A.J., Newsome, D.N., 2003. Environmental performance reporting for natural area tourism: contributions by visitor impact management frameworks and their indicators. Journal of Sustainable Tourism 11, 348–375.

More, T.A., Averill, J.R., 2003. The structure of recreation behavior. Journal of Leisure Research 35, 372–395.

Morgan, D., 2006. Analyzing the risk of drowning at surf beaches. Tourism Review International 10, 125–130.

Morgan, D., Fluker, M., 2006. Risk management for Australian commercial adventure tourism operations. In: Mansfield, Y., Pizam, A. (Eds.), Tourism, Security and Safety: From Theory to Practice. Elsevier, Burlington, pp. 153–168.

Moscardo, G., 2007. One-day boating adventures. In: Jennings, G. (Ed.), Water-based Tourism, Sport, Leisure, and Recreation Experiences. Elsevier, Oxford, pp. 187–206.

Moscardo, G., Taverner, M., Woods, B., 2006. When wildlife encounters go wrong: tourist safety issues associated with threatening wildlife. In: Mansfield, Y., Pizam, A. (Eds.), Tourism, Security and Safety: From Theory to Practice. Elsevier, Burlington, pp. 209–228.

Mosisch, T.D., Arthington, A.H., 2004. Impacts of recreational power-boating on freshwater ecosystem. In: Buckley, R. (Ed.), Environmental Impacts of Ecotourism. CAB International, Wallingford, pp. 171–186.

Moss, L.A., 2004. Amenity migration: global phenomenon and strategic paradigm for sustaining mountain environmental quality. In: Taylor, L., Ryall, A. (Eds.), Sustainable Mountain Communities. The Banff Centre, pp. 19–24.

Moss, L.A., 2005. Introduction. In: Moss, L.A. (Ed.), The Amenity Migrants. CAB International, Wallingford (this volume).

Moss, L. (Ed.), 2006. The Amenity Migrants. CAB International, Wallingford.

Moss, L.A.G., Glorioso, R.S., 1999. Baguio Bioregion, Philippines: formulating a strategy for tourism, amenity migration and urban growth. In: Price, M.F., Wachs, T., Byers, E. (Eds.), Mountains of the World: Tourism and Sustainable Mountain Development, Creating Opportunities in the 21st Century, Mountain Agenda, Centre for Development and Environment. University of Berne, Berne.

Muir, F., 1993. Managing tourism to a seabird nesting island. Tourism Management 14, 99–105.

Mundet, L., Ribera, L., 2001. Characteristics of divers at a Spanish resort. Tourism Management 22, 501–510.

Musa, G., 2003. Sipadan: an over-exploited scuba-diving paradise? An analysis of tourism impact, diver satisfaction and management priorities. In: Garrod, B., Wilson, J.C. (Eds.), Marine Ecotourism: Issues and Experiences. Channel View, Clevedon, pp. 122–137.

Nathanson, A., Haynes, P., Galanis, D., 2002. Surfing injuries. American Journal of Emergency Medicine 20, 155–150.

National Association of Underwater Instructors, (2005). Dive Safety Through Education. NAUI Worldwide. <http://www.naui.org> (accessed 27.5.09).

Natural Habitat Adventures, 2009. The nature people. <http://www.nathab.com/> (accessed 25.02.09).

Neil, D., 1990. Potential for coral stress due to sediment resuspension and deposition by reef walkers. Biological Conservation 52, 221–227.

Neumann, P.W., Merriam, H.G., 1972. Ecological effects of snowmobiles. Canadian Field Naturalist 86, 207–212.

Newby, E., 1986. A Book of Travellers' Tales. Collins, London.

Newbery, B., 1997. In League with Captain Nemo. Geographical 69 (2), 35–41.

Newsome, D., Cole, D.N., Marion, J.L., 2004a. Environmental impacts associated with recreational horse-riding. In: Buckley, R.C. (Ed.), Environmental Impacts of Ecotourism. CAB International, Wallingford, pp. 61–82.

Newsome, D., Dowling, R., Moore, S., 2005. Wildlife Tourism. Channel View, Clevedon.

Newsome, D., Lewis, A., Moncrieff, D., 2004b. Impacts and risks associated with developing, but unsupervised, stingray tourism at Hamelin Bay, Western Australia. International Journal of Tourism Research 6, 305–323.

Newsome, D., Milewski, A., Philips, N., Annear, R., 2002. Effects of horseriding on national parks and other natural ecosystems in Australia. Journal of Ecotourism 1, 52–74.

Newsome, D., Smith, A., Moore, S.A., 2008. Horse riding in protected areas: a critical review and implications for research and management. Currents Issues in Tourism 11, 144–166.

Nichols, C., Stone, G., Hutt, A., Brown, J., Yoshinaga, A., 2000. Observations of interactions between Hector's Dolphins (Cephalorhynchus hectori), boats and people at Akaroa Harbour, New Zealand. In: Science for Conservation, vol. 178. Department of Conservation, Wellington, New Zealand.

North Island, 2009. <www.north-island.com/>; (accessed 25.02.09).

Northeast Natural Resources Center (NNRC), 1997. Wet, Wild, and Profitable. A report on the economic value of water-based recreation in Vermont. NNRC, Vermont.

Notzke, C., 2004. Indigenous tourism development in Southern Alberta, Canada: tentative engagement. Journal of Sustainable Tourism 12, 29–54.

Nowacek, S.M., Wells, R.S., Solow, A., 2001. Short-term effects of boat traffic on bottlenose dolphins, Tursiops truncatus, in Sarasota Bay, Florida. Marine Mammal Science 17, 673–688.

Nowacek, S.M., Wells, R.S., Owen, E.C.G., Speakman, T.R., Flamm, R.O., Nowacek, D.P., 2004. Florida manatees, Trichechus manatus latirostris, respond to approaching vessels. Biological Conservation 119, 517–523.

Olindo, P., Whelan, T., Whelan, T., 1991. The Old Man of Nature Tourism: Kenya. Nature Tourism: Managing for the Environment. Island Press, Washington, DC.

Ollenburg, C., 2006. Horse riding. In: Buckley, R.C. (Ed.), Adventure Tourism. CAB International, Wallingford, pp. 305–323.

Ollenburg, C., 2007. Regional signatures and trends in the farm tourism sector. Tourism Recreation Research 33, 13–23.

Orams, M., 2004. Why dolphins may get ulcers: considering the impacts of cetacean-based tourism in New Zealand. Tourism in Marine Environments 1, 17–28.

Ospina, G.A., 2006. War and ecotourism in the National Parks of Colombia: some reflections on the public risk and adventure. International Journal of Tourism Research 8, 241–246.

Outdoor Industry Association, 2005. Outdoor recreation participation in the United States, seventh ed. <http://www.outdoorindustry.org/research.current. html> (accessed 01.12.05).

Outdoor Industry Association, 2007. <http://www.outdoorindustry.org/gov. communications.php?sortyear=2007> (accessed 15.04.08).

Professional Association of Dive Instructors, (2009). PADI – The way the world learns to dive. <http://www.padi.com> (accessed 27.5.09).

Page, S.J., Steele, W., Connell, J., 2006. Analysing the promotion of adventure tourism: a case study of Scotland. Journal of Sport and Tourism 11, 51–76.

Page, S.J., 2007. Tourism Management: Managing for Change. Elsevier, London.

Page, S.J., Dowling, R.K., 2002. Ecotourism. Pearson Education, Harlow.

Page, S.J., Bentley, T., Walker, L., 2005. Scoping the nature and extent of adventure tourism operations in Scotland: how safe are they? Tourism Management 26, 381–397.

Parsons, E.C.M., Warburton, C.A., Woods-Ballard, A., Hughes, A., Johnston, P., 2003. The value of conserving whales: the impacts of whale-watching on the economy of rural west Scotland. Aquatic Conservation 13, 397–415.

Patterson, I.R., Pan, R., Jenkins, J., 2007. The motivations of baby boomers to participate in adventure tourism and the implications for adventure tourism providers. Annals of Leisure Research 10, 26–53.

Pearce, P.L., Foster, F., 2007. A "University of travel": backpacker learning. Tourism Management 28, 1285–1298.

Pechlaner, H., Fischer, E., Hammann, E.M., 2006. Leadership and innovation processes – development of products and services based on core competencies. Journal of Quality Assurance in Hospitality and Tourism 6, 31–57.

Peeters, P. (Ed.), 2007. Tourism and Climate Change Mitigation: Methods, Greenhouse Gas Reductions and Policies. Stichting NHTV Breda, Breda, Netherlands, p. 207.

Peeters, P., Gössling, S., Lane, B., 2009. Moving towards low-carbon tourism: new opportunities for destinations and tour operators. In: Gössling, S., Hall, C., Weaver, D. (Eds.), Sustainable Tourism Futures. Routledge, New York, pp. 240–257.

Pesant, A.R., 1987. Snowmobiling impact on soil properties and winter cereal crops. Canadian Field Naturalist 101, 22–32.

Petreas, C.P., 2003. Scuba diving: an alternative form of coastal tourism for Greece? In: Garrod, B., Wilson, J.C. (Eds.), Marine Ecotourism: Issues and Experiences. Channel View, Clevedon, pp. 215–232.

Pickering, C.M., Buckley, R.C., in press. Shortcomings of snowmaking as a response to climate change in the Australian ski industry. Ambio.

Pickering, C.M., Bear, R., Hill, W., 2007. Indirect impacts of nature based tourism and recreation: the association between infrastructure and the diversity of exotic plants in Kosciuszko National Park, Australia. Journal of Ecotourism 6, 146–157.

Pigram, J.J., Jenkins, J.M., 1999. Outdoor Recreation Management. Routledge, London, p. 329.

Pigram, J.J., Jenkins, J.M., 2006. Outdoor Recreation Management, second ed. Routledge, London, p. 426.

Pigram, J.J., Sundell, R.C. (Eds.), 1997. National Parks and Protected Areas: Selection, Delimitation and Management. University of New England, Armidale, p. 469.

Pitt, L.F., Opoku, R., Hultman, M., Abratt, R., Spyropoulou, S., 2007. What I say about myself: communication of brand personality by African countries. Tourism Management 28, 835–844.

Pizam, A., 2008. Space tourism: new market opportunities for hotels and cruise lines. International Journal of Hospitality 27, 489–490.

Pomfret, G., 2006. Mountaineering adventure tourists: a conceptual framework for research. Tourism Management 27, 113–123.

Prados, M-J., 2005. Territorial recognition and control of changes in dynamic rural areas: analysis of the naturbanization process in Andalusia, Spain. Journal of Environmental Planning Management 48, 65–83.

Prall, J., Winston, K., Brennan, R., 1995. Severe snowboarding injuries. Injury 26, 539–542.

Price, M.F., Moss, L.A.G., Williams, P.W., 1997. Tourism and amenity migration. In: Messerli, B., Ives, J.D. (Eds.), Mountains of the World A Global Priority. Parthenon Publishing, London, New York.

Prideaux, B., Cooper, M., 2009. River Tourism. CAB International, Wallingford.

Priest, S., Gass, M.A., 2005. Effective Leadership in Adventure Programming. Human Kinetics, Champaign, p. 328.

Prior, M.R., Ormond, R., Hitchen, R., Wormald, C., 1995. The impacts on natural resources of activity tourism: a case study of diving in Egypt. International Journal of Environmental Studies 48, 201–209.

Priskin, J., 2004. Four-wheel drive vehicle impacts in the Central Coast region of Western Australia. In: Buckley, R. (Ed.), Environmental Impacts of Ecotourism. CAB International, Wallingford, pp. 339–348.

Pullin, A.S., Knight, T.M., Stone, D.A., Charman, K., 2004. Do conservation managers use scientific evidence to support their decision-making? Biological Conservation 119, 245–252.

Rainbow, J., Buckley, R.C., Byrnes, T., Warnken, J., 2000. Green Guide to Blue Seas. CRC Tourism. Griffith University, Gold Coast.

Rainbow, J., Warnken, J., Buckley, R.C., 2002. Green Guide to Scuba Diving Tours. CRC Tourism. Griffith University, Gold Coast.

Raschi, A., Trampetti, S. (Eds.), 2008. Management for Protection and Sustainable Development. Consiglio Nationale della Ricerche, Montecatini, Italy.

Reisinger, Y., Steiner, C., 2006. Reconceptualising interpretation: the role of tour guides in authentic tourism. Current Issues in Tourism 9, 481–498.

Requa, R.K., Toney, J.M., Garrick, J.G., 1977. Parameters on injury reporting in skiing. Medicine and Science in Sports 9, 185–190.

Richins, H., 2007. Motorized water sports. In: Jennings, G. (Ed.), Water-based Tourism, Sport, Leisure, and Recreation Experiences. Elsevier, Oxford, pp. 69–94.

Riegl, B., Velimirov, B., 1991. How many damaged corals in Red Sea reef systems? A quantitative survey. Hydrobiologia 216/217, 249–256.

Ritchie, J.R., 1998. Managing the human presence in ecologically sensitive tourism destinations: insights from the Banff-Bow Valley Study. Journal of Sustainable Tourism 6, 293–313.

Rodger, K., Moore, S.A., 2004. Bringing science to wildlife tourism: the influence of managers' and scientists' perceptions. Journal of Ecotourism 3, 1–19.

Rodger, K., Moore, S.A., Newsome, D., 2007. Wildlife tours in Australia: characteristics, the place of science and sustainable futures. Journal of Sustainable Tourism 15, 160–179.

Roe, M., Benson, J.F., 2001. Planning for conflict resolution: jet-ski use on the Northumberland Coast. Coastal Management 29, 19–39.

Rogers, C.S., 1990. Responses of coral reefs and reef organisms to sedimentation. Marine Ecology Progress Series 62, 185–202.

Rogerson, C.M., 2006. Creative industries and urban tourism: South African perspectives. Urban Forum 17, 149–166.

Rogerson, C.M., 2007. The challenges of developing adventure tourism in South Africa. Africa Insight 37, 228–244.

Ronning, R., Gerner, T., Engebretsen, L., 2000. Risk of injury during alpine and telemark skiing and snowboarding. American Journal of Sports Medicine 28, 506–508.

Ronning, R., Ronning, I., Gerner, T., Engebretsen, L., 2001. The efficacy of wrist protectors in preventing snowboarding injuries. American Journal of Sports Medicine 29, 581–585.

Rouphael, A.B., Inglis, G.J., 2001. Increased spatial and temporal variability in coral damage caused by recreation scuba diving. Ecological Applications 12, 427–440.

Russell, C.L., Ankenman, M.J., 1996. Orangutans as photographic collectibles: ecotourism and the commodification of nature. Tourism Recreation Research 21, 71–78.

Russell, S.V., Lafferty, G., Loudoun, R., 2008. Examining tourism operators' responses to environmental regulation: the role of regulatory perceptions and relationships. Current Issues in Tourism 11, 126–143.

Ryan, C., 1998. Saltwater crocodiles as tourist attractions. Journal of Sustainable Tourism 6, 314–327.

Ryan, C., 2003. Recreational Tourism: Demand and Impacts. Channel View, Clevedon.

Ryan, C., 2007. Surfing and windsurfing. In: Jennings, G. (Ed.), Water-based Tourism, Sport, Leisure, and Recreation Experiences. Elsevier, Oxford, pp. 95–111.

Ryan, C., Harvey, K., 2000. Who likes saltwater crocodiles? Analysing socio-demographics of those viewing tourist wildlife attractions based on saltwater crocodiles. Journal of Sustainable Tourism 8, 426–433.

Sanecki, G.M., Green, K., Wood, H., Lindenmayer, D., 2006. The implications of snow-based recreation for small mammals in the subnivean space in south-east Australia. Biological Conservation 129 (4), 511–518.

Scarpaci, C., Dayanthi, N., 2003. Compliance with regulations by swim-with-dolphins operations in Port Phillip Bay, Victoria, Australia. Environmental Management 31, 342–347.

Scarpaci, C., Bigger, S.W., Corkeron, P.J., Nugegoda, D., 2000. Bottlenose dolphins, *Tursiops truncatus*, increase whistling in the presence of "swim-with-dolphin" tour operators. Journal of Cetacean Research and Management 2, 183–186.

Schaefers, J., 2006. Mountain biking. In: Buckley, R.C. (Ed.), Adventure Tourism. CAB International, Wallingford, pp. 324–331.

Schaeffer, T.N., Foster, M.S., Landrau, M.E., Walder, R.K., 1999. Diver disturbance in kelp forests. California Fish and Game 85, 170–176.

Schleyer, M.H., Tomalin, B.J., 2000. Damage on South African coral reefs and an assessment of their sustainable diving capacity using a fisheries approach. Bulletin of Marine Science 67, 1025–1042.

Schoen, R.G., Stano, M.J., 2002. Year 2000 whitewater injury survey. Wilderness and Environmental Medicine 13, 119–124.

Schott, C., 2007. Selling adventure tourism: a distribution channels perspective. The International Journal of Tourism Research 9, 257.

Schrader, M.P., Wann, D.L., 1999. High-risk recreation: the relationship between participant characteristics and degree of involvement. Journal of Sport Behaviour 22, 426–441.

Scott, N., Laws, E., 2004. Whale watching – the roles of small firms in the evolution of a new Australian niche market. In: Thomas, R. (Ed.), Small Firms in Tourism: International Perspectives. Elsevier Science, Amsterdam, pp. 153–166.

Sekhar, N.U., 2003. Local people's attitudes towards conservation and wildlife tourism around Sariska Tiger Reserve, India. Journal of Environmental Management 69, 339–347.

Shackley, M., 1995. The future of gorilla tourism in Rwanda. Journal of Sustainable Tourism 3, 61–72.

Shackley, M., 1996a. Community impact of the camel safari industry in Jaisalmar, Rajasthan. Tourism Management 17, 213–218.

Shackley, M., 1996b. Wildlife Tourism. International Thomson Business Press, London.

Shackley, M., 1998a. 'Stingray City' – managing the impact of underwater tourism in the Cayman Islands. Journal of Sustainable Tourism 6, 328–338.

Shackley, M., 1998b. Visitor Management: Case Studies from World Heritage Sites. Butterworth-Heinemann.

Shangri-La River Expeditions, 2009. Exploring the rivers of Western China. <http://www.shangri-la-river-expeditions.com/> (accessed 03.02.09).

Sharpe, R., 2005. "Going above and beyond:" the emotional labor of adventure guides. Journal of Leisure Research 37, 29–50.

Shumway, J.M., Otterstrom, S.M., 2001. Spatial patterns of migration and income change in the Mountain West: the dominance of service-based, amenity-rich countries. Professional Geographer 53, 492–502.

Sicklebill Safaris, 2009. Specialists in birdwatching tours to New Guinea, Australia and throughout the Pacific region. <http://www.sicklebillsafaris.com> (accessed 03.02.09).

Siderelis, C., Moore, R.L., 2006. Examining the effects of hypothetical modifications in permitting procedures and river conditions on whitewater boating behavior. Journal of Leisure Research 38, 558–575.

Simmons, D.G., Becken, S., 2004. The cost of getting there: impacts of travel to ecotourism destinations. In: Buckley, R.C. (Ed.), Environmental Impacts of Ecotourism. CAB International, Wallingford, pp. 15–24.

Simpson, R., 1996. Recreation and tourism in Europe's protected areas: threat or opportunity? Ecodecision 20, 40–43.

Singh, S., 2008. Destination development dilemma – case of Manali in Himachal Himalaya. Tourism Management 29, 1152–1156.

Slanger, E., Rudestam, E., 1997. Motivation and disinhibition in high risk sports: sensation seeking and self efficacy. Journal of Research in Personality 31, 355–374.

Smith, V.L., 2006. Adventure cruising: an ethnography of small ship travel. In: Dowling, R.K. (Ed.), Cruise Ship Tourism. CAB International, Wallingford, pp. 240–250.

Snyder, J., Stonehouse, B., 2007. Prospects for Polar Tourism. CAB International, Wallingford, p. 318.

Sournia, G., 1996. Wildlife tourism in West and Central Africa. Ecodecision 20, 52–54.

Spenceley, A., 2008. Responsible Tourism: Critical Issues for Conservation and Development. Earthscan, London, p. 432.

Spradley, J.P., 1980. Participant Observation. Rinehart and Winston, New York, Holt, p. 195.

Stabler, M., 1997. Tourism and Sustainability: Principles to Practice. CAB International, Wallingford, p. 380.

Stewart, S.I., 2002. Amenity migration. In: Luft, K., McDonald (Eds.), Trends 2000: Shaping the Future. Proceedings of the Fifth Conference Outdoor Recreation and Tourism Trends. Department of Park, Recreation and Tourism Resources, Lansing, MI, pp. 369–378.

Straadas, W., 2009. Sustainable transportation guidelines for nature-based tour operators. In: Gössling, S., Hall, C., Weaver, D. (Eds.), Sustainable Tourism Futures. Routledge, New York, pp. 258–281.

Stronza, A., Durham, W.H. (Eds.), 2008. Ecotourism and Conservation in the Americas. CAB International, Wallingford.

Stynes, D.J., White, E.M., 2006. Reflections on measuring recreation and travel spending. Journal of Travel Research 45, 8–17.

Summer, R.M., 1980. Impact of horse traffic on trails in Rocky Mountain National Park. Journal of Soil and Water Conservation 35, 85–87.

Summer, R.M., 1986. Geomorphic impacts of horse traffic on montane landforms. Journal of Soil and Water Conservation 41, 126–128.

SunChaser Eco-Tours, 2009. <http://www.sunchasercharters.ca/> (accessed 26.05.09).

Sung, H., 2007. Classification of adventure travelers: behavior, decision making, and target markets. In: Weed, M. (Ed.), Sport and Tourism: A Reader. Routledge, New York, pp. 224–251.

Suzuki, M., Kawamura, M., 1994. Studies on recreational behaviours in the national park. I. mountaineering in the National Park "Daisen". Tottori University Forest. Research Bulletin 22, 83–114.

Swarbrooke, J., Beard, C., Leckie, S., Pomfret, G., 2003. Adventure Tourism: the New Frontier. Butterworth-Heinemann, London.

Symmonds, M.C., Hammitt, W.E., Quisenberry, V.L., 2000. Managing recreational trail environments for mountain bike user preferences. Environmental Management 25, 549–564.

Tabata, R.S., 1989. The use of nearshore dive sites by recreational dive operations in Hawaii. Coastal Zone 89, 2865–2875.

Taj Safaris, 2009. Hotels, resorts and palaces. <www.tajsafaris.com/news>; (accessed 03.02.09).

Talge, H., 1993. Impact of recreational divers on scleractinian corals at Loo Key, Florida. In: Proceedings of the Seventh International Coral Reef Symposium, Pacific Science Association, pp. 1077–1082.

Tarazi, F., Dvorak, M.F.S., Wing, P.C., 1999. Spinal injuries in skiers and snowboarders. American Journal of Sports Medicine 27, 177–180.

Tatchu Surf Adventures, 2009. <http://www.tatchuadventures.com/> (accessed 06.04.09).

Taylor, D.M., O'Toole, K.S., Ryan, C.M., 2003. Experienced scuba divers in Australia and the United States suffer considerable injury and morbidity. Wilderness and Environmental Medicine 14, 83–88.

Thurston, E., Reader, R.J., 2001. Impacts of experimentally applied mountain biking and hiking on vegetation and soil of a deciduous forest. Environmental Management 27, 397–409.

Tisdell, C., 2001. Tourism Economics, the Environment and Development. Edward Elgar, Cheltenham, p. 320.

Tisdell, C.A., 2005. Economics of Environmental Conservation. Edward Elgar, Cheltenham, p. 288.

Tonderayi, D., 1999. Amenity migration and tourism in the Eastern Highlands Bioregions of Zimbabwe: policy, planning and management considerations. In: Godde, P.M., Price, M.F., Zimmerman, F.M. (Eds.), Tourism and Development in Mountain Regions. CAB International, Wallingford, pp. 297–323.

Townsend, C., 2003. Marine ecotourism through education: a case study of divers in the British Virgin Islands. In: Garrod, B., Wilson, J.C. (Eds.), Marine Ecotourism: Issues and Experiences. Channel View, Clevedon, pp. 138–154.

Tran, X., Ralston, L., 2006. Tourist preferences influence of unconscious needs. Annals of Tourism Research 33, 424–441.

Tratalos, J.A., Austin, T.J., 2001. Impacts of recreational SCUBA diving on coral communities of the Caribbean island of Grand Cayman. Biological Conservation 102, 67–75.

Trauer, B., 2006. Conceptualizing special interest tourism – frameworks for analysis. Tourism Management 27 (2), 183–200.

Travel Industry Association of America, 2009. <http://www.tia.org> (accessed 04.02.09).

Trevett, A.J., Forbes, R., Rae, C.K., Sheehan, C., Ross, J., Watt, S.J., Stephenson, R., 2001. Diving accidents in sports divers in Orkney waters. Scottish Medical Journal 46, 176–177.

Tsang, N.K., Ap, J., 2007. Tourists' perceptions of relational quality service attributes: a cross-cultural study. Journal of Travel Research 45, 355–363.

UNWTO-UNEP-WMO, 2008. Climate Change and Tourism: Responding to Global Challenges. UNWTO, Madrid.

Vail, D., Heldt, T., 2004. Governing snowmobilers in multiple-use landscapes: Swedish and Maine (USA) cases. Ecological Economics 48, 469–483.

Vaske, J.J., Carothers, P., Donnelly, M.P., Baird, B., 2007. Recreation conflict among skiers and snowboarders. In: Weed, M. (Ed.), Sport and Tourism: A Reader. Routledge, New York, pp. 252–270.

Verbeek, D., Bargeman, B., 2008. The sustainability chain is as strong as its weakest link. In: Ken, T., Tukker, A., Vezzoli, C., Ceschin, F. (Eds.), Sustainable Consumption and Production: A Framework for Action. Flemish Institute for Technological Research, Brussels, pp. 135–148.

Waitt, G., 1997. Selling paradise and adventure: representations of landscape in the tourist. Australian Geographical Studies 35, 47–60.

Waldvogel, J., 2007. Greetings and closings in workplace email. Journal of Computer-Mediated Communication 12, 456–477.

Walle, A.H., 1997. Pursuing risk or insight: marketing adventures. Annals of Tourism Research 24, 265–282.

Walpole, M.J., Goodwin, H.J., 2000. Local economic impacts of dragon tourism in Indonesia. Annals of Tourism Research 27, 559–576.

Walters, R.D.M., Samways, M.J., 2001. Sustainable dive ecotourism on a South African coral reef. Biodiversity and Conservation 10, 2167–2179.

Warnken, J., Byrnes, T., 2004. Impacts of tourboats in marine environments. In: Buckley, R.C. (Ed.), Environmental Impacts of Ecotourism. CAB International, Wallingford, pp. 99–124.

Watkins, W.A., 1986. Whale reactions to human activities in Cape Cod waters. Marine Mammal Science 2, 251–262.

Watson, A., Moss, R., 2004. Impacts of ski-development on ptarmigan (Lagopus mutus) at Cairn Gorm, Scotland. Biological Conservation 116, 267–275.

Weaver, D., 2008. Ecotourism, second ed. Wiley, Milton.

Weaver, D.B., 2001. The Encyclopedia of Ecotourism. CAB International, Oxford.

Weaver, T., Dale, D., 1978. Trampling effects of hikers, motorcycles and horses in meadows and forests. Journal of Applied Ecology 15, 451–457.

Webber, P. (Ed.), 2004. Trail Solutions. International Mountain Biking Association, Boulder, CO.

Webber, P. (Ed.), 2007. Managing Mountain Biking. International Mountain Biking Association, Boulder, CO.

Weber, K., 2007. Outdoor adventure tourism: a review of research approaches. In: Weed, M. (Ed.), Sport and Tourism: A Reader. Routledge, New York, pp. 57–71.

Whinam, J., Cannell, E.J., Kirkpatrick, J.B., Comfort, M., 1994. Studies on the potential impact of recreational horseriding on some alpine environments of the Central Plateau, Tasmania. Journal of Environmental Management 40, 103–117.

Whinam, J., Chilcott, N., Bergstrom, D.M., 2005. Subantarctic hitchhikers: expeditioners as vectors for the introduction of alien organisms. Biological Conservation 2, 207–219.

White, N.R., White, P.B., 2007. Home and away: tourists in a connected world. Annals of Tourism Research 34, 88–104.

Wikelski, M., Foufopoulous, J., Vargas, H., Snell, H., 2004. Galapagos birds and diseases: invasive pathogens as threats for island species. Ecology and Society 9.

Wild Women on Top, 2009. Ordinary women doing extraordinary things. <www.WildWomenOnTop.com>; (accessed 02.03.09).

Wilderness Travel, 2009. Extraordinary cultural, wildlife and hiking adventures since 1978. <http://www.wildernesstravel.com/itins/exploratories.html> (accessed 03.02.09).

Wiley, D.N., Moller, J.C., Pace, R.M., Carlson, C., 2008. Effectiveness of voluntary conservation agreements: case study of endangered whales and commercial whale watching. Conservation Biology 22 (2), 450–457.

Wilks, J., 1999. Scuba diving safety on Australia's Great Barrier Reef. Travel Medicine International 17, 17–21.

Wilks, J., Davis, R.J., 2000. Risk management for scuba diving operators in Australia's Great Barrier Reef. Tourism Management 21, 591–599.

Wilks, J., Pendergast, D., Leggat, P.A., 2006. Tourism in Turbulent Times: Towards Safe Experiences for Visitors. Elsevier, p. 357.

Williams, I.D., Polunin, N., 2000. Differences between protected and unprotected reefs of the western Caribbean in attributes preferred by dive tourists. Environmental Conservation 27, 382–391.

Williamson, J.E., 1999. Accidents in North American Mountaineering. American Alpine Club, Boulder, CO.

Winn, P., 2009. Exploring the Rivers of Western China, second ed. (DVD), Earth Science Expeditions and Shangri-La River Expeditions, Grand Junction CO.

Woods-Ballard, A., Parsons, E.C.M., Hughes, A., Velander, K.A., Ladle, R.J., Warburton, C.A., 2003. The sustainability of whale-watching in Scotland. Journal of Sustainable Tourism 11, 40–55.

World Travel and Tourism Council (WTTC), 2007. <http://www.wttc.org/> (accessed 10.12.07).

Wu, S., Wei, P., Chen, J., 2008. Influential factors and relational structure of Internet banner advertising in the tourism industry. Tourism Management 29, 221–236.

Wyder, T., 1987. 175 years of mountaineering in Switzerland. The Finsteraarhorn. Magglingen 44, 2–4.

Xiao, H., Smith, S.L.J., 2006a. The maturation of tourism research: evidence from a content analysis. Tourism Analysis 10, 335–348.

Xiao, H., Smith, S.L.J., 2006b. The making of tourism research: insights from a social sciences journal. Annals of Tourism Research 33, 490–507.

Xiao, H., Smith, S.L.J., 2007. The use of tourism knowledge: research propositions. Annals of Tourism Research 34, 310–331.

Xiaoli, W., 2007. Construction of the security assurance system of adventure tourism in China. Journal of Anhui Agricultural Sciences 35 (7) (188), 2100–2102.

Yamakawa, H., Murase, S., Sakai, H., Iwama, T., Katada, M., Niikawa, S., Sumi, Y., Mishimura, Y., Sakai, N., 2001. Spinal injuries in snowboarders: risk of jumping as an integral part of snowboarding. Journal of Trauma 50, 1101–1105.

Zakai, D., Chadwick-Furman, N.E., 2002. Impacts of intensive recreational diving on reef corals at Eilat, northern Red Sea. Biological Conservation 105, 179–187.

Zurick, D.N., 1992. Adventure travel and sustainable tourism in the peripheral economy of Nepal. Annals of the Association of American Geographers 82, 608–628.

Index